Reading Freud's Patients

What would the story of analysis look like if it were told through the eyes of the analysand? How would the patient write and present the analytic experience? How would the narrative as written by the analysand differ from the analytic narrative commonly offered by the analyst? What do the actual analytic narratives written by Freud's patients look like?

This book aims to confront these intriguing questions with an innovative reading of memoirs by Freud's patients. These patients—including Sergei Pankejeff, known as the Wolf Man; the poet H. D.; and the American psychoanalyst Abram Kardiner—all came to Vienna specially to meet Freud and embark with him on the intimate and thrilling journey of deciphering the unconscious and unraveling the secrets of the psyche. A broad psychoanalytic and literary-historical reading of their memoirs is offered in this new entry to the popular Routledge History of Psychoanalysis Series, with the purpose of presenting the analysands' narratives as they themselves recounted them. This makes it possible to re-examine the links among psychoanalysis, literature, and translation and sheds new light on the complex challenge of coming to know oneself through the encounter with otherness.

This book is unique in its focus on multiple memoirs by patients of Freud and presents a fresh, even startling, close-up look at psychoanalysis as a clinical practice and as a rigorous discourse and offers a new vision of Freud's strengths and, at times, defects. It will be of considerable interest to scholars of psychoanalysis and intellectual history, as well as those with a wider interest in literature and memoir.

Anat Tzur Mahalel (Ph.D.) is a practicing psychoanalytically-oriented clinical psychologist, and a post-doctoral researcher in the interdisciplinary program in psychoanalysis, University of Haifa; staff member at the advanced school for psychoanalytic psychotherapy, University of Haifa; and in private practice in Haifa, Israel. She has published papers on the history of psychoanalysis, psychoanalysis and literature, translation theory, and autobiography.

The History of Psychoanalysis Series
Series Editors
Professor Brett Kahr and Professor Peter L. Rudnytsky

This series seeks to present outstanding new books that illuminate any aspect of the history of psychoanalysis from its earliest days to the present, and to reintroduce classic texts to contemporary readers.

Other titles in the series:

Reading Freud's Patients
Memoir, Narrative, and the Analysand
Anat Tzur Mahalel

Rediscovering Pierre Janet
Trauma, Dissociation, and a New Context for Psychoanalysis
Edited by Giuseppe Craparo, Francesca Ortu, and Onno Van der Hart

Freud/Tiffany
Anna Freud, Dorothy Tiffany Burlingham and the 'Best Possible School'
Edited by Elizabeth Ann Danto with Alexandra Steiner-Strauss

Freud at Work
On the History of Psychoanalytic Theory and Practice, with an Analysis of Freud's Patient Record Books
Ulrike May

What is this Professor Freud Like?
A Diary of an Analysis with Historical Comments
Edited by Anna Koellreuter

Corresponding Lives
Mabel Dodge Luhan, A. A. Brill, and the Psychoanalytic Adventure in America
Patricia R. Everett

For further information about this series please visit https://www.routledge.com/The-History-of-Psychoanalysis-Series/book-series/KARNHIPSY

Reading Freud's Patients

Memoir, Narrative, and the Analysand

Anat Tzur Mahalel

LONDON AND NEW YORK

First published 2020
by Routledge
2 Park Square, Milton Park, Abingdon, Oxon OX14 4RN

and by Routledge
52 Vanderbilt Avenue, New York, NY 10017

Routledge is an imprint of the Taylor & Francis Group, an informa business

© 2020 Anat Tzur Mahalel

The right of Anat Tzur Mahalel to be identified as author of this work has been asserted by her in accordance with sections 77 and 78 of the Copyright, Designs and Patents Act 1988.

All rights reserved. No part of this book may be reprinted or reproduced or utilised in any form or by any electronic, mechanical, or other means, now known or hereafter invented, including photocopying and recording, or in any information storage or retrieval system, without permission in writing from the publishers.

Trademark notice: Product or corporate names may be trademarks or registered trademarks, and are used only for identification and explanation without intent to infringe.

British Library Cataloguing-in-Publication Data
A catalogue record for this book is available from the British Library

Library of Congress Cataloging-in-Publication Data
A catalog record has been requested for this book

ISBN: 978-0-367-02714-8 (hbk)
ISBN: 978-0-367-02715-5 (pbk)
ISBN: 978-0-429-39824-7 (ebk)

Typeset in Times New Roman
by Integra Software Services Pvt. Ltd.

To my family, Elad, Itamar, Talia, and Yael

Contents

Series editor's foreword   x
Prologue   xiv

1 Psychoanalytic space and writing space   1
Introduction 1
Psychoanalytic writing and case studies 3
Analytic narratives from the patient's point of view 5
Psychoanalysis, translation, and writing 11

2 *Fragments of an Analysis with Freud* by Joseph Wortis: criticism and longing   18
Introduction to Wortis's Fragments *18*
Resistances in the analytic encounter 22
Longing for an unattainable object 27
The work of memory and mourning in intertextual contexts 30
Impasse and a momentary encounter 36

3 *Diary of My Analysis with Sigmund Freud* by Smiley Blanton: from a deadlock of silence to the act of writing   39
Introduction to Blanton's Diary *39*
The inspiring figure of the analyst 42
Freud as the writer of The Interpretation of Dreams *49*
Analytic and textual dialog on areas of controversy 52
Blanton's narrative of separation 58
The search for the fragmented voice 61
The need for love and recognition 65

4 *My Analysis with Freud: Reminiscences* by Abram Kardiner: memory, mourning, and writing 71
  Introduction to Kardiner's Reminiscences 71
  Kardiner's work of memory 72
  The challenge of reminiscence 74
  The termination phase of analysis 78
  The absence of the mother 83
  Work of memory and mourning through writing 86

5 *An American Psychiatrist in Vienna, 1935–1937, and His Sigmund Freud* by John Dorsey: "My Sigmund Freud" 90
  Introduction to Dorsey's Sigmund Freud 90
  Enchantment and separation in transference 93
  The representation of a muted termination 101
  Telling a story in psychoanalysis and in writing 105

6 *The Wolf Man and Sigmund Freud* by Sergei Pankejeff: between a case study and a memoir 112
  Introduction to Pankejeff's The Wolf Man and Sigmund Freud 112
  One book, four authors 114
  Lifting the veil 116
  A retranslation of the case study 121
  Separation from Freud as an analyst and as a biographer 128
  Termination from an interminable analysis 131

7 *Tribute to Freud* by Hilda Doolittle (H. D.): between the analytic and the poetic 137
  Introduction to H. D.'s Tribute to Freud 137
  The memoir as a call to memory 141
  The gift of the memoir 146
  Analysis as home 150
  Freud and H. D.: paternal and maternal transference 153
  Two poets, two lost children: H. D. and Mignon 163

8 The creation of voice in psychoanalysis and literature 173
  Writing and psychoanalysis as a work of memory 173
  Writing and psychoanalysis as a work of mourning 175

Freud: paternal and maternal transference 178
Translating the enigmatic messages of the other 181

Epilogue: psychoanalysis terminable and interminable   187
References   192
Index   199

Series editor's foreword

Nothing is more important in psychoanalysis than the patient's experience. It follows that, however valuable the innumerable case histories written by analysts may be, there are no more precious documents in our literature than patients' chronicles of their own journeys into the interior, which must include a reckoning of their relationships with their guides.

Under no circumstances is this truer than when that guide is Freud himself, and the patients' memoirs are written with an awareness that they will be of interest to readers primarily as a contribution to the vast archive of primary sources on the life and work of the founder of psychoanalysis. Surprisingly, however, until the present contribution by Anat Tzur Mahalel, the sole extant study of the book-length narratives by Freud's patients has been that by Beate Lohser and Peter M. Newton (1996), and it may be said that their collective significance for our understanding of the history of psychoanalysis has only begun to be appreciated.

In advancing her thesis that "this distinct literature can be seen as a work of translation of the analytic experience, which includes the work of memory and the work of mourning," Tzur Mahalel approaches the narratives by Freud's patients not simply for what they reveal about his analytic technique, but as texts of creative nonfiction that demand to be read with the tools of literary criticism. In thus expanding the conceptual framework of Lohser and Newton, Tzur Mahalel simultaneously enlarges their canon by devoting a chapter to the memoirs of the Russian Sergei Pankejeff—better known as the "Wolf Man"—as well as to those by Joseph Wortis, Smiley Blanton, Abram Kardiner, John Dorsey, and Hilda Doolittle, all five of whom happened to be Americans.[1]

Tzur Mahalel quotes Dorsey's (1976) avowal that "all I can mean by describing Sigmund Freud must really refer to *my* image of my Sigmund Freud" (xvi). Notwithstanding his leaden style, Dorsey's statement contains a truth that pertains to the readers of these works no less than it does to their authors' experiences with Freud. I imagine that almost everyone will share my amusement at Freud's comparison of his reticence at the outset of Dorsey's analysis to "the Japanese gardener who was reproached, after being hired, for sitting for several days and doing no work," but "rejoined that he *was* working: the first step in building the garden being to take in the landscape" (53), and will also join me in smiling at his mockery of "the American who boasted of making the complete tour of the Louvre in one hour and three-quarters, and who then added, 'And if I had my roller-skates on I could have made it in an hour and a half'" (68).

But while appreciation of Freud's wit is unlikely to arouse controversy, those who are enticed by Tzur Mahalel's thoughtful and engaging book to read or reread these vital contributions to the history of psychoanalysis are bound to diverge widely in the image of Freud they construct from this Rashomon-like compilation of perspectives on the same human being. For myself, not only did I come away convinced that a far more troubling picture of Pankejeff's four and a half years on Freud's couch, as well as of his status as a protégé of the psychoanalytic establishment, emerges from the interviews he granted late in life to Karin Obholzer than it does from the authorized version of his memoirs in the volume published by Muriel Gardiner, but I was also perturbed by the degree to which Freud allowed himself to be swayed by the attitudes of his patients. On the one hand, he showed unabashed favoritism to those who were awestruck and submissive, including both Blanton (1971), who told him that *The Interpretation of Dreams* was "my bible. I carry it and reread it every year" (93), and the even more lightweight Dorsey (1976), for whom "my Professor Freud attained preeminently [*sic*] my revered father figure" (23), while on the other he belittled the intellectually formidable but skeptical Wortis (1954) in truly appalling fashion, informing him that "you are ignorant and I am here to teach you" (50), and "you must learn to absorb things and not answer back. You must change that habit" (114).

Of particular interest to me is the testimony of Kardiner (1977), who credits Freud with uncovering his fear of his father in childhood, but takes Freud to task for failing to see that "*the one whom I feared now was Freud himself,*" so that, ironically, "the central fact in the transference situation was overlooked by the man who had discovered the very process of transference itself" (58, 100). In comparing notes with other analysands, Kardiner learned that, "as with the Oedipus complex, unconscious homosexuality was a routine part of everyone's analysis" with Freud, not just of his own, and that Freud believed the male patient "could do nothing but reconcile himself to it" (61, 99), a point of view wholly in accord with his fatalistic outlook in "Analysis Terminable and Interminable." With the benefit of hindsight, Kardiner explains the consequences of Freud's refusal to confront the "aggression and hostility" concealed beneath his submissiveness in the following fashion:

> I made a silent pact with Freud. "I will continue to be compliant provided that you will let me enjoy your protection." If he rejected me, I would lose the chance to enter this magical professional circle. This tacit acceptance on my part sealed off an important part of my character from scrutiny.
>
> (59)

That Freud had failed to analyze his negative transference was also at the heart of Ferenczi's critique of Freud, and there is an uncanny convergence between Kardiner's testimony in his memoirs and that furnished by Ferenczi in his *Clinical Diary*, where he describes his own "silent pact" in which he played the role of "a blindly dependent son" to Freud, in return for which he was rewarded with "membership in a distinguished group guaranteed by the king, indeed with the rank of field marshal for myself (crown-prince fantasy)" (Dupont 1985, 185). What makes the perspective of both Kardiner and Ferenczi so compelling is that they combine an outward posture of compliance like that wholeheartedly adopted by Blanton and Dorsey with the internal critical awareness of a Wortis, so that when they do finally cast off their inhibitions and reject their Faustian bargains, their indictments of Freud are that much more searing since they come from disillusioned adherents who had gained admission to his "magical professional circle," rather than from outright opponents of psychoanalysis.

The fact remains, however, that by the end of his journey Ferenczi came to recognize that "it was only adoration and not independent judgment that made me follow him" (Dupont 1985, 185), just as Wortis (1954) dared to tell Freud to his face that he "did not generally stand in awe of a name simply because it was famous, but tried to judge for myself," which led Freud to wash his hands of him completely: "If anybody asked me about a certain talented Wortis who came to study with me, I will say he learned nothing from me, and I will disclaim all responsibility" (120, 128). Even Pankejeff, after Freud had explained the free association technique to him at the outset of his analysis, when he responded that he would give it a try but wanted to verify the results for himself, was, as he informed Obholzer (1980), met with the reproof: "Don't start that. Because the moment you try to view things critically, your treatment will get nowhere," as a result of which Pankejeff "naturally gave up the idea of any further criticism" (31). Despite Freud's adjuration that he proceed with blind faith, however, especially with respect to the primal scene that he allegedly witnessed at the age of one and a half, Pankejeff concludes in retrospect, "He maintains I saw it, but who will guarantee that it is so? That it is not a fantasy of his?" (31). Pankejeff's criticism of Freud for too energetically riding his own hobby horses—for forcing the evidence to fit his preconceived theories—is, moreover, independently echoed by both Wortis (1954) and Kardiner (1977), the former of whom castigates his "general foraging in a false direction" (185), while the latter details how Freud erroneously used his "extraordinary insight" to "put me on a wild goose chase for a problem that did not exist" (98).

As it turns out, at least in my reading, the seemingly divergent perspectives on Freud that may be gleaned from the narratives of his patients actually add up to a coherent and, in the main, far from flattering portrait, one that is the mirror image of his notorious declaration to Ferenczi that "neurotics are a rabble, good only to support us financially and to allow us to learn from their cases: psychoanalysis as a therapy may be worthless" (Dupont 1985, 186). To be sure, I believe that I have sound reasons and solid evidence to support my conclusions, but I recognize that others are bound to see things differently. Indeed, although Tzur Mahalel argues that "the writings of Freud's patients express admiration for him as an intriguing researcher and gifted writer," she declines to join the debates over Freud's character or the quality of his analytic work. She chooses instead to focus on what matters most in the end—the experience of his patients during and after their analyses, including the intense attachments fostered by regression, as well as the retrospective work of mourning and translation. In so doing, Anat Tzur Mahalel highlights our good fortune that this unique genre of autobiographical narratives—to which Ferenczi's *Clinical Diary* forms the indispensable seventh seal—has preserved the therapeutic relationship with Freud "not only in the analytic, but also in the textual, space."

Peter L. Rudnytsky
Gainesville, Florida

Note

1 Also available in the History of Psychoanalysis Series is Anna Guggenbühl's diary of her analysis with Freud in 1921 (Koellreuter 2016), but this extremely interesting raw material lacks the narrative form that would lend itself to a literary analysis. Paul Roazen's *How Freud Worked* (1995) offers a characteristically gossipy retrospective tour of his interviews with ten of Freud's former patients.

References

Blanton, S. (1971). *Diary of My Analysis with Sigmund Freud*. New York, NY: Hawthorn Books.
Dorsey, J. M. (1976). *An American Psychiatrist in Vienna, 1935–1937, and His Sigmund Freud*. Detroit, MI: Center for Health Education.
Dupont, J., ed. (1985). *The Clinical Diary of Sándor Ferenczi*. Translation: Michael Balint and Nicola Zarday Jackson. Cambridge, MA: Harvard University Press, 1988.
Kardiner, A. (1977). *My Analysis with Freud: Reminiscences*. New York, NY: Norton.
Koellreuter, A., ed. (2016). *What Is This Professor Freud Like? A Diary of an Analysis with Historical Comments*. London: Karnac.
Lohser, B. and Newton, P. M. (1996). *Unorthodox Freud: The View from the Couch*. New York, NY: Guilford Press.
Obholzer, K. (1980) *The Wolf-Man: Conversations with Freud's Patient—Sixty Years Later*. Translation: Michael Shaw. New York, NY: Continuum, 1982.
Roazen, P. (1995). *How Freud Worked: First-Hand Accounts of Patients*. Northvale, NJ: Aronson.
Wortis, J. (1954). *Fragment of an Analysis with Freud*. New York, NY: Simon & Schuster.

Prologue

Case studies are the most central and prominent window into psychoanalytic work, both for professionals and for the broader public. Psychoanalysis is represented by and studied through case studies, which offer a glimpse into the intimacy of analytic work. The starting point of this book is that not enough attention has been paid to the fact that case studies are written exclusively by analysts. This is an intriguing state of affairs because psychoanalysis is by its nature dialogical, based as it is on a dialog between different worlds, concretely between the worlds of analysand and analyst and broadly speaking between the conscious and unconscious and between self and other.

The main interest of this book is therefore the voice of the analysand. The writing subject in psychoanalysis is the analyst, whose voice in the analytic literature is well represented. But what is the voice of the analysand? What are its distinct characteristics? Is it the voice we hear second-hand through the analyst? Is it the voice heard when a certain analysand is asked to write a memoir? Is it the voice we hear when reading stories written by analysands? These questions, which are not often raised, bring us to the notion of the muteness of the analysand. This muteness has hardly been mentioned in academic discussions and can be considered a blind spot of psychoanalysis. This is an allusive muteness, for one of the primary aims of psychoanalysis has always been to bring forth the analysand's repressed memories, and aspects of the self that have not yet found expression. I want to emphasize that I am not arguing that analysands do not write, for memoirs written by analysands have existed for many decades. Nevertheless, this literature has always been situated in the margins of psychoanalytic literature, and these margins are the main concern of the present book.

Literature written by analysands has followed the psychoanalytic literature from its very beginning, yet has been mainly overlooked in the field's academic and theoretical writings. Texts by analysands have tended to be treated as no more than personal stories, anecdotal in their theoretical importance. This stance has pushed these texts aside and made them transparent. The challenge of tying together memoirs written by Freud's patients, for example, as a distinct corpus and offering them a united reading has been taken up mainly by Lohser and Newton (1996). A textual collection of oral reports and interviews gathered from Freud's patients also appeared in Roazen (1995). These books were significant in bringing forth the voices of the analysands and, in some cases, analyzing them. Nevertheless, the main concern of these attempts was gathering information about Freud as analyst and persona, rather than characterizing the analysand as a writing subject. Drawing attention to the analysand as author brings forth questions that have until now been overlooked, such as their motivations for writing, the content and form of the texts, and the dialog that these texts create with psychoanalytic literature. In addressing these questions, I aim to treat these memoirs as distinct texts that deserve their own targeted reading and not to be treated only as footnotes to the canon.

The main concern of the present book is not memoirs written by analysands in general, but memoirs written by a specific group of analysands, Freud's analysands. This corpus is constructed of six memoirs, which were written over two decades, after Freud's death. Interestingly, they were all written by foreign, not Austrian, analysands. The author-analysands of this corpus consist of American psychiatrists, an American woman poet, and a Russian aristocrat who later became an émigré. They came to Freud at different phases in their lives and went through various analyses, different in duration and character. The times of writing the memoirs and their writing styles also distinguish the memoirs: some of them were written during analysis, as diaries that were later edited, and others were written long after analysis terminated; some of the memoirs try to stay close to the case study genre and to the actual events that took place in the analytic sphere, while others emphasize poetic and symbolic aspects of the encounter with Freud. Even among the group of American psychiatrists, four in number, that seem similar in their motivation for undergoing analysis, as part of their professional ambitions, there are salient differences in their level of identification with the new discipline and in the transference relationships each one of them creates with Freud. Two of them were first-generation Eastern Europe Jewish immigrants to New York City, while the other two were Southerners from Christian farm-owning families.

As a psychoanalytically-oriented psychotherapist and clinical psychologist, one of the central impressions I take away from reading the texts written by analysands is the diversity that characterizes them, including diversity in the points of view they offer on the analytic situation. Reading these texts brings into focus the common ground we expect to find in literature about analysis, a common ground based on shared theoretical and technical premises and language, i.e., analysis as presented from the point of view of the analyst. This is the point of view from which the analytic situation—in terms of psychic life, analytic interpretations and processes, and the achievement of psychic transformation—has been exclusively presented and learned.

Texts written by analysands are actually autobiographical case studies. Reading these texts makes it clear that the analytic situation has been represented in a biased way because of the one-sided authorship that has predominated. There is something of a paradox here, as psychoanalysis, that field that is so profoundly occupied with liberating the analysand's repressed reminiscences and muted inner voices, has collaborated in the analysand's literary silence. Even though contemporary psychoanalytic thought tends to emphasize the relational aspects of the analytic encounter as a mutual "meeting of minds," as suggested by Lewis Aron (1996), the psychoanalytic literature has remained much more conservative. This insistence on one-sidedness creates a situation in which only one subject is given the authority to become an author in psychoanalytic literature.

I should note that stories of analysis written by analysands are by no means rare. Analysands have been writing moving, intriguing stories of analysis since the beginning of psychoanalysis. They have appeared as memoirs of the analyst or of the transformative process of analysis, or as part of their authors' autobiographies. They have appeared on the initiative either of the writing analysand, the analysand's colleagues, or the analyst. The present book's innovation is in gathering the memoirs written by Freud's patients, specifically, and in looking at this collection as a distinct group of texts.

This process is valuable for a couple of reasons. First, it offers an opportunity to shed light on psychoanalysis in its initial evolution. The writing analysands arrived in Vienna from various locations for the singular purpose of meeting Freud and his innovative thought. They write about their initial encounters with his thought, which usually took place in the textual realm, when they read his writing. They describe reading Freud's texts as a revelation of new realms of knowledge and experience, an innovative and yet-to-be-discovered path. Subsequently, they felt the urge to follow their curiosity and come to Vienna, full of hope and expectations for the opening of new personal and professional horizons. When we look into the experience of being an analysand of Freud's, we need to bear in mind the intensely structured setting, involving five to six analytic sessions a week. During analysis, patients were instructed not to make any significant life decisions, whether personal, familial, or professional. They came alone or with their families and made the hotel near Freud's residence their temporary home. We can imagine how much hope and enthusiasm was involved in this journey, hope for a turning point in life, an internal and external transformation. Freud's patients chose to leave their homes, their familiar habits, and every framework of affiliation that they had in order to go on an adventurous journey that revolved almost exclusively around the analytic sessions and the transference relationship. They went with the aim of discovering this revolutionary field and being part of the recently discovered path to the mysterious realms of the psyche.

Second, this collection of texts was written by analysands who were in analysis with the most famous analyst of all, whose writing has become a canonical and inseparable part of modern thought. The very act on the part of his analysands of writing memoirs about him can be understood, as I bring forth, as a brave and even subversive act of presentation. In literary theory, Gilles Deleuze and Félix Guattari offer the concept of *minor literature*, literature that emerges from canonical literature and gives voice to the voices that had been left muted, that were not even presented as voices. Because minor literature has to do with giving a voice to the voiceless, it is understood as a political act that involves subversion. Deleuze and Guattari characterize this distinct process of writing as "writing like a dog digging a hole, a rat digging its burrow. And to do that, finding his own point of underdevelopment, his own *patois*, his own third world, his own desert" (1986 [1975], 18, emphasis in original). Understanding the memoirs written by Freud's patients as minor literature is not only a result of their relationship to Freud's canonical stance, but also has to do with the writers' initiative to transform themselves to the active stance of the writer, or author. By writing, the analysand is given the authority to offer a textual sketch of Freud, and this authority is not an act that should be taken for granted, especially not at the time these analyses took place.

Therefore, this book offers two new perspectives on this collection of writing by Freud's analysands: first, in terms of the importance of the collection for psychoanalytic and memoir literature; and second, in terms of its significance as minor literature that has been set aside or overlooked in relation to the canon of psychoanalytic literature.

It gives me great pleasure to thank those whom I have been privileged to meet and work with on this book. First and foremost, I am thankful to Vered Lev Kenaan at the Department of Hebrew and Comparative Literature and Emanuel Berman of the Department of Psychology at the University of Haifa, my supervisors, and academic parents. I feel extremely privileged to have met Vered and Emanuel, both leading scholars in their fields, who guided me wisely and safely from the very beginning of my dissertation. In this intriguing interdisciplinary field of psychoanalysis and literature, they helped me to discover my own voice and stay attuned to it. I thank Routledge and my editor, Russell George, for the wonderful opportunity they have given me to explore the generous space that is offered by a book. I am grateful to the late Lewis Aron, who expressed interest in my research throughout its evolution and whose death is a great loss to the psychoanalytic community. I wish to thank Dana Amir, the head of the interdisciplinary research track in psychoanalysis, for her inspiration as a scholar in psychoanalysis and her brilliant reading. I thank Michal Ben Naftali for her remarkable voice as author and philosopher and for her wise insights into my writing. My gratitude to the late Beatriz Priel, who was my masters' thesis supervisor and first truly opened my eyes to psychoanalytic literature, challenging me never to look at things just as they were. I want to thank the research group of the interdisciplinary research track in psychoanalysis and the scholars of the Department of Hebrew and Comparative Literature at the University of Haifa, who helped me think about my research in its different phases. I am grateful to my dear patients from all times and places, and my dear students through the years at the University of Haifa, all of whom made me think about psychoanalysis in new ways. I thank Marie Deer, my dedicated language editor, for our mutual professional path together.

I am eternally grateful to my beloved family, my parents, Nava and David Mahalel, for always believing in me, to my brothers Adi and Amit, and to my late grandparents Gila and Michael Dana, Ahuva and Shachar Mahalel.

Finally, my deepest thanks to my close family, who are my earth and sky, my home and path, body and soul. To my husband and closest companion, Elad, for his wisdom and patience, for our mutual learning of the craft of living. To my children: Itamar for teaching me the art of listening; Talia for her sight and insight; and Yael for her laughter and vibrance. Thank you for the love; the whole wide world is captured within it.

Chapter 1

Psychoanalytic space and writing space

Introduction

Psychoanalysis, from its very beginning, is intertwined with text and writing. The psychoanalytic space is created and developed by various aspects of textuality as much as it is created and developed by the encounter between two subjects in the clinic. At the heart of both psychoanalysis and writing are self-reflection and the exploration of the unconscious. Within this space, the subject recreates the subject's life narrative, self, and singular voice.

On the verge of the twentieth century, the modern world adopted psychoanalysis with great enthusiasm. It became a central and curious entity, supplying innovative understandings of intrapsychic, intersubjective, and cultural phenomena. The challenge that psychoanalysis offered to the modern enlightened subject, governed by logic and intellect, was profound. Accepting the centrality of the unconscious transformed how we understand subjectivity and one's relations with his inner world and surroundings. It was suggested that we turn our attention from an omnipotent, divine, outer entity toward an inner entity that carries the individual's reservoir of psychic energy, private history, and way of remembering.

Psychoanalysis calls for a new kind of listening to the human voice, a very fine tuning of one subject to self and other, in an attention that is both concentrated and free-floating, analytic and sensual, aiming to explore the unconscious but not forcing it to be revealed. This is an attention that requires a vast space of time and effort in order to be fully and truly productive. It is also the unique attention received from the analyst that gradually creates, in turn, a similar attention within the analysand. For Freud, the meaning of contenting oneself "with studying whatever is present for the time being on the surface of the patient's mind" (1914a, 147) lies in putting the focus on listening to the subtle nuances of expression, voice, and body gestures, the distinguished narrative brought to the analytic setting and its weaving during the process. At the outset of analysis, Freud used to say, "Before I can say anything to you I must know a great deal about you; please tell me what you know about yourself" (1913a, 134). In these words, the abstinent analyst, who may be experienced as frustrating at times, is brought to light in his generosity, the generosity of true listening.

An area of psychoanalytic exploration that has not yet received the attention it deserves is the literature written by analysands. In this book I offer a unique collection of texts written by analytic patients, in fact by patients of the father of psychoanalysis himself, Sigmund Freud (1856–1939). The specific choice of texts presented here allows an alternative point of view on the history of psychoanalysis, on the psychoanalytic setting as introduced and created by Freud, and on his patients' encounters and relationships with him. Freud's patients felt themselves to be participants in the historical moment of the creation of a new scientific field that suggested an innovative way to understand the human psyche, development, motivations, pathology, and cure. This new field suggested revolutionary paths for exploring the unconscious and understanding enigmatic phenomena such as dreams, parapraxis, and perversion.

The writings of Freud's patients express admiration for him as an intriguing researcher and gifted writer, which was the main reason they all made great efforts to overcome important challenges and become his analysands. Another thing that makes this collection of texts unique is that the therapeutic relationship with Freud existed not only in the analytic, but also in the textual, space. The authors of these texts read Freud vigorously before, during, and after their analytic encounters with him, and experiences of reading and writing received a prominent place in those encounters. Freud used to talk freely with his patients about literature, books, and the experience of reading and writing, and his rich library played an important role in analysis, as Freud would approach it, open one book or another, and read from it or check some point in the book. He used to loan books to his patients and present copies of his own literary works to them as gifts.

Freud's writing created a new literary genre, weaving together the poetic and the scientific, the mythic and the autobiographical, and offering a continuous search for the various languages of the psyche. His use of canonical literature is characterized by deep emotional participation and intimacy, expressing his profound attachment to literature and textuality. The classical poets and authors, including Shakespeare, Dostoyevsky, Lessing, Schiller, and his most beloved Goethe, had served as central figures of admiration and identification for Freud since childhood. Poetry was a source of inspiration, both personal and professional, for Freud in various stages of his life. The image of the poet appears in his writing as a mentor, a source of consolation and guidance, and a voice expressing his deepest fantasies and longings (Anzieu 1986 [1959], 118–121, 146, 292–294, 309–314; Frankland 2000, 6–62; Nägele 1987, 23–45). An example of Freud's deep ties to the literary world can be found in his literary self-portrait, *An Autobiographical Study*. He states there that the main inspiration for his decision to study medicine was Johann Wolfgang von Goethe's essay *Nature* (which we now know to have been written, in fact, by a friend of Goethe's and erroneously attributed to Goethe himself) (Freud 1925a, 8). Freud identified most deeply with Goethe's education and formation (*Bildung*), as presented in Goethe's autobiography, *Aus Meinem Leben:*

Dichtung und Wahrheit, to which Freud dedicated an essay (Freud 1917a). Freud was especially inspired by the apprenticeship period through which the young Goethe had to go in order to find his place in society, and the way in which Goethe, as author and poet, used his own personal reminiscences as an *exemplum*. Freud also took profound inspiration from Goethe's dedication to science and poetics and his attraction to the unknown as an enigma waiting to be solved, but whose secrets are never completely revealed (Anzieu 1986 [1959], 119, 370–371).

Freud's affinity for the literary realm gave his patients the opportunity to create a multi-layered dialog with him that included rich and profound literary aspects. They read his writings and usually also the literary corpus that inspired him. Their psychoanalytic-poetic dialog with Freud continued to develop even after their separation from him and even his death, finding its expression in the memoirs they wrote and published about him. The patients' narratives are autobiographical texts, for they center on the narrative of transformation and development of the self. They can also be regarded as a collection of memoirs on Freud, for his figure, as an analyst, scholar, and author, stands in the center of the texts. These texts are also influenced by the genre of the psychoanalytic case study and by Freud's own distinguished writing. Nevertheless, they cannot, obviously, be regarded as case studies, for the point of view they suggest is different, and this is also what makes them distinct and subversive.

Psychoanalytic writing and case studies

Case studies are a distinguished and unique genre created by psychoanalysis. They offer the story of a single analysis or psychotherapy, with an emphasis on the subject's history, the sources of the development of the distress or illness, and the therapeutic process and its results. Case studies are the most central and prominent window into psychoanalytic work, both for professionals and for the broad public. Because this genre first appeared in Freud's writing, the case studies were mainly read and used as texts aimed at conveying knowledge of scientific and cultural importance about psychoanalytic work. Nevertheless, these texts were, from the outset, also regarded as stories, telling the tales of people's lives and psychic transformations. In Freud's book, *Studies in Hysteria*, from 1895, which was written in collaboration with Joseph Breuer, the genre of the psychoanalytic case study was introduced solemnly, with a slightly apologetic tone,

> I have not always been a psychotherapist. Like other neuropathologists, I was trained to employ local diagnoses and electro-prognosis, and it still strikes me myself as strange that the case histories I write should read like short stories and that, as one might say, they lack the serious stamp of science. I must console myself with the reflection that the nature of the subject is evidently responsible for this, rather than any preference of my own.
>
> (1895, 160)

These words express Freud's complex stance toward the revolutionary aspects of his revelations, which were profound but not necessarily in accordance with the scientific zeitgeist of his time.

The genre of the case study originally strived to offer a scientific observation of the analytic process, but the text can by no means avoid the subjective point of view, for the process by its very essence strives for subjectivity and the creation of the subject. The case study genre, therefore, at its core, represents a bold turning away from the empirical dogma of the objective scientist and a movement toward hermeneutics, wherein the psychoanalyst resembles an investigator of ancient texts and forgotten languages; *this* investigation, however, cannot be carried out without the active participation of the analysand.

Today, psychoanalytic writing is explicitly situated between referential writing, which remains loyal to the actual events that took place, and fiction. The final text of a case study contains aspects of the psychodynamics of the analysand in the context of the analytic encounter and of the analyst's psychodynamics, as well as the working through of these aspects as processed in the analytic encounter and its transformation into text (Ogden 2005). The case study is therefore the product of a complex and vast work of translation, first from the inner discourse of the analysand to the analytic discourse created with the analyst, and then from the analytic discourse to text.

The case study is obligated to tread a path between the referential and the fictional, the actual and the fantasmatic, the ethical demand for truth and the need to tell a story. The referential aspect of the case study entails a loyalty to the need to give voice to the patient's narrative. The fictional aspect of the text reveals the analytic experience in its emotional and sensual richness, which cannot be delivered using facts. Hermeneutic readings of Freud's classical case studies allow us to evaluate their multi-layered richness, including the intertextual links they create with other genres (Cohn 1999). I want to suggest that although Freud's intention was to offer a narrative, in which the source of pathology is revealed in full through psychoanalysis, the texts that were finally produced expressed a complex matrix of points of view on different subjects in various contexts. The analytic process is presented as a work of art woven together from the threads and patches of its various narratives and interpretations. What the case study offers is not, finally, a mimetic documentation of the therapeutic process but rather a translation into text of continuous chains of events, experiences, and interpretations. In the work of translation offered in the case study, the biographical narrative of the analysand is reconstructed and the subject is transformed and re-created as a protagonist. The analyst is also transformed in the process of writing, becoming the author of the analysand's biography. In this respect, the case study always contains both biographical aspects of the analysand-protagonist and autobiographical aspects of the analyst-author (Anderson 2001, 60–65).

Analytic narratives from the patient's point of view

In the early days of psychoanalysis, the crucial assumption about authorship was that there is a certain truth in the psychic cure, and that this truth is held by the analyst. The analyst conveys this truth to the patient in the analytic setting and to the broad scientific community in writing. Contemporary relational psychoanalysis no longer seeks the truth as an ontological entity; instead, the truth that is sought is a relational entity created in the intersubjective experience of exploration. As a result, there has been a vast development in the thematic and stylistic aspects of contemporary case studies, mainly in relation to the importance of psychic transformation to the experiential and intersubjective aspects of the process, as well as the mutual aspects of the transference relationship. Nevertheless, the literary transformation of the analytic process is still loyal to the classical assumption, continuing to offer a narrative written by only one of the two participating subjects.

A crucial concept in the examination of the analysand's writing is the concept of voice. As pointed out by Ogden (1998), psychoanalytic literature is profoundly and consistently devoted to the development of the self, in the sense of the psychic potential of the subject. The concept of voice, on the other hand, which can be understood as the actualization of the self in active expression, has been overlooked. Voice is the experience of the self as created in the act of speech and includes the collection of linguistic expressions of the self; voice is "the way the self is created through the use of language" (428). So, in contrast to thought, which has the familiar quality of an inner experience, the voice we use for talking and writing has a quality of otherness. A person experiences his or her own speaking differently from how that person experiences his or her own thought. Speaking and writing therefore create a unique experience of attention to the self, of listening and reflecting. This different experience invites new questions in regard to voice, including: How do I sound? Is this how I want to sound? What makes me sound this way? In contrast to the self, which is evaluated as being true or false, voice is evaluated in terms of the extent to which it expresses a live experience, the extent to which its use of language awakens lost or repressed experiences. Both the analytic setting and writing offer the conditions in which a subject can hear herself or himself speak, sometimes for the first time: "in the very act of speaking, inner was becoming outer, thinking was becoming talking, unthinkable context was becoming thinkable content, experience was being turned inside out" (Ogden 2009, 147).

These ideas call for a unique and distinct language created between analysand and analyst in the analytic setting. This language is a mutual creation, constructed from the various languages of both participants and a new language that is created in the process of exploring the unconscious and of psychic transformation. The notion of a distinct and unique language created in analysis raises intriguing questions: What happens to it after the analysis ends, after the analytic couple separates? What happens to it in a new relationship that the analysand creates (an intimate relationship, a new analysis)? What happens to it after the analyst dies, and after the analysand dies? Is this language forgotten, extinct, does it disappear?

After the analysis terminates, the analysand faces the challenge of preserving and continuing the process of psychic transformation without the actual daily encounter with the analyst. In terms of language, this challenge can be articulated in the questions: How can one promise the continuation of the language created in psychoanalysis? How can one continue to think and speak it? What linguistic transformations does the termination of analysis create? And How can it remain alive? These questions occupied me in my reading of the writing of Freud's analysands: in other words, to what extent do these texts express the private language created between Freud and the authors, any late understandings and interpretations, and a translation of the messages received from him?

One of the fascinating transformations offered in these texts is the movement from the position of analysand and reader to the position of author. This transformation holds dialectic qualities, for, on the one hand, it continues and resonates with the affinity between literature and psychoanalysis, as well as with Freud as a father figure, and, on the other hand, it serves as an act of differentiation and even subversion. The analysands' writing continues the psychoanalytic striving to create and recreate new and forgotten languages. The analytic language is distinct from everyday language in its loyalty to the exploration of the unconscious not only thematically, but also in the attention given to the various and mysterious ways the unconscious reveals itself, as Freud writes in *Fragment of an Analysis of a Case of Hysteria*:

> He that has eyes to see and ears to hear may convince himself that no mortal can keep a secret. If his lips are silent, he chatters with his fingertips; betrayal oozes out of him at every pore. And thus the task of making conscious the most hidden recesses of the mind is one which it is quite possible to accomplish.
>
> (1905a, 77–78)

In articulating the first law of psychoanalysis, Freud makes a pivotal distinction between psychoanalytic communication and ordinary conversation,

> You will notice that as you relate things various thoughts will occur to you which you would like to put aside on the ground of certain criticisms and objections. You will be tempted to say to yourself that this or that is irrelevant here, or is quite unimportant, or nonsensical, so that there is no need to say it. You must never give in to these criticisms, but must say it in spite of them—indeed, you must say it precisely *because* you feel an aversion to doing so … say whatever goes through your mind.
>
> (Freud 1913a, 135, emphasis in original)

Freud describes this unique kind of communication using the well-known yet inspiring image of the train journey: "Act as though, for instance, you were a traveler sitting next to the window of a railway carriage and describing to someone inside the carriage the changing views which you see outside" (ibid.). The patient then "reads" this opening text that he or she receives from the analyst and offers back the patient's own private translation of it, according to the patient's inner world, thoughts, memories, fantasies, and linguistic expressions. Thereafter, both participants dedicate themselves to the reading and interpreting of the various texts the analytic encounter offers them. Transforming the analytic process into a story by writing can be understood as a continuation of these mutual processes of reading and writing, expressing and interpreting, while retranslating reminiscences from analysis and the author's history.

Writing, in the literary-textual sense, has to do with leaving a mark, one that remains alive even after the author disappears. Writing the story of analysis has to do with creating a record of the analytic process and its implications, so that even long after the process is terminated, it still leaves a mark. Writing promises the everlasting existence of analysis and of the specific language created in the analytic process (Amir 2014, 2018).

In the specific context of the memoirs written by Freud's analysands, the transformation from the patient's and reader's position to the author's position also has a revolutionary aspect. This has to do with Freud's position as the ultimate father figure. For them, the movement to the author's position can be understood as a transformation from their passive admiration toward Freud, as his analysands and readers, to the active subjectivity of the author. The writing of the analysand can be regarded, therefore, as minor literature, as described by Deleuze and Guattari, in terms of the search for a distinct literary voice. This voice is destined to be muted within the existing major literature, and it therefore faces an ontological challenge. The breakthrough of minor literature from the known canon is a political act that changes existing power relations. Because of the subversiveness of the analysand's writing, it should be emphasized that its value lies not only in the innovative point of view it offers. This literature should also be evaluated in terms of expressing the unexpressed, speaking the muted, representing the unrepresented, and drawing attention to various blind spots in the obvious. In evaluating the unique literature of Franz Kafka, Deleuze and Guattari state the following:

> We might as well say that minor no longer designates specific literatures but the revolutionary conditions for every literature within the heart of what is called great (or established) literature. Even he who has the misfortune of being born in the country of a great literature must write in its language, just as a Czech Jew writes in German, or an Ouzbekian writes in Russian.
> (1986 [1975], 18)

This definition of the analysand's literature as minor may come as a surprise, for psychoanalysis identifies itself with the continuous and determined striving to dig beneath the obvious and common foundations of language, politics, and culture, and with an aspiration toward the wild, the repressed, and the condemned. In this respect, a paradox is revealed here in terms of the concepts of major and minor literature: if psychoanalytic literature in general can be understood as minor, in the expression it offers to the dark, repressed, and muted aspects of human life, can the analysand's literature be regarded as the minor literature that stems from within the major literature? I want to argue that it is exactly this representation of psychoanalysis as revolutionary and minor that contributes to the ongoing avoidance of any investigation into the analysand's literature, and possibly of other questions of authorship arising in the psychoanalytic context.

Deleuze and Guattari stress the uneasiness that characterizes the encounter with minor literature, as compared with major literature, which is so commonly read and referenced:

> The problem of minor literature, but also a problem for all of us: how to tear a minor literature away from its own language, allowing it to challenge the language and making it follow a sober revolutionary path? How to become a nomad and an immigrant and a gypsy in relation to one's own language? Kafka answers: steal the baby from its crib, walk the tightrope.
> (Deleuze and Guattari 1986 [1975], 19)

According to the two scholars, this uneasiness, which tempts the reader to avoid the work, is an opportunity for a new point of view, an innovative dialect, moving us away from the usual way in which we look at and respond to events and phenomena. I want to stress here, again, that I am not referring to any lack of literature written by analysands, but rather to the lack of regard for this literature as relevant to our understanding of psychoanalysis. These texts have been treated as marginal personal narratives, and thus their potential to enrich psychoanalytic literature has been overlooked. The literature of the analysand can therefore be regarded as minor mainly because of its distinctly minor place within the major language of psychoanalysis. This literature can be regarded as the product of a struggle, a literature that by its very existence offers a voice to the muted and a representation to the unrepresented, a voice who's very muting itself has been overlooked.[1]

The six memoirs that stand at the center of the present book were published from the 1950s through the 1970s. They were all written by patients of Freud, and the author's analytic encounter with him stands at the center of each in one way or another. All six books were published after Freud's death in 1939, but the temporal relationship between their publication and the analysis was different for each. Four of the writers were American psychiatrists who were privileged to be accepted into analysis with Freud and came to live in Vienna for this purpose. These analyses were defined as didactic, as a continuation of the analytic training of these psychiatrists. Because Europe was the only place where didactic analysis took place until the 1930s, the American professionals had to travel to Europe in order to complete their training. The four American doctors were in analysis with Freud between the 1920s and the 1930s, after they had gathered the necessary recommendations and capital in each case. Loyal to the tradition of psychoanalytic writing, the four texts written by them bear the imprint of the case study genre. Nevertheless, each of the texts tells a different story of a unique personal encounter with Freud.

The first of these books to be published was *Fragments of an Analysis with Freud* (1954), by Joseph Wortis. This is a remarkable text in terms of the criticism it expresses of psychoanalysis in general and of the encounter with Freud specifically. Wortis was also the only one among the group of American psychiatrists who did not finally pursue psychoanalytic training. It may be that it was his professional position as an outsider to the psychoanalytic community that made it possible for him to publish his controversial memoir of Freud relatively early. The three subsequent books were published approximately two decades after Wortis's book, and these memoirs, in contrast to Wortis's, are characterized by a sympathetic tone toward their well-known psychoanalyst. The second book published was *Diary of My Analysis with Sigmund Freud* (1971), by Smiley Blanton. This book consists of a diary that was written during analysis and later edited, with the intention of publishing it as a memoir of Freud, but Blanton never accomplished his goal, and the book was eventually published by his wife. The third book, *My Analysis with Freud: Reminiscences* (1977), was written by the relatively well-known New York psychoanalyst Abram Kardiner, following a series of interviews he gave in the 1960s. The last and the least known of the books written by the American psychiatrists is John Dorsey's *An American Psychiatrist in Vienna, 1935–1937, and His Sigmund Freud* (1976). This book offers a retrospective reading by the author of the diary he kept during analysis.

There are two other important books in the collection of books written by Freud's patients presented here, in addition to the four just mentioned. The first, *The Wolf-Man by the Wolf-Man*, was written by Sergei Pankejeff, known as the Wolf Man, and appeared in 1971 under the name of its editor, Muriel Gardiner. "The Wolf Man" is the name Pankejeff received in the world of psychoanalysis from the famous case study written about him by Freud, *From the History of an Infantile Neurosis* (1918). The pairing of Freud's text with Pankejeff's offers an intriguing look at a historic analysis from two different points of view. The double narrative of the Wolf Man's analysis offers us an opportunity to examine a pivotal and historic analytic process that occurred in the first years of psychoanalysis and the relationship that the relatively minor text written by the patient creates with the canonical text of the analyst. And last but not least in the collection of texts written by Freud's patients is *Tribute to Freud* (1974), by the poet and author Hilda Doolittle, known as H. D. This remarkable book is written as a quest for a new and distinguished poetic voice. The writer reconstructs her memories from the analytic encounter and recreates them in the literary sphere. Thus, a dialectic connection is created between the analyst–analysand relationship and the author–addressee or protagonist. For H. D., the act of reconstructing the past inevitably involves recreation.

In recent decades, innovative hermeneutic readings of the classical psychoanalytic case study have been offered. These readings consider psychoanalytic literature and the case study as literature that was influenced by ancient literature (Lev Kenaan 2019; Armstrong 2005), and by modern literary genres such as the detective story (Brooks 1984, 264–285; Nägele 1987, 14). Linda Anderson (2001) presents Freud's case studies as a cornerstone in the development of the autobiographical genre. She reads the case study as a genre that labors under the conscious premises of the text itself. The classical case study strove to present a scientific record and an exemplum of an analytic process from the analyst's point of view, but a modern reading of it shows that the narrator's point of view is far from objective:

> Freud became a novelist, or at least a short story writer, despite himself, and a short story writer, we may add, of a particularly modernist bent. In order to tell his patient's story and interpret it, Freud is forced to tell a story of his own, one which necessarily implicates him as narrator/author. If the theory is that the patient should in the end come into possession of their own story, what the case histories demonstrate is a more ambiguous and inconclusive dialog between the patient's version and Freud's own.
>
> (62)

According to this interpretation, the classical case study offers a complex dialog between two subjects as well as a dialog between the subjects' expectations, fantasies, and unconscious, and the actual events that took place. What was intended as the analysand's biography turns out to be the analyst's autobiography. The patient's story, as presented in the case study, is limited to the part of that story that is seen through the eyes of the analyst. The analyst's point of view is limited, as is every singular point of view.

The writing patient can be seen as the silent literary participant in this psychoanalytic discourse. From a literary point of view, the patient is the muted subject whose voice is heard only as a borrowed voice created by the analyst. But if we pay attention to the texts written by the patients themselves, giving them new readings as texts situated on the periphery of the discourse, we can see them as offering psychoanalysis an innovative point of view, one that is less obligated to the norms of psychoanalytic writing and which, in various ways, creates a new language.

It is worth asking why memoirs about Freud written by his patients have been mostly overlooked by literary and psychoanalytic research. Rather than being considered as a distinguished corpus, they have generally received only individual readings, or even partial readings of specific aspects, usually concerning what we can learn from them about Freud as an analyst. The main research on a collection of texts written by Freud's patients was Beate Lohser and Peter M. Newton's *Unorthodox Freud*, published in 1996 (one can also add the reading offered by Luciana Nissim Momigliano, in her 1987 paper, which offered an intriguing yet personal reading of some of Freud's patients' texts). Lohser and Newton's book centered on a primary reading of this otherwise neglected collection. Nevertheless, the reading offered by the researchers treated these texts as possessing mainly documentary value, as a record of how Freud worked. The main focus of their research was therefore a new look at Freud's technique, based not on how he presented it in his own writing but on how he actually applied it as depicted by his patients. This choice of focus also led to a decision to limit the selection of texts examined to those that actually describe Freud's analytic setting. This limitation led to the omission of Pankejeff's intriguing memoir, which, for reasons I discuss later, does not offer a detailed description of how Freud worked with him. The main thing that is neglected in the readings offered in *Unorthodox Freud* is the essence of these texts as narratives that create a literary representation of the psychoanalytic experience, and that do that by providing an innovative point of view. They express the narrator's process of transformation from analysand into author, who has the authority to tell the story from the narrator's own point of view.

The patients' memoirs that I examine here are historically significant, as they bring to life analytic processes as practiced when they were first created, and by their founder himself. These texts open up a world of experience, pointing to the uniqueness of the analytic encounter in the early days of psychoanalysis. All the writers came to Vienna as foreigners; analysis demanded both personal and professional sacrifices. The analysis involved five to six sessions a week, and their whole lives revolved around it. They had to leave their homes and their work, collect the necessary funds, and move to a temporary residence in Vienna for at least a couple of months, sometimes even years. Freud's patients developed a particular shared culture, including meetings with other patients in cafés and participation in cultural and psychoanalytic events. The memoirs reflect the patients' sense of having been part of a historic moment, at the birth of an essential new discipline. Most of the texts are dominated by the authors' appraisal of Freud as an extraordinary analyst, scientist, and trailblazer.

Psychoanalysis, translation, and writing

These narratives written from the patients' point of view can be seen as works of translation. The transformation of the analytic experience into a literary narrative involves a translation from the language of the analytic experience into autobiographical literature.

Translation served Freud as a pivotal metaphor for the psychoanalytic process, which he represents in his writing as a work of translation from the unconscious realm into consciousness. He sees the analytic work of translation as an intrapsychic introspective process, as well as an interpersonal process taking place within the analytic dyad (Priel 2003). This is how he uses the metaphor of translation to describe psychoanalytic work: "We fill in what is omitted by making plausible inferences and translating [the unconscious] into conscious material. In this we construct, as it were, a sequence of conscious events complementary to the unconscious psychical processes" (Freud 1938, 159). It is only through conscious language that unconscious language can be brought to consciousness. This transformation from unconscious to conscious occurs through psychoanalytic interpretation, which offers a translation of the unconscious language.

The image of the revelation of the unconscious as a work of translation appears constantly in Freud's writing and is connected to the notion of *Nachträglichkeit*, translated as deferred action, afterwardsness, or *après coup*. This concept first appears in a letter from Freud to Wilhelm Fliess, dated December 6, 1896. There he expresses his new insights on the seduction theory:

> I am working on the assumption that our psychical mechanism has come into being by a process of stratification: the material present in the form of memory-traces being subjected from time to time to a *re-arrangement* in accordance with fresh circumstances—to a *re-transcription*.
> (Freud in Laplanche and Pontalis 1973 [1967], 112, emphasis in original)

Jean Laplanche (1924–2012) and Jean-Bertrand Pontalis (1924–2013), in their wide-ranging project *The Language of Psycho-Analysis*, offer the following definition of *Nachträglichkeit*,

> [A] term frequently used by Freud in connection with his view of psychical temporality and causality: experiences, impressions and memory-traces may be revised at a later date to fit in with fresh experiences or with the attainment of a new stage of development. They may in that event be endowed not only with a new meaning but also with psychical effectiveness.
> (111)

Later, they add that "the first thing the introduction of the notion does is to rule out the summary interpretation which reduces the psychoanalytic view of the subject's history to a linear determinism envisaging nothing but the action of the past upon the present" (111–112). *Nachträglichkeit* illustrates the hermeneutic aspect of Freudian thought, wherein the past is continuously interpreted, constructed, and retranslated by present interpretations. This concept can be understood as a delayed discharge, as suggested in the translation "deferred action," offered by James Strachey in the *Standard Edition*. Laplanche and Pontalis point out that for Freud, *Nachträglichkeit* means a real working over, a "work of recollection" that is not the mere discharge of accumulated tension but a complex set of psychological operations (ibid., 114). This notion appears in *Studies in Hysteria*: "Every day [the patient] would go through each impression once more, would weep over it and console herself— at her leisure, one might say" (Breuer and Freud, 1895, 162). The very act of recollection involved in *Nachträglichkeit* carries with it the process of remembering, re-experiencing, mourning, and consoling. The reliving of the past allows it to be translated as a new yet familiar experience, which gives the subject the leisure of experiencing the self in new contexts.

Nachträglichkeit is a concept that deals with the relationship between past and present and between experience and recollection. Translation theories draw similar lines of thought, as they deal with the relationship between the mother tongue and foreign languages and between the original text and the translated text. The French hermeneutic philosopher Paul Ricoeur (1913–2005) suggests an understanding of the translator's work as situated between two masters: author and reader; self and other. Translation, for Ricoeur, resembles the psychoanalytic "working through" (*Durcharbeitung*) in that it involves both the work of memory and the work of mourning. All translation involves some aspect of dialog between self and stranger and therefore demands the memory of both the original text in its original language and the language of translation. At the same time, translation requires us to acknowledge the finite limits of language and the multiplicity of different tongues. Ricoeur follows Walter Benjamin (1892–1940), in his classic essay "The Task of the Translator" (1968 [1955]), on the importance of loyalty to the language into which the text is being translated. In contrast to Benjamin, he does not find the search for a pure language fruitful. For him, translation represents and expresses the inevitable gap between languages and between self and other, both within and outside the self.

The work of memory, or remembering, is defined by Ricoeur as follows: "this work, which one can also liken to a parturition, is concerned with the two poles of translation. In one way, it attacks the view that the mother tongue is sacred, the mother tongue's nervousness around its identity" (2006 [2004], 4). Ricoeur uses the psychoanalytic understanding of resistance, expressing the inhibitions to allow the return of the repressed, for thinking about the challenge of translation. In psychoanalysis, the repressed is experienced dialectically as familiar and foreign, foreign because it is situated in the unconscious and familiar because of its archaic roots. In analogy to the work of remembering involved in translation, resistance means "this deceitful refusal to have the language of reception subjected to the test of the foreign" (5). The translated text is therefore experienced as familiar–foreign, as translation maintains a tight affinity with the original text and, at the same time, bears a transformation of it, a transformation that creates ambivalence: "On the psychological level, the translator is ambivalent. He wants to force the two sides, force his language so that it is filled with incongruity, force the other language so that it is interned [*se dé-porter*] in his mother tongue" (Berman 1984, in

Ricoeur, 8). Translation has a dialectic essence, for it bears with it a quality of uniting and giving birth with fragmenting and mourning. The work of memory in translation touches the conflict between fidelity and treason in relation to language, which the translator struggles to overcome: "the work of translation, won on the battlefield of a secret resistance motivated by fear, indeed by hatred of the foreign, perceived as a threat against our own linguistic identity" (23).

The melancholic recognition of the inherent foreignness present in every essence brings Ricoeur to the work of mourning involved in translation, mourning "applied to renouncing the very ideal of the *perfect translation*" (23, emphasis in original). The perfect translation is based on the "messianic expectation" (9) of pure language. It follows the archaic fantasy of perfection and familiarity in order to avoid the painful acknowledgment of the inherent gaps between languages, which is also the internal breakage of language. Clinging to the universal ideal and the denial of the foreign leads, paradoxically, to narrowing the familiar, to the verge of suffocation:

> Recaptured universality would try to abolish the memory of the foreign and maybe the love of one's own language, hating the mother tongue's provincialism. Erasing its own history, the same universality would turn all who are foreign to it into language's stateless persons, exiles who would have given up the search for the asylum afforded by the language of reception. In short, errant nomads.
>
> (9–10)

The work of mourning, involving recognition of the untranslatable and the foreign foundation inherent in all language and between languages, eventually holds an enriching potential. The challenge of accepting the foreign brings with it the reward of "the recognition of the impassable status of the dialogicality of the act of translating" and "the happiness associated with translating" (10). Alongside the inherent gap between self and other in the linguistic realm, the desire to translate is given partial satisfaction in "linguistic hospitality," "where the pleasure of dwelling in the other's language is balanced by the pleasure of receiving the foreign word at home, in one's welcoming house" (10).

Thinking about psychoanalysis and translation evokes the image of psychoanalysis as a quest for language. Psychoanalysis seeks psychic cure through the process of revealing the unconscious. Yet the unconscious can, paradoxically, only be revealed in the medium of consciousness. Thus, the search for the language of the unconscious is actually a search for an innovative language that can in some way speak this reservoir of memories, experiences, and thoughts hidden in the unconscious. The work of translation inevitably involves mourning the fantasy of wholly revealing the psyche, historically and dynamically, and also the fantasy of being wholly known by the psychoanalyst. The challenge of accepting foreign aspects of self and other, which forever remain somewhat obscure, allows a genuine and pleasurable acquaintance with, acceptance of, and intimacy with self and other.

These ideas may be linked to the intriguing fact that Freud's analysands who wrote about their analysis and published their texts were all foreigners in Vienna. As mentioned, they had all had to leave their homes and familiar habitats in order to undergo analysis with Freud. The foreign aspects of the encounter with Freud were even more salient for his American patients. Freud's dislike of and contempt for American culture was well-known. In the years after his 1909 visit to the United States, Freud used to express this contempt bluntly, even directly, to his American patients, as will be shown later. Freud was also impassioned about the German language and, even though he spoke impeccable English, he had a heavy accent and would express his annoyance at the necessity of holding analysis in English with his foreign patients. He would also express his pleasure when a foreign patient knew German and would demand mostly facetiously, but with some seriousness, that the patient learn the language as quickly as possible. Moreover, these foreign patients were also experiencing the challenge of entering the analytic process, with the intensity of its six sessions a week, in the greatly heightened context of foreign surroundings, far from their family and friends, professional community, and known culture. The patients who wrote these memoirs had to dedicate their time to the encounter with psychoanalysis and Freud, learning the new language of the field and putting effort into free association, dream documentation, and self-reflection, either alone or with other patients. Analysis thereby became their temporary home, and their transference to Freud included a transference to the encounter with Vienna and Viennese culture. Thus, the familiar–foreign aspect already present in every encounter was much more profound in the case of Freud's foreign writing analysands.

The reading I offer in this book of the collection of texts written by Freud's patients is based on the notion that this distinct literature can be seen as a work of translation of the analytic experience, which includes the work of memory and the work of mourning. I refer to the work of memory because this collection of texts can be understood as a return to the analytic experience, offering it a new life or a new voice in retrospect. The essence of the work of remembrance for Ricoeur is the rebirth of experience in a new medium, context, or perspective. This innovative platform of expression inevitably gives rise to new and previously obscure meanings. The essence of writing about the analytic experience is reviving reminiscences, including the inevitable resistance to the return of the repressed. Resistance arises as a result of the familiar–foreign quality of memory, familiar because it is the writer's own narrative that the writer is creating, and foreign because the process of writing is understood as a recreation of memory in a new medium. This recreation embodied in the text includes familiar and unfamiliar layers of experience, obscure meanings, and repressed memories. The work of mourning that is part of translation refers, as we have seen, to the inherent foreignness involved in the encounter with the other. The other exists outside the self but also inside it; therefore, otherness is an inevitable part of every encounter and essence. Nevertheless, the self primarily reacts to otherness with anxiety. The other is in essence an obscure and undeciphered foreigner, and thus the encounter with the other means an encounter with the self's limitations of knowledge and acquaintance.

The collection of texts written by Freud's patients situates Freud at its center and is therefore a collection of memoirs about him. The work of mourning embodied in the text is expressed in aspects of the transference relations that were not worked through in analysis. As a figure of transference, Freud occupies a central position in the analysand-authors' lives and plays a crucial role in their expectations of growth and health. Freud's presence, which signifies the parent in childhood, is represented in their writing as having a familiar–foreign quality, expected and surprising, gratifying and frustrating, known and enigmatic. This paradoxical presence of Freud as a protagonist in the patients' memoirs represents the two dialectical poles of selfness and otherness.

In Jean Laplanche's conceptualization, translation is the basis for the formation of unconscious processes and the psychoanalytic dialog (1999). The communication between parent and child is built on what Laplanche conceptualizes as messages that are enigmatic for both participants. They are enigmatic because of their libidinal source and seductive quality, and translation is the child's attempt to bind aspects of the adult's enigmatic messages. This process is always incomplete, and its remainders are constitutive of the unconscious; that is, the untranslatable aspects of the adult messages are repressed. Laplanche addresses the deterministic and hermeneutic aspects of psychoanalysis, adding to them a third aspect, "the message of the other person" (265). The analyst's interpretations are carried out on already translated contents. The transference thus involves the analysand's attempt to decipher the analyst's enigmatic messages both in realtime and in a series of *après coup* attempts. The analytic experience is thereby presented as an endless work of translation (Birksted-Breen 2010). This intriguing line of thought is profound for the reading of texts written by analysands, following the point of view that sees them as works of translation of the analytic process. The familiar–foreign encounter in the analytic setting with Freud invited communication that included enigmatic messages.

The patients' narratives tell the story of a literary voice evolving through the process of writing about the analytic experience and the work of translation involved in writing. The work of translation is especially valuable for the process of working through separation, because separation is the breaking point of independence for the patient, and the termination process that continues after analysis ends is, at least partially, undertaken individually. The abruptness of the separation in analyses conducted by Freud and the incompleteness of his understanding or recognition of its psychic implications made this working through even more challenging.

The theories of translation proposed by Ricoeur and Laplanche suggest that the analysands' writings are works of translation in three ways: a translation of the analytic experience as a reconstruction of the past (the work of memory); a translation of the termination phase of analysis, including the residues of unresolved conscious transference, which may have been strengthened by the short term of the process and the abrupt separation (the work of mourning); and, finally, an attempt to translate and decipher Freud's enigmatic messages, which were repressed during analysis and aroused again later, in *Nachträglichkeit*.

In this book, I present this literary collection as a work of translation in which analysis is represented as a mythical womb that nourishes the predeveloped parts of the psyche and gives them new life. In this unique process of birth, labor becomes a never-ending process of psychological meanings. Freud serves at the same time both as the symbolic mother figure who carries the patient as an embryo and delivers it into the world and as the father figure against whom the patient needs to rebel in order to accomplish independence and self-fulfillment. After the separation from Freud, the termination of the analysis, and Freud's own subsequent death, his patients continued to speak with and relate to him. Their writing expresses their desire to relive the analytic encounter, to develop and transform it. In this respect, the main addressee of these texts is Freud, and the texts themselves represent the fantasy of reuniting with him in the literary sphere.

I now turn to a reading of the six memoirs written by Freud's analysands. Each chapter involves its own distinct narrative of psychoanalysis and encounter with Freud. The reading offered here will take an intimate and thorough look into each narrative, following the ideas presented in this introduction. In the closing chapter, these ideas will be discussed together from a broader standpoint.

Note

1 Although Freud tended to encourage his student analysands to put down their analytic thoughts in writing, he also recommended, and sometimes even demanded, that they avoid keeping an analytic journal. As H. D. notes in her memoir (H. D. 1974, 185, 187). Another example of this kind of discouragement is D. W. Winnicott, who regarded Margaret Little's writing during analysis as an expression of her false self. In his "Mind in Its Relation to the Psycho-Soma," Winnicott describes the patient's cessation of keeping a diary as the result of an analytic achievement: "It happened that on the day on which this work reached its climax that patient stopped writing her diary. This diary had been kept throughout the analysis, and it would be possible to reconstruct the whole of her analysis up to this time from it. There is little that the patient could perceive that has not been at least indicated in this diary. The meaning of the diary now became clear—it was a projection of her mental apparatus, and not a picture of the true self, which, in fact, had never lived till, at the bottom of the regression, there came a new chance for the true self to start" (Winnicott 1949, 251–252); Little did not finally publish her analytic journal until after Winnicott's death (Little 1990).

Chapter 2

Fragments of an Analysis with Freud by Joseph Wortis
Criticism and longing

Introduction to Wortis's *Fragments*

Wortis's memoir of Freud was among the first texts written by an analysand. Whereas most of the memoirs written by Freud's analysands were published in the 1970s, Wortis published his first reminiscences in article form only about five years after the analysis ended and only several months after Freud's death (Wortis 1940). In addition to this agility in publishing, there is another salient and distinct characteristic of this text, and that is its critical tone.

The biggest challenge this memoir presents to the reader is remaining neutral. Its polemical tone and the intensity of the disagreements and disputes described in it almost coerce the reader to take an active part in the struggle and join one side or the other. A more careful look at the text, however, allows other, more obscure voices to be heard. Such a reading of Wortis's memoir will reveal it as a text in which the dominant critical voice against Freud and psychoanalysis overcomes other voices that are also present in the text.

Fragments of an Analysis with Freud was published in 1954, telling the story of the author's analysis, which had taken place approximately two decades earlier, in Vienna, from October 1934 to January 1935. Joseph Wortis (1906–1995) was an American psychiatrist, born in Brooklyn to a family of secular Jewish immigrants. His father was Russian and his mother came from French origins; in their home they spoke English. The memoir, however, does not reveal the author's origins or early history. The story begins when the author is a young student, aged 20. When asked about his childhood in a late interview, he revealed that he had been raised in a neighborhood of Italian and Polish immigrants, "as an orthodox atheist." As a result of this environment, he had "no religious identification" and "very little ethnic identification" (Dufresne 1996, 590–591). After completing his academic education in the United States, Wortis moved to Europe to attend medical school. He graduated in 1932 in Vienna and started his psychiatric internship back in America. At that point, he received a mysterious offer to become an expert in the psychology of sexuality, with an emphasis on homosexuality. He could construct his study program in Europe as he liked and would receive a generous scholarship during that time. This offer was relayed to him by the British doctor Havelock Ellis (1859–1939). The circumstances of the offer were to be handled discreetly and were left out of the memoir. Ellis's biography, published in 1980, reveals that the offer actually came from the widow of a doctor who had taken his own life after hiding his homosexual tendencies. After his death, the widow decided to give money for the promotion of research into and awareness of the subject of homosexuality in the United States (Grosskurth 1980, 417–422). The scholarship afforded Wortis the funds and affiliation to study with the scholars of his choice, and his request was to study with Havelock Ellis in England and with Freud in Vienna. His professional patrons disapproved at first of his wish to seek psychoanalysis, but eventually agreed. Wortis's analysis with Freud started at the beginning of October 1934 and lasted for four months. Wortis then returned to New York but did not pursue psychoanalytic training, a decision that had to do with the fact that he did not receive the expected recommendation from Freud. His time in Vienna did eventually result in recognition for him, however, for bringing insulin shock treatment for schizophrenia from Vienna to the United States. In 1950 he published his first book, *Soviet Psychiatry*. The memoir of his analysis was published four years later. He was the editor of the *Biological Psychiatry Journal* for several decades and published many papers in the field.

The memoir begins with the challenges Wortis faced on being accepted for analysis with Freud: he admits that he was not keen on the area of expertise offered to him, but decided to accept the offer for the opportunity to work with Freud; he faced resistance from his patrons, the American psychiatrist Adolf Meyer and Havelock Ellis, to his request to enter into analysis; and he also had to raise funds to pay for the analysis and leave his home and familiar environment. He emphasizes the hardships he went through in order to meet Freud, and yet the motivation for this goal remains obscure. Other than the general remark that he was intrigued by Freud's thought, the reader is left in the dark with respect to the deeper reasons for Wortis's desire for psychoanalysis. Moreover, the memoir expresses harsh criticism for the field, overall. Wortis presents himself, explicitly, as a solid, objective scientist who is only drawn to psychoanalysis out of intellectual curiosity. And although he asked to go through analysis, Wortis declares that he would have preferred to study psychoanalytic theory with Freud intellectually, not as an analysand. Nevertheless, the memoir reveals that Wortis's desire to remain an objective and neutral scientist, even as an analysand, was not fulfilled, and that the analytic encounter stimulated intense emotional responses in him.

Another factor that contributed to the complexity of the relationship between Wortis and Freud was the complicated nature of the relationship between Freud and Havelock Ellis. Ellis was a British doctor who had won recognition for his research on the psychology of sex. Over the years 1897 to 1928, he published his *Studies in the Psychology of Sex*, a six-volume investigation of the field. When he began his work, he was considered a trailblazer in this innovative field, but as time went on he had to witness a gradual decline in the prestige of his theory, while Freud's theory climbed to the central position. In her biography of Ellis, Grosskurth claims that Ellis's attitude toward Freud came to be governed by competitiveness and jealousy. Ellis had initially seen himself as Freud's colleague, but later began to express explicit criticism of psychoanalysis and especially of its scientific value. In a 1919 paper, Ellis claimed that Freud should not be regarded as a scientist but as an artist (Ellis 1919), and Freud told Wortis during analysis that this paper caused "a great deal of harm to psychoanalysis" (Wortis 1954, 64–65). In her biography of Ellis, Grosskurth shows that crucial developments in Ellis's theory were created as a response to Freud's thought, in an attempt to challenge and dispute psychoanalytic theory (Grosskurth 1980, 291–293, 359–363). Wortis's memoir quotes from letters he received from Ellis during his analysis that reveal Ellis's negative stance toward psychoanalysis and his criticism of his student's wish to enter into an analytic process. As I will show later in more detail, Ellis tended to warn Wortis during his analysis not to trust Freud and to cling to his critical scientific thinking as an analysand.

But these were not the only factors that complicated the encounter between Freud and Wortis from the outset. In the chapter in which Wortis describes the circumstances of his analysis with Freud, he reveals that there had been an earlier, initial exchange between the two that had taken place two years before the actual analysis. This is how it is mentioned in the book: in 1932, Wortis studied medicine in Vienna, and before he left, he wrote to Freud with a request to meet him in person:

> At the end of the summer we moved to Vienna, where I at once wrote to Freud. It was not my first attempt to meet with him. Two years before, after a prolonged residence in Vienna, I had written a note to him, telling him how much helpful stimulus I had from his books and how much I would have liked to meet him before I left, but added that I did not think it right for a student to presume upon the time of so busy a man. He had answered (in German):
> *Thank you for the friendly note, and for your willingness to forego a visit.*
> But this time, under different circumstances, his response was different.
>
> (Wortis 1954, 6–7)

Even though this story is brought up in the text in a matter-of-fact way, I want to suggest that it is by no means minor. Freud's early rebuff of Wortis's request stands in contrast not only to the present "different circumstances," but to Havelock Ellis's response to a similar suggestion from Wortis. Ellis is presented at the outset of the memoir as the "literary and scientific hero" of Wortis's college days (1). Unlike Freud, Ellis had accepted Wortis's invitation immediately and willingly, and since their first encounter the two had kept up a warm and friendly connection. In other words, at the outset of his career, the author had contacted two different people whose writing he had read and admired. The responses he received from both of them, markedly different as they were, remained etched in Wortis's memory, for when asked to construct a plan for the study of homosexuality, he asked to meet and study with both Ellis and Freud.

During his first face-to-face encounter with Freud, Wortis does not mention their previous exchange two years earlier. Nevertheless, the memory of that past refusal structures the relationship with him from its very beginning. Even though it has been emphasized that the professor is very punctual, Wortis arrives at their first encounter late: "This time I kept Freud waiting, for I came a minute late, and noticed him standing at the window looking out to the gate when I passed through" (15–16).

As the meeting progresses, Wortis's ambivalent attitude toward analysis is expressed explicitly and is accompanied by what is described as a conflict of loyalties:

> "I ought perhaps to say at the outset," I told Freud, "that I am acting against Ellis's advice." And I read the passage from Ellis's letter, telling me to follow Freud's *example* rather than his *precept*, and go my own independent way. Freud listened with interest and said, "Ellis, in a fundamental sense, has rejected psychoanalysis."
>
> (16, emphasis in the original)

This last remark refers to Ellis's criticism of Freud, who did not go through analysis himself and carved his own way independently, yet required his students to follow his way as "a Freudian" and become analysands as a prerequisite to becoming analysts (11–12). To his letter to Wortis, Ellis had attached Freud's own letter to Ellis in which he writes that due to his unstable economic state, he cannot offer Wortis a discount (13–14).

Wortis, whether intentionally or unconsciously, attempts to alleviate his conflict of loyalties between Ellis and Freud, and eventually finds himself defending Ellis. His resentment arises as a response to Freud's remark about Ellis's rejection of psychoanalysis, and especially in response to his conclusion that "a man can only accept so and so much of psychoanalysis." He describes his response by saying, "I rather resented the implication that psychoanalysis stood high and perfect, like divine revelation, and only those could share its secrets who enjoyed grace" (17). He expresses his resistance by saying to Freud that it may very well be that in the end he will reject analysis too, "and I may as well say at the outset that the implication that something is wrong with me for that reason is not very agreeable" (17).

Thus, this first encounter between Freud and Wortis does not present a very good prospect for a positive relationship based on trust and intimacy. From the outset, a conflict of loyalties is presented for both of them. Wortis has ties of loyalty to Ellis, his academic father figure, whose attitude toward Freud is complex. Freud, on the other hand, it seems, is attached to his theory and fails to see more deeply into Wortis's criticism or to work through his resistances. This tragic dynamic is repeated time after time in analysis, as expressed in the memoir. Even in their first encounter, the dialog between the two continues in the following way:

> Freud had once written in some essay that those who haven't been analyzed have no right to criticize, and those who are analyzed and then criticize do so because some special sensibilities were stirred. "I shouldn't like that to be said of me," I said. "It could be," said Freud, and he then added, whether in regard to himself or me, I don't know, "It is perfectly natural for a person to defend his own opinions."
>
> (17)

The question of Freud's intention touches on a pivotal complexity in regard to Freud's and Wortis's ability to see the other beneath their own subjectivity. The memoir suggests that for the writer, Freud is an authoritative father figure who wields intellectual and personal power ("I ... had read Freud with fascination and was very eager to meet and work with him," 12), yet expresses condescension and strictness. For Freud, meanwhile, Wortis, besides being his analysand, also represents critical voices from the medical community who doubt the scientific value of his theory.

The first encounter between Wortis and Freud ends with a gesture that prefigures their future relationship. The scene is described as follows: "He rose and gave me his hand, held stiffly, and bent in strangely at the wrist; whether this was a surgical contracture or a mannerism, I did not know. I left" (18). At the time, Freud indeed suffered from some distortion of his wrists, as also documented by Smiley Blanton, another analysand, whose memoir is discussed later in this book (Blanton 1971, 65). What is striking here, in my view, is the contrast between the two interpretations of Freud's bent wrist, between weakness and false nature. Here, Freud's gesture of trust and a new beginning carries with it a message of danger for Wortis.

Resistances in the analytic encounter

The explicit narrative the memoir tells is the story of an analysis that failed. Freud is presented as an authoritative and detached analyst, overly confident in his theory and technique, while Wortis presents himself as a critical and unsatisfied analysand. This narrative is constructed out of dialogs between the two characters, who fail, every time, to create fruitful communication. The impression that the reader takes away is that Wortis is alert to every opportunity to criticize Freud and psychoanalysis. He tells Freud that the interpretations he receives seem far-fetched (40); he criticizes their scientific value and their bourgeois nature (56–77); and he is keen to point out every inconsistency in

Freud's theoretical assumptions. Freud's character, as the protagonist of the text, is ironically constructed, as an elderly and sullen man, hard of hearing, detached from scientific developments, conservative, sensitive to criticism, and keen for money. The author, in contrast, is presented as a talented and promising young man, speaking in the voice of the future and backed up by the scientific community. The moments when Wortis succeeds in getting through to Freud and arousing his anger are presented with explicit satisfaction. For example, one full paragraph of the text is dedicated to a dream interpretation suggested by Freud that revolves around Wortis's alleged wish to skip sessions and thereby also the money he would otherwise have paid Freud for those sessions. This is followed by a sarcastic description of Freud insisting on this interpretation, in response to Wortis's alleged confusion, and finally by Freud, still convinced of his own interpretation, turning to Wortis and checking again with him whether he has sufficient funds (48, 56–77). This description is given in an allegedly objective and neutral tone, but the reader can notice a certain effort to ridicule Freud, his pursuit of funds, and his intolerance of criticism.

At the outset of the analysis, Wortis presents his desire to meet Freud as an intellectual curiosity about the man and his theory. As for self-introspection and revealing his unconscious, Wortis expresses resentment and a lack of interest. In moments of candor, Wortis admits anxiety over possible harm to his functioning and sanity. He expresses his fear of mental illness and the reviving of the dysphoric feelings in which he was absorbed for a short time prior to the analysis. After the first session, he concludes that the analysis "threatened to revive unpleasant introspective thoughts which led me nowhere and hampered my free activity" (22). Even though Wortis was well aware that he would be expected to enter into analysis with Freud, the encounter, with its demand for "a degree of honesty which is unusual and even impossible *in der bürgerlichen Gesellschaft* (in bourgeois society)" (22), leaves him desolate. The reading suggests that the defense that the writer used against psychic turmoil was radical projection: instead of being the subject of analytic research, he is determined to be the researcher, and his object of research will be Freud himself. Writing was thus Wortis's way of giving voice to this unusual choice. For example, after the first session, Wortis is in tremendous discomfort due to his impression of Freud as a figure of great power. He describes his discomfort as a response to the demand to reveal himself, as mentioned earlier, and to

> the unpleasant prospect of developing what Freud called *Widerstand*, or resistance, against him, my present lord and master; who sat in quiet judgement while I talked, like a stern Old Testament Jehovah, and who seems to take no special pains to act with hospitality or reassurance, but had instead needlessly disturbed our friendly association by what seems to me to be an over-emphasis on money matters.
>
> (22)

The great anxiety of the analysand with respect to the demand to look into his psyche, and his intense occupation with self-control, are naturally reflected in great difficulty on his part in free-associating. At the beginning of the analysis, Wortis warns Freud about his inability to be authentic and free in the presence of the other, and especially the authoritative other:

> I said to Freud that it was impossible, I thought, to let my thoughts flow freely, since I was undoubtedly influenced by Freud's presence, and what he brought to mind: sex and neuroses. He made no comment but said I was just to go on.
>
> (24)

A couple of weeks into analysis, Wortis admits that he still finds it difficult to let his thoughts flow freely in the presence of Freud:

> "It seems to me," I said, "a great many things have occurred to me in your presence, and I have said a great many things, because I felt it would *accord* with your ideas or interests. I know you are interested in neurotic material. When I am with a friend who is interested in socialism, for an example, I think and talk socialism with him." "But you ought not to care what I think," said Freud.
>
> (62, emphasis in original)

Freud's lack of insight into Wortis's inability to express himself freely in the presence of the authoritative other creates a tragic impasse in this complex analysis. Wortis has an obscure notion that if he had been able to feel affection from Freud, that might have made it easier for him to reveal himself. In some moments of honesty, he even expresses this notion to Freud. Freud, on the other hand, fails to hear his analysand's wish beneath the dominant voice of criticism and devaluation. Instead, he reprehends Wortis for his continual resistances, insisting that Wortis should not be interested in his analyst's attitude toward him and that their relationship is not a relevant subject for discussion. Freud refuses, rather rigidly, to acknowledge his part in his analysand's stubborn resistances. In response to Wortis's request for a recognition for his abilities, Freud reproaches him for positioning the personal relationship between them at the center of attention. At some point during analysis, Wortis claims that he hears too much criticism from Freud: "I said that, considering what I had heard of myself up to now, I was not inclined to think much of myself" (61). Freud's response is consistent with his general analytic stance toward Wortis: "I had forewarned you at the outset that a neurosis can be revived in an analysis. But the interesting thing is how you turn everything into a judgement on you, as if that were the only thing that mattered." Wortis answers, "I don't like to lower my opinion of myself, without getting something in return." Freud concludes this dialog sharply by saying, "That is not a scientific attitude. You have not yet completed the transition from the pleasure principle to the reality principle." Here, Freud is criticizing Wortis in his own language, which reappraises empirical science. He also continues to maintain an analytic stance of abstinence toward his analysand. When, sometime later, Wortis brings up the importance of the analyst's sympathy in the analytic process, Freud responds severely:

> No. I am glad you brought the question up, because I can clear up the misunderstanding: the positive transference is not part of the psychoanalytic therapy. The psychoanalytic cure consists in bringing unconscious material to consciousness; to this end the positive transference is used, but only as a means to an end, not for its own sake.
>
> (64)

Freud apparently did not keep notes on this analysis, but a documentation of the frustration he felt toward Wortis is expressed in a letter that H. D., who was also in analysis at the time, wrote to a close friend. Speaking of Freud, she writes: "he told me about a new patient that Dr. Ellis had sent—who has been most disappointing—and how was he to have known that Dr. E. would send such a dud?" (H. D. to Bryher, October 30, 1934 [Friedman 2002, 438]). Wortis's memoir describes two occasions on which Freud lost his temper in analysis and invited him to quit the analysis before the scheduled time for termination. On one of these occasions, Freud said to Wortis: "At any rate, up to now I have not been able to tell you anything you didn't know yourself." He then quoted Shakespeare to the effect that "to hear something you already know will never make you wise" (Wortis 1954, 80).

Wortis's memoir suggests that the most challenging moments for Freud are the occasions on which Wortis expresses approval of critical opinions toward psychoanalysis and of people who hold such opinions, such as Havelock Ellis or Wilhelm Steckel, or when he mentions controversial points about psychoanalysis, such as its orientation only toward certain social classes, especially the intellectual and wealthy. Faced with Freud's rage on these occasions, Wortis presents an explicit response of remorse, but the sarcastic tone of the text leaves open the question of whether this remorse is authentic. Freud himself is apparently skeptical of this remorse and tends to ignore it. Freud's outbursts, which are described by Wortis with implicit joy, emphasize the assumption I made earlier that Freud does not understand Wortis's critical stance as being independent from the criticism held in the scientific community of his time. This bias is apparent on these occasions in Freud's difficulty to see Wortis beyond his outward confidence and self-assurance. "You belong to the group of happy people," he says to Wortis in what seems like an ironic tone (45). Later on in analysis Freud becomes more explicit in his hostility, "I have told you the truth to the point of rudeness. It is people like you who are responsible for all the theories that are floating around, and confusing the scientific world" (128). Freud makes explicit the connection he sees between Ellis's and Wortis's criticism, "Ellis has had a bad effect on you, because he spoiled you, because Ellis makes too few judgements, as I told you before, and here you come and feel free to air your opinions in spite of your ignorance" (129).

This dialog of power instead of intimacy leaves the analysis and both of the subjects at an impasse. An example of this tragic dynamic appears in a transference dream that Wortis reports and their different interpretations of the dream:

> I had a dream in which I felt I was going to die from a cancer of my face, and interpreted it in accordance with what I supposed was psychoanalytic theory, by saying that I was feeling injured by the analytic procedure, but Freud thought it meant that I wished he would die from his cancer (for which he had actually already undergone several operations) because of the unpleasant things he said.
>
> (86)

In the dream, Wortis is suffering from the same illness that Freud has in real life, and whereas Wortis emphasizes the injuries caused to him by the analysis, Freud emphasizes the hostility the analysand feels toward his analyst. These interpretations illustrate the shared experience of a hostile relationship with a harmful potential. In this relationship, each person felt as though he was the victim of the other's aggression.

In reading Wortis's memoir, one gets an uneasy impression of tendentiousness behind the regular construction of the narrative. The text invests great literary and rhetoric effort in convincing the reader to see Freud as grotesque and ludicrous. Freud is situated at the center of the text, constantly lit with an intrusive, unflattering light, while the writer remains in the protective shadow of an objective witness. The memoir opens with the following statement: "This is a book about Sigmund Freud and his theories, and not about me"; it continues: "My main purpose is to give a picture of Freud as I saw him, and an account of some of his methods and views." Wortis presents his record as being "accurate and complete" (ix). He then describes his fragile state as an analysand, "being a young man closely influenced by three very distinguished old men, each of whom held to quite distinctive points of view." He refers here to Freud, Ellis, and the American psychiatrist Adolf Meyer, who was also involved in Wortis's scholarship. Because his American mentors "maintained a certain critical detachment from the psychoanalytic movement," Wortis felt at that time "badly battered by the pressures and uncertainties" (ix–x).

Although his emotional state was fragile at the time, the writer states that he does not intend to tell his story from his personal point of view, but from an objective one, "accurate and complete":

> I have no intention of perpetuating the discussion of my own person. If I am to be dissected, I prefer on general humane principles to have it done

as a post-mortem. I also have no wish to achieve distinction by posing naked in the street.

(x)

For the writer, self-reflection and autobiographic writing are interpreted here in a determinedly concrete way, equated with exposing one's genitals. It is therefore only the one subject in the story of this analysis, the explicit protagonist of Wortis's memoir—namely Freud—who is subjected to this kind of exposure.

An interesting interpretation of this aspect of the memoir was presented in a satirical column published on February 19, 1955, in the *New Yorker* by Wolcott Gibbs. The text, *A Couch of My Own*, offers a tragicomic look at Wortis's memoir and presents Wortis as an opportunist, seeking to encounter Freud for the sole purpose of writing a book about him. This aim is soon identified by Freud, who thereafter develops a hostile attitude toward Wortis. Gibbs opens his text with Wortis's supposed text, where he states that his "first few interviews with Dr. Sigmund Freud were not very illuminating." According to his impression, Freud was not in sympathy with his purpose as an analysand, which was to embody his findings in a book for the layman. Freud "made little attempt to hide his distaste." Gibbs's Wortis presents his analysis ironically, not as an analytic process but as a series of interviews. At the end, he concludes that they "were basically unsympathetic," therefore he went home. He concludes that he never returned to Freud, for he had about all he needed for his book at that time. Centering on Freud while putting oneself safely in the shadows is a distinct characteristic of Wortis's text. There still remains an unanswered question, however, regarding the curiosity, even yearning, that Wortis had toward Freud, as evidenced by the fact that he insisted on going through analysis even at the price of being "badly battered" by his American mentors.

Longing for an unattainable object

Between the cracks of the defensive attitude of the writer, there are other, more obscure, voices that enrich the text. These voices express longing for affection and recognition, fragile requests and bitter disappointments. For example, in response to Freud's reprimand over Wortis's sensitivity to criticism, he says, "It was not so much your criticisms I minded, as the feeling that I was not liked" (Wortis 1954, 51). At other times, Wortis lets go of his vexation and intrusive curiosity and expresses regret over their continuous arguments and fighting. For example, he says to Freud toward the end of analysis, "I am sick of fighting, and I don't know why we have so much of it" (158). This question raises a broader question, concerning the pattern of relationships Wortis tends to create in his life, and he says to Freud, "I always seem to find myself too much admired and too seldom liked" (75); and in the following session, "Sometimes I think I may antagonize people on purpose. Maybe I like to fight too much" (78). At these moments of recognition, Wortis promises Freud to change his faulty ways and overcome his "narcissistic conceit" (115): for example: "I promised again to try to be good... 'I will do what I can'" (58–59). Toward the end of the analysis, Wortis expresses his ongoing discomfort over the feeling that Freud does not like him. He says, "Sometimes in the course of this analysis I have become so remorseful, self-reproachful and self-concerned that I was no good for anything" (117).

It is conspicuous that Wortis, as an analysand and as a writer, emphasizes his critical and argumentative voice and only obscurely expresses his fragility and deprivation. This tendency, which serves a defensive role, leaves him continuously deprived of affection. Reading the memoir raises the notion that for Wortis the paternal representation overshadows the maternal one. Even though his actual father is only mentioned briefly toward the end of the memoir, Wortis is constantly preoccupied with father figures and sees his condition as an analysand mainly as being "badly battered" among three distinctive "fathers." In contrast, the maternal representation is salient in its absence: Wortis's actual mother is not mentioned at all, and relationships with women and femininity remain obscure. In this context, a conclusion can be drawn that the dynamic with Freud, with its over-competitiveness and lack of tenderness, reflects a preoccupation with phallic characteristics as a compensation for maternal absence. Thus, deprivation and fragility become associated with humiliation and therefore denied.

Wortis's conflict over his evolving dependency on Freud is presented metonymically through Freud's strong bond with his dog, a chow chow, and its presence in the study: "I lay on the couch, Freud behind me, his dog sitting quietly on his haunches at the foot of the bed... a large dog... a big chow I thought it was ... I didn't notice exactly" (23, ellipses in original). Freud and his chow chow are connected here, creating a somewhat joint persecutory parental representation. The image of Freud and his dog hovering over the helpless Wortis as he lies on the couch continues to occupy him, and he later sends Havelock Ellis a humorous sketch of it: "Our New Year's greetings card carries a rough sketch of myself on the analytic couch with Freud peering over the end and his big chow sitting on his haunches beside us" (132).[1] Freud's bond with his dog also arouses competitiveness for Freud's affection in Wortis, which is soon followed by a feeling of humiliation. For example, Wortis describes himself entering Freud's study:

> Freud's dog, the handsome chow, was in the hall when I came in, and the maid told me it is the Professor's great favorite. "The Herr Professor is very much attached to it," she said; "when the dog doesn't eat, the Herr Professor is unhappy." The dog and I were both admitted at the same time.
>
> (32)

Wortis's sarcastic tone in describing Freud's identification with his dog is evident here. Underneath that tone, one can identify the insult he feels over losing his potential position as Freud's protégé to a dog. It is interesting to note that

Wortis misidentifies the chow as male, in concert with Wortis's denial of the feminine, whereas it was in fact a female chow.

At Wortis's last analysis session with Freud, the two return to one of their favorite subjects of dispute, between socialism or communism on the one hand and capitalism on the other. Wortis was a socialist; Freud, meanwhile, saw socialism as yet another characteristic of the American lack of culture. Freud completely rejected the criticism of psychoanalysis as allegedly representing capitalist or bourgeois values. Moreover, Freud claimed, the prohibition on private property deprives a man of the private space required for creativity. In their last session, as they return to these arguments, Freud speaks of "the necessity of having a private room and the right to be alone occasionally" and adds, "That in itself is enough to make Communism impossible for me." Wortis replies, in an uncharacteristic way, "my father could never enjoy such privacy because he had to work fourteen hours a day all his life in his shop" (165). The dispute over communism, which until this point has been regarded as an intellectual or cultural dispute (Freud even explains their fighting as stemming from cultural reasons, 158), is revealed, on the verge of their separation, as being a very personal debate. Freud confesses his need for solitude and Wortis speaks for the first time of his actual father. For the first time, the reader hears something of Wortis's background, which until now seems to have started at the age of 20, when he was allegedly reborn as a European medical student. This knowledge enriches the complexity of Wortis's relationship with Freud, because it reveals his sense of inferiority and longing in relation to what he experiences as a higher social and intellectual class. Wortis's attraction to brilliant and powerful father figures may have served as a compensation for the inferiority he felt because of his own father. Moreover, the relation to the adopted father figure reveals his inner conflict in regard to inferiority. Paradoxically, the challenging connection with Freud, filled with criticism and fighting, may have aroused his denied identification with the father, who, while he was not an admired intellectual or scientist, was devoted to his children's well-being.[2]

The fantasy of finding a compensating father figure and the conflict this wish arouses are expressed in a dream Wortis brings to this last session. In the dream, Wortis appears as

> saying good-bye to Freud in a friendly informal way. A grandson of [Freud's] in the dream declares his intention of studying medicine, then analysis, but I told him, 'The name of Freud is sufficient. You don't have to do anything more.' In the dream I felt as a schoolboy, and I suggested that the guilt feelings came from the sense that I did not do well in the analysis.
>
> (163–164)

In this dream, which appears on the verge of the termination of the analysis, Wortis allows himself to put aside his armor and, in a relatively explicit way, express his feeling of deprivation and longing for a potent father figure who will lead him on the right path and save him all the hardship involved in carving out one's own path. Moreover, this dream gives expression to a more worked-out form of aggression: his usual attacks on Freud are replaced here by a more developed form of jealousy that is directed in the dream toward Freud's actual descendants. This development allows for authentic regret for not having created the benevolent relationship he had wished for, and thereby failing to receive Freud's affection. For the first time, Wortis's fantasies are revealed authentically and explicitly.

The work of memory and mourning in intertextual contexts

As was discussed in the first chapter, autobiographical writing revolves around the work of memory or remembrance and the work of mourning. In Wortis's memoir, these aspects are revealed through obscure allusions to two canonical texts, which I look at more closely here as a way of enriching the narrative. The first text is Freud's case study *Fragment of an Analysis of a Case of Hysteria*, which recounts an unsuccessful and nevertheless canonical analysis. The second text is the historical memoir *Conversations with Goethe*, by Johann Peter Eckermann; the choice of this text is an obscure expression of Wortis's wish for affection and recognition.

Freud's 1905 case study *Bruchstück einer Hysterie-Analyse* was translated into English as *Fragment of an Analysis of a Case of Hysteria*. Wortis's memoir bears the name *Fragments of an Analysis with Freud*, a literary allusion to Freud's text. The fact that the memoir has a name that is similar to Freud's canonical case study implies an ironic stance toward psychoanalytic literature, because while the case study emphasizes the patient's pathology, hysteria, the memoir's name obscurely implies that the patient's pathology stems from the analytic encounter itself. Moreover, both Dora's case study and Wortis's text tell the story of an unsuccessful analysis. In Dora's case study, Freud concludes:

> Nor is the case of whose history and treatment I have published a fragment in these pages well calculated to put the value of psycho-analytic therapy in its true light. Not only the briefness of the treatment (which hardly lasted three months) but another factor inherent in the nature of the case prevented results being brought about such as are attainable in other instances, where the improvement will be admitted by the patient and his relatives and will approximate more or less closely to a complete recovery.
>
> (Freud 1905a, 115)

And in Wortis's case, Freud wrote a letter to Wortis several months after the termination of analysis, stating, "It is true that your analysis with me was *no immediate success*" (Wortis 1954, 168; the emphasized words were originally written by Freud in English). Furthermore, there lies within both texts an obscure assumption that one of the possible reasons for the unsuccessful analysis was Freud's authoritative stance, the fact that he tended to rigorously insist on a certain line of interpretation and thereby somewhat frustrate his patient. The texts also present similarities between the two patients themselves. In the case study, Dora is presented as a young woman in search of an anchor of stability, and whose caretakers are rather inadequate. Her mother is shown as being preoccupied with obsessive cleaning, while her father obscurely encourages her into a love relationship with a married elder man. Dora is described as an innocent young woman who finds herself prematurely exposed to adult passion, a dynamic that is repeated in Freud's intrusive interpretations (Langs 1976). Wortis obscurely presents himself, similarly, as an innocent young man who is, in analysis, prematurely exposed to interpretations of sexual content that he cannot identify with and yet within which he finds himself imprisoned.

Wortis states at the outset of the memoir that he was determined to meet Freud after finding himself deeply intrigued by his writing, as he had written to Freud two years before their actual first encounter (describing, as mentioned earlier, "how much helpful stimulus I had from his books" [Wortis 1954, 6]), but he does not elaborate on what it was that so deeply intrigued him. I would like to propose an answer to this question. Freud's writing is distinct in the explicit and direct language it uses to express issues concerning sexuality. Freud assesses his assumptions about and articulates his interpretations of sensual and sexual experiences, and, moreover, creates distinct and original ties between sexual life and the dynamics of fantasy and the psyche. He writes about genitals, masturbation, sexual arousal, and seduction in both childhood and adulthood, and even about the greatest taboo, namely incest, both as actual experiences and as fantasies. The use of such explicit language in regard to sexuality and the associations that it creates between the physical and the psychological is one of the pivotal innovations of psychoanalysis. In this context, we are reminded of Wortis's opening statement about his unwillingness to pose naked in the street. As an analysand, Wortis consistently and rigorously rejects interpretations regarding his sexuality. Is it possible that through the obscure allusion to Dora, the text is in fact implying the deep effect that psychoanalysis had on the writer? Is it possible that beneath the conscious condemnation, the possibility of being present in a sphere that allowed open and uncritical speculating about sexuality was therapeutic for him? It should be mentioned that although Wortis explicitly and contemptuously denies sexual interpretations, the text is filled with sexual dreams of his, which tend to include figures from Freud's close circles. For example, in one of his dreams he hugs Freud's governess Paula, and Freud in the dream is "scandalized" (33). The dream may suggest a dilemma about being scandalized, whether it involves Wortis himself being scandalized by the direct expression of sexuality, or Freud being scandalized by his patient's fantasies and lack of inhibitions. The work of memory involved in writing suggests that although the direct language about sexuality and its importance to psychic development has been furiously rejected by Wortis in analysis, it may hold a deep and lasting therapeutic value for him after all.

The memoir *Gespräche mit Goethe* (Conversations with Goethe), by Johann Wolfgang von Goethe's personal editor and assistant, Johann Peter Eckermann, appeared in 1847, a few years after Goethe's death. Eckermann (1792–1854) met Goethe when Eckermann was a poor young poet from an insignificant background and Goethe was already very well-known. The relationship between the two men developed into a tight, profound bond, as Eckermann's memoir suggests. The text opens with the first encounter between the two. At the outset of their relationship, Goethe reads Eckermann's poetry and praises it generously. Soon afterward, Goethe proposes that Eckermann live nearby and serve as his personal editor. The memoir ends with Goethe's death, shortly before which he has asked to leave his last writings in Eckermann's hands. The memoir is woven through with the evolving acquaintance, dialogs, and encounters between the two subjects. Through Eckermann's writing, Goethe is presented as an elderly genius, looking back on his life's achievements and occupied with the question of the eternity of his poetry. These are the years in which Goethe wrote his mature literature, including the second part of *Faust*; his autobiography, *Poetry and Truth*; and *Elective Affinities*; and their writing process is described in the memoir. Eckermann's memoir also suggests his own development and growth (his *Bildung*) from an inexperienced poet into Goethe's editor and personal assistant.[3]

At one point, Wortis's memoir explicitly alludes to Eckermann's canonical memoir. In one of the analytical sessions, the discussion is, characteristically, followed by an argument about the fact that Wortis's curiosity is drawn to Freud instead of to himself. Freud expresses his frustration at Wortis's resistances and suggests that he might end the analytic process immediately ("it may be just as well if we make this our last session," 58). Wortis persuades him not to give up on him, and Freud agrees, but with a warning,

> you ought to be ashamed of yourself for acting that way, grumbling and growling for three days because I said this or that to you. You will have to give up your sensitivity. You ought to understand that I am not interested in passing judgement on you. If I say anything it is only for the sake of the analysis, and you ought not to worry what motives I have.
>
> (58)

As the session continues, on the subject of his curiosity about Freud, Wortis says:

> "I was just curious to know how you approached a problem and tackled it."
>
> "But this is not what an analysis is for," said Freud. "You are not here to get things out of me, wise words and the like; all that has nothing to do with the analysis."

"But it is tempting," I said, "because you are a great man, and I know how interesting Eckermann's conversations were"—an allusion to Eckermann's *Conversations with Goethe*.

I thought there was a brief approving silence at this point, but Freud said, "I am not acting differently from the way any other analyst would act in the same situation, no matter who he was."

(58)

Aside from the explicit motivation of the analysand–writer to write a canonical memoir, as was suggested in Gibbs's satirical text, there is another intriguing analogy between the two relationships. A comparative reading of the two memoirs presents two father–son relationships, each time between an elderly, well-known figure and a young apprentice, approximately four decades younger. The comparison between the two texts reveals interesting parallels.

At the outset of Eckermann's memoir there appears a scene that forms the basis of the deep and long-lasting bond between Goethe and the writer. In the scene, Eckermann asks Goethe to read a manuscript he has written, to which Goethe turns immediately. When he finishes, he returns to Eckermann with the warmest appraisal: "I have just come from *you*. I have been reading your writing all the morning; it needs no recommendation—it recommends itself" (Eckermann 1949 [1836–1848], 10, emphasis in original). Goethe promises to forward the text immediately and ensure its publication. This warmth toward the inexperienced poet arouses in Eckermann the deepest gratitude and affection, enchantment even:

> We sat a long while together, in a tranquil, affectionate mood. I was close to him; I forgot to speak for looking at him—I could not look enough. His face is so powerful and brown! Full of wrinkles, and each wrinkle full of expression! And everywhere there is such nobleness and firmness, such repose and greatness! … I was extremely happy near him; I felt becalmed like one who, after many toils and tedious expectations, finally sees his dearest wishes gratified.
>
> (11)

Wortis's memoir offers a scene that makes intriguing allusions to Eckermann's scene of elevation, yet presents a contrasting experience. One month into analysis, Wortis brings to Freud a manuscript he has written and, as with Eckermann's request to Goethe, Wortis asks Freud to read it:

> I had brought along my Observations of a Psychiatric Interne, an account of my first assignment in a psychiatric hospital, which I thought Freud might want to read, but he politely declined, saying it was bad policy to use written material in an analysis. There was another reason, he added, but he would not tell me now.
>
> (Wortis 1954, 65–66)

When Wortis arrives for the following session, he enters with a feeling of emptiness and no dreams to report, saying to Freud, "It was as if I had tried all night, and brought nothing to light for my pains" (66). I want to suggest that Wortis is obscurely forming his request to Freud in the form of Eckermann's request to his own father figure. The allusion emphasizes the pain of Freud's refusal, which stands in contrast to Goethe's generosity and the positive feelings that aroused in Eckermann. Freud's rigorous adherence to rules on which he does not even adequately elaborate leaves Wortis feeling like an empty vessel, in strong contrast to Eckermann's feeling of enrichment.

Another example of an allusion that Wortis's memoir makes to Eckermann's text is the possibility of the "son" serving as the father figure's assistant and close ally. In *Gespräche mit Goethe*, Eckermann is offered the chance to become Goethe's editor at the very beginning of their relationship, following Goethe's appraisal of Eckermann's writing:

> With respect to poetry and criticism, you are in the best possible condition. You have a natural foundation for them. They are your profession, to which you must adhere, and which will soon bring you a good livelihood.... You shall have the best of everything; because the best means are in my hands. Thus you will have laid a firm foundation for life. You will have attained a feeling of comfort, and will be able to appear anywhere with confidence.
>
> (Eckermann 1949 [1836–1848], 16)

Goethe's proposal embodies all of Eckermann's wishes, and he responds to it whole-heartedly. Eckermann's memoir of Goethe is dedicated to the transformative effect that his acquaintance with Goethe had on Eckermann as a poet and a man. Wortis's memoir offers a completely different kind of acquaintance between Freud and the writer, but an obscure fantasy of the writer's is gradually revealed in the text, namely the wish to receive recognition from "the father"; however, that fantasy remains unfulfilled. For example, in one of the sessions, Wortis expresses his need to become an analyst in order to make a living and gain a better understanding of the field. Freud responds furiously:

> "You know nothing about it—you are just a *bloody beginner*." (Freud used the English phrase) ...
>
> "But I can't unfortunately study forever," I said. "I have a research fellowship and have to do some research of my own. What will I live on otherwise!"
>
> "I recognize all that but it has nothing to do with analysis. You have a right to live, but not as an analyst.... If anybody asked me about a certain

talented Wortis who came to study with me, I will say he learned nothing from me, and I will disclaim all responsibility."

"I don't seem to have made much of a personal success with you," I said.

"Decidedly not," said Freud.

(Wortis 1954, 128)

Wortis is conscious of Freud's affinity with Goethe, and connects to it during analysis. He borrows Goethe's *Collected Works* from Freud's library and speaks about it often during the sessions. The allusions that his memoir of Freud make to Eckermann's classic memoir of Goethe, written a century previously, bring to the surface the tragic aspect of Wortis's analytic encounter with Freud. It is at the end of the same session in which Freud suggests that Wortis should leave the analysis prematurely that Wortis asks whether he could translate one of his works: "For some reason I had occasion to say I would consider it an honor to translate a work of Freud's." Freud rejects the offer immediately and without hesitation, saying: "But everything has been translated already." Wortis does not give up and asks whether he could translate a new work, but Freud rejects this offer as well, saying, "I don't expect there will be any more" (132). This dialog of a fantasized bond and its rejection creates another allusion to Eckermann's memoir, wherein the father figure invites the younger protagonist to be his assistant and possibly an apprentice. With the request to translate the father figure's writing, Wortis may be expressing his fantasy of becoming the intellectual and literary apprentice to the great father figure. The act of writing the memoir on Freud later on could also have been a late fulfillment of this fantasy, although only a partial one, because it was carried out without Freud's consent. This aspect may also give another meaning to the text's vengeful tone, as an expression of the pain and rage of Freud's rejection. On the explicit level, this dialog between Freud and Wortis contributes to the ironic aspect of the analytic relationship, of this dance that never succeeds in finding a mutual and graceful flow. Yet on the obscure level, and given the allusion to Eckermann's memoir, the dialog expresses mourning over unfulfilled fantasies regarding the admired father figure.

The allusion to Eckermann's memoir is an implicit indication of Wortis's fantasy of creating a bond with Freud outside the analytic setting. This fantasy is expressed in one of Wortis's dreams during analysis: "I came upon a scrapbook full of literary essays by an ambitious acquaintance, Dr. B., written under an assumed name. This was an identification with myself for I hoped to write literary essays some time too, perhaps under a pseudonym" (155). Wortis is primarily drawn to Freud as a writer, being deeply moved and impressed by Freud's courage and his potent voice, and was determined to meet him. During analysis, it becomes somewhat clear that it is not introspection or the revelation of his unconscious that he seeks, but to become Freud's literary and intellectual apprentice. Freud's insistence on the analytic setting and on centering their attention on Wortis's thoughts does not accord with Wortis's fantasy and is therefore interpreted by him as intolerable rejection.

The two memoirs both end with the death of the father figure, but they offer two very different, even opposite images of that death. In Eckermann's memoir, Goethe's death is described as a continuation of his benevolent, potent, and enriching presence:

> Stretched upon his back, he reposed as if asleep; profound peace and security reigned in the features of his sublimely noble countenance.... A perfect man lay in great beauty before me; and the rapture which the sight caused made me forget for a moment that the immortal spirit had left such an abode.
>
> (Eckermann 1949 [1847], 394)

Wortis's memoir, in contrast, shows Freud's death as being accompanied by the death of a whole generation of father figures, leaving the generation of sons defenseless and solitary. Soon after Freud, Ellis and Meyer also passed away, and "Schilder, Stekel, Rank, Adler, Brill—all passed on. A new generation of psychiatrists moved forward, with no one to lean upon any longer but themselves" (Wortis 1954, 181).

As a continuation of the allusion to Eckermann's memoir as a work of mourning the writer's unfulfilled fantasy of his encounter with Freud, the allusion to Dora's case study can be understood as a work of mourning the writer's unfulfilled fantasy of becoming his analyst's textual protagonist, of being in the center of his thoughts, doubts, and arguments in the process of writing, possibly as a compensation for an analytic encounter that ended ambivalently and prematurely.

Impasse and a momentary encounter

This chapter has presented Wortis's memoir as a narrative of unfulfilled expectations. On the explicit level, this critical/comic text offers an encounter between an admired and well-known figure who is revealed as conservative, authoritative, and strict, and an intelligent analysand who is much more curious about his analyst's weaknesses than he is interested in revealing his own unconscious. On the implicit level, the text expresses mourning for the analyst and analysand's shared inability to rise above the negative aspects of the transference and work through the hidden fantasies of dependence, which were felt as dangerously harmful to both participants in analysis and brought them continuously to an impasse.

Wortis's text, then, in addition to and beyond his explicit defiance, expresses the work of remembering a bitter and ambivalent analysis. The experience of disappointment and rejection does not leave much space for more complexity on the explicit level. The textual work of mourning finds its expression only obscurely, and must be deciphered beneath the layers of explicit criticism and resistance. Beneath the bitter taste of an encounter that does not evolve into a meaningful meeting of minds, there appears in the text a different scene, which expresses a surprisingly honest dialog. A month after his analysis begins, Wortis receives a letter from Havelock Ellis that saddens him, for in it Ellis "spoke of his failing energies" (70). Freud responds by identifying with Ellis and says to Wortis, "When one is old, what can one expect?" Breaking with the usual criticism and aggression between them, Wortis then continues in the same vein as Freud, saying:

> It is a sad world, everything is topsy-turvy and rotten; all that Ellis stands for is forgotten, and war may come any minute. What has a young man to look forward to? What chance has he to feel he can do useful work against the background of this huge rottenness—this *Scheusslichkeit*?
>
> (70)

Freud expresses his sad consent, and Wortis continues by opening up about "my feelings about being a Jew, my views on Anti-Semitism, and my not infrequent thoughts about death" (70). These are issues that constantly occupied Wortis in analysis but had tended to be brought to the dialog in an argumentative way that created conflict.[4] At this particular moment in the analysis, the two subjects become an analytic couple, a unit of joint thinking and experiencing. In this session, Freud is generous enough to encourage his analysand to enter into the analytic state of mind:

> There was not much more to say. Freud told me to speak of anything, "Just let your mind drift," he said in English. "You don't have to speak of things that happen now," he added. "Anything will do, past or present, since it is all of one piece, and our purpose is to see the structure of your mind, like an anatomist."
>
> (71)

These beautiful words of the analyst are brought to the text as is, with no criticism, argumentation, or ridicule. In the experience of reading, these words come through as therapeutic, a respite from the hostility and envy that dominate the text. This is the only place in the text where explicitly benevolent mutual feelings are presented.

I want to suggest that this moment, paradoxically, sharpens the pain of the missed encounter, of the potential father–son relationship, education, apprenticeship, and affection. This moment highlights the analytic relationship as a relationship that had the potential to serve as a shelter against the fear of the upcoming war, of old age, of loss and death, but that potential was not fulfilled and the analytic moment therefore turned out to be only a momentary pause before the usual confrontations between them continued. Nevertheless, the moment was not entirely lost, for it is brought to the text as a live experience which made a significant mark on the writer. Writing, in this context, serves as a way to signify the fantasy embodied in the analytic encounter and to show where its momentary fulfillment left its stamp.

In an epilogue that Wortis wrote to a late edition of the memoir, three decades after it first appeared, he reviews the reception of his text, which had first been disappointingly rejected but then gradually drew the attention of readers around the world. In retrospect, he states, "Ironically, I may be best remembered as The Man Who Was Analyzed by Freud" (Wortis 1984, 205–206). Indeed, it is interesting to see the transformation of this critical and resistant analysand into one of psychoanalysis's storytellers, a position that he attained with his decision to write his story as analysand, along with all the work of memory and mourning that that entails.

What Wortis's memoir explicitly offers is the story of a bad analysis, filled with wounds and battles. In retrospect, this text can be read as an invitation to think about the profound spectrum of fantasies with which one comes to analysis, the limited ability to communicate it, and the ongoing effort invested in this urge to create internal and external connections to these fantasies, during and after the analytic encounter, both in the sessions and in writing.

Notes

1 Wortis quotes Ellis's response letter: "We enjoyed your clever and lifelike sketch of the psychoanalysis and laughed heartily. I hope it [analysis] is now over!" (Wortis 1954, 132).
2 It is interesting to note, in this context, Freud's well-known conflict over his own father's lack of potency and Freud's attraction to strong father figures such as Hannibal and Goethe (Breger 2000, 160–162; Anzieu 1986 [1975], 198–201).
3 One of the English editions of *Gespräche mit Goethe* included an introduction written by Havelock Ellis (Eckermann 1930 [1836–1848]), thereby possibly strengthening Wortis's affinity with the memoir.
4 A couple of weeks later in analysis, for example, Wortis refers to his Jewishness with alienation and states that he has "no strong Jewish feelings" and "would like to see the Jews become assimilated and disappear" (144). When Freud argues for the advantages of Jewish identity, such as "Jewish family life and intellectual life," Wortis responds with an air of disgust, "Jews have bad manners, especially in New York" (145).

Chapter 3

Diary of My Analysis with Sigmund Freud by Smiley Blanton

From a deadlock of silence to the act of writing

Introduction to Blanton's *Diary*

Smiley Blanton's analytic diary tells his story as Freud's analysand. Written during the analysis and edited continuously afterward, it was not published until after Blanton's death. He left a bequest of a 120-page typewritten manuscript; according to Margaret Gray Blanton, his wife and editor, the plan had been to add supplementary material in order to create "a rounded historical document of both general and scientific interest" (Gray Blanton 1971a, 6). In her preface, Gray Blanton discusses the fact that Blanton had not met this goal and points out a "natural hesitancy about including even the minimum of intimate personal history that one can hardly avoid setting down in a work of this kind" (6). She concludes her preface by saying, "It is my hope that this book will also be of special interest as one observer's personal sidelight on the great founder of psychoanalysis in the last years of his life" (10).

Blanton's book is introduced as a minor text, but it then reveals itself as surprising in its richness and uniqueness, offering relatively detailed analytic work on dreams and moments of intimacy. The story tells of an analysis filled with disruptions, amputations, and continuations. The analysis first began in September of 1929 and ended in June of 1930, then resumed for three subsequent sequences of sessions, in the summers of 1935, 1937, and, finally, 1938, the next-to-last summer of Freud's life. Even for the main period of analysis, the first nine-month sequence, the narrative offered in Blanton's text is not always continuous, as there were several periods of weeks, sometimes even months, in which Blanton avoided writing. These silent periods correspond to disruptions and changes in the analytic setting. In their very first analytic session, Freud informed Blanton that he would be leaving for Berlin in two weeks for some crucial medical procedures; the termination of the first analytic sequence, in June 1930, took place in a sanatorium in Tegel. Thus, from the very beginning of the analysis, it was marked by dramatic changes in the analytic setting. The implications of these changes are not given explicit expression in the text and it is unclear to what extent they were worked through in analysis, but I want to propose that these changes echoed ghosts from

Blanton's history and found their expression in the breaks in continuity of the narrative and writing process during analysis. The periods during which Blanton followed Freud in his travels abroad are not described in the diary, and the setting of those analytic sessions therefore remains obscure.

Much like other books written by Freud's patients, this book has been read mainly as a source of information about Freud's work and character rather than as an independent literary text. Lohser and Newton suggest that Blanton's positive, cooperative attitude toward Freud overshadowed various resistances to psychoanalysis (1996, 119). Momigliano mentions the obscurity of Blanton's nature, along with his sense of foreignness in Vienna, both of which taken together made it difficult for him to reveal his experience in its entirety (1987, 378).

Smiley Blanton (1882–1966) was an American psychiatrist from the southern United States. He lost his mother to tuberculosis at the age of 3, and shortly thereafter his father married his sister-in-law (Blanton's aunt). Blanton studied English at Harvard, then went to medical school at Cornell, where he specialized in psychiatry. In 1914, after serving an internship, he founded the Speech and Mental Hygiene Clinic at the University of Wisconsin, where he treated and researched speech defects and stuttering. In 1929, after he was turned down for a position as the head of a nursery school, he decided to enter analysis with Freud in Vienna. At the time Blanton met Freud, he was 47 and Freud was 71. Blanton lived in Vienna with his wife for nine months while he was in analysis with Freud there; after returning home, he settled in New York and completed his psychoanalytic training. Over the next decade, he became increasingly interested in the possibilities of combining religion and psychiatry. In 1937, he established The Blanton-Peale Institute and Counseling Center in New York City with Dr. Norman Vincent Peale (1898–1993), the pastor of Marble Collegiate Church. The center, next door to the church, was a religious and psychiatric outpatient clinic where Blanton and Peale developed a therapeutic method combining psychiatry, psychoanalysis, and Christianity. The two men also wrote books together, notably *Faith Is the Answer: A Psychiatrist and a Pastor Discuss Your Problems* (1940). During his career, Blanton himself wrote approximately ten books and many articles in his own areas of research. Margaret Gray Blanton (1887–1973), his wife, was an independent researcher in the fields of education and history. The couple had no children. Five years after Blanton died at age 84, his wife published his memoir of his analysis with Freud.

The story of the initial meeting between Freud and Blanton begins with a delay. Blanton found himself arriving 20 minutes late at Freud's summer residence, "much chagrined to being late" (1971, 19), because his taxi driver, who had assured him he knew the location, proved not to know it after all. Blanton arrived at his session with Freud quite anxious and troubled, and this is how he describes Freud's reaction: "'I thought the appointment was at three o'clock.' There was no irritation in his voice, but I felt that he was sizing me up, wondering what sort of person I was and why I should keep him waiting" (20). This reaction, holding both the boundaries of the analytic setting and the lack of any condemnation or punishment by Freud, paves the way for Blanton's analytic process, establishing a path between contrasting possibilities and describing the figure of Freud as both rigorous and generous, both potent and fragile. These dialectics find yet another expression in the image offered of Freud's room, which, alongside the paternal aspects of discipline and hierarchy practiced there, is also described as a maternal womb: "To the right of the desk and against the wall was a comfortable couch with blankets on it and a shawl or soft woolen blanket folded on the head end" (20). Freud's presence and attentiveness are a pleasant surprise to Blanton:

> At all times he seemed in close touch with what I was saying. I felt he was interested, that he was taking in what I was giving him. There was none of that cold detachment which I had imagined was the attitude an analyst is supposed to take.
>
> (21)

In the next session, Blanton reveals to Freud his love for dogs and explains this love as, among other things, a compensation for not having children. Freud responds by saying, "The feeling for dogs is the same as we have for children; it is of the same quality. But do you know in what way it differs?... There is no ambivalence, no element of hostility" (24, ellipsis in original). Blanton finds it hard to agree, for in his view there indeed can be hostility in this relationship, "as when the dog wanted to go out and I was tired and did not want to," yet Freud insists, concluding, "This feeling of hostility is not such as we have toward our children" (24).

Blanton tells the story of his analysis as an encounter characterized by both fragmentation and continuity. It contains terminations and reunions, common grounds and disputes. From early on in the analysis, Blanton expresses his wish to write and publish his analytic story, a task with which he remains occupied, to some extent, for the rest of his life. Any reading of the memoir should bear in mind that it was a writing process that took place mainly during the analytic experience, with some later editorial work by both Blanton himself and his wife, Gray Blanton (Gray Blanton mentions having omitted some of Blanton's dreams from the original manuscript, because she found them too revealing, 6). The text therefore lacks the retrospective point of view on the analytic experience that comes through the prism of the passage of time, along with the work of memory and mourning that it entails. Nevertheless, the writing process covers an analysis that continued for approximately ten years and four analytic episodes, with each reunion with Freud including a retrospective view of past encounters. The work of translation expressed in Blanton's memoir touches on the process of creating a voice of his own, a process inspired by Freud as both analyst and writer. At the beginning of the text, we meet a Blanton who is apprehensive of Freud's authority; as the analysis progresses, we notice a gradual construction of independence and of the distinct voice of the author.

The inspiring figure of the analyst

A crucial layer in Blanton's memoir is the author's gradual evolution into an independent psychoanalyst with his own distinct views and methods of treatment. This process is presented as occurring thanks to Freud's constant presence in the author's life, in analytic sessions over the years as well as through the inspiration of his persona as analyst. In London, in 1938, as their final separation nears, when Freud is on the verge of death and Blanton is a mature and well-established analyst, Blanton turns to Freud to express what he sees as the essence of their prolonged encounter:

> I feel that a lot of the benefit of psychoanalysis is due to the character of the analyst.... I think a great deal of the benefit I have had from my analysis is the association with you and the appreciation of your courage, your scientific manner, and your sympathy.
>
> (112, ellipsis in original)

At the beginning of analysis, in the fall of 1929, the Blanton we meet is a very insecure and anxious man. After he begins to give Freud "a brief account of my life and training," Freud interrupts, asking him, "Have you prepared this?" Blanton answers in the affirmative, and Freud says, "But you must not prepare what you are to say but give freely what comes into your mind. That is the classical method." Blanton reacts with several moments of silence, whereupon Freud says, "You may go ahead and give me what you have prepared!" (23). Following this pivotal moment, Freud's ongoing line of interpretation with Blanton is to invite him to put aside his inhibitions and restrictions and express himself more freely. Freud often uses the word "perhaps" in his interpretations, as if he were, with this word, softening his authoritative stance. The silence described here, the muting of the voice in response to an invitation to free expression, is an expression of the very neurotic inhibitions from which Blanton wishes to liberate himself. During analysis, Blanton does not usually respond actively to Freud's invitations. Interestingly, though, he keeps returning to these interpretations in his writing, as if the very act of writing them were keeping alive the message to free his mind and express himself.

In stark opposition to Wortis's analysis, in which Freud took a mainly reproachful stance, with Blanton Freud takes a caring stance, as a concerned caretaker who wishes his child to overcome his anxieties and gain self-confidence. The frustration that Blanton tends to feel as an analysand invited to free-associate, along with the inspiration he feels at being with Freud, who is a model of bravery and self-determination to Blanton, paves the way for a prolonged period of growth.

The experience of frustration as an inhibited analysand finds expression in dreams that Blanton brings to analysis. A pair of transferential dreams appear after the following events. At a session in early March of 1930, Freud talks about himself as a writer, the developer of a new science, and says,

> In developing a new science one has to make its theories vague. You cannot make things clear-cut. But when you write, the public demands that you make things definite, else they think that you do not know what you are saying.
>
> (47–48)

Especially in the matter of the papers on technique, Freud feels that they "are completely inadequate." He states that in regard to technique, analysts "need something to start with," but later, "they must learn to develop their own technique" (48). At the end of this session, after the two also talk about Freud's upcoming death, Freud says to Blanton, "Perhaps you may have something more to say about your attitude toward analysis" (49).

To this session, which carries with it the message of the necessity of growing out of inhibitions and apprehension, Blanton responds with two dreams with Freud at their center:

> In the first, I am sitting in a chair and Freud is facing me. I am just talking. During the hour, a secretary comes into the room, a woman with many cards. Later, a man comes into the room with some manuscript. I feel this is a very poor way to carry on an analysis. I feel I am not getting my money's worth.

The second dream follows the first one and can therefore be regarded as a further transformation of similar ideas:

> In the second dream, I am about to make a speech about psychoanalysis and education. The crowd is waiting. Freud, dressed in a black suit, comes from a rear room, and I realize that he is to hear my speech. Although he goes back into his room, I know that he can hear me, and I feel embarrassed about this.
>
> (49)

In the first dream, Blanton appears as an analysand under the control of the analyst. During the session in the dream, Freud sets the analytic setting and changes it according to his needs. The room turns into an office, in which the analyst and analysand are seated in chairs facing one another, and people who work with Freud enter the room, ignoring Blanton and occupied with activities and chores that exclude him. Blanton is apparently expected to submit to these conditions without complaining. In the dream, the analytic setting, so crucial to the process, is violated in numerous ways. This transformation of Freud's room into an office where various workers come and go may be referring obscurely to the violation of the analytic setting at the very outset by its removal to Berlin for Freud's medical procedures after the first two weeks of analysis. As mentioned, Blanton did not write anything during the weeks when the analysis took place in Berlin, and this dramatic change in setting is only mentioned in the entry for the initial session, when Freud notified Blanton of his planned travel and casually invited Blanton to join him, offering to continue the analysis but in this very different context. Another aspect that is implied in the first dream is the fact that the intrusions into the room relate to Freud's position as an important man, a writer. The first to enter is "a woman with many cards," and then "a man comes into the room with some manuscript." The turning point in the dream is Blanton's disapproval. In contrast to his actual response, as expressed in his immediate acquiescence to Freud's suggestion to join him in Berlin, in the dream he objects to these changes in the setting. Around him, everyone treats them as unimportant, yet Blanton begins to develop an independent and critical attitude. He distinctly feels that "this is a very poor way to carry on an analysis."

In the second dream, Blanton has emerged from the nurturing hatching grounds of Freud's room into the bright lights of the stage. He is about to give a lecture in a field that has the potential to become his expertise, given that he worked in education for many years prior to his analysis and had expressed to Freud his wish to establish a school based on psychoanalytic principles. While the first dream revolves around intrusions on the analytic setting, the second dream revolves around Freud as a figure of authority and rigor, to whom Blanton responds with embarrassment. This dream expresses Blanton's wish to create an independent voice, a conflicted wish, because, alongside the empowerment that it entails, it also creates self-doubt and apprehension. While free-associating about this pair of dreams in analysis, Blanton mentions an American doctor who is also temporarily living in Vienna at that time and who argues that the talks that he regularly has with another doctor can be regarded as analysis. Blanton thinks that "he is just fooling himself" (50). He concludes, "On the whole, the dream means that I repudiate analysis that is not carried on according to rule. Also, I have some doubts about my being able to present analysis in the best light" (50). In response to the critical stance toward psychoanalysis, and possibly also toward himself as analysand, that Blanton is suggesting, Freud offers an appeasing voice:

> Perhaps you are too optimistic about getting analysis accepted. Take the word of an old man like me—analysis necessarily raises resistance. The fact that we have an unconscious means the presence of resistance. And you cannot present analysis in such a way as not to arouse resistances. It is only in analysis—with difficulty, with much patience, and with much repetition—that we can overcome this resistance.
>
> (50)

To this, Blanton responds with silence.
Three weeks later, Freud presents Blanton with the following insight:

> You know that boys, after they have been passive, always become active. For example, a boy just had a visit from the doctor, who opened the boy's mouth and looked in his throat. As soon as the doctor was gone, the boy tried to look in his sister's throat. Boys always take an active role after they have had to take a passive role.
> (53)

Following this input, Blanton dreams a dramatic dream:

> Last night I dreamed that Bobs, my dog, found a porcupine in a hollow tree. He flung the porcupine out. At first I thought it was a coon. Then Bobs swallowed the porcupine. I cut it out of Bobs' throat, but in so doing I got some quills in my thumb.
> (56)

The dream echoes Freud's story about the boy drawn to an active position and, I suggest, gives it a blunter interpretation. In the dream, Blanton transforms himself from the passive position of observing the interaction between his dog and the porcupine to the active position of cutting his dog's throat.

Blanton offers his associations with the dream:

> Associations: The night before, Dr. Lippman had been telling us about a baby that had cried for hours. The mother brought the child to him, but he could find nothing. Finally the mother called his attention to the baby's swollen thumb.
> (56)

A triad of reminiscences is joined together to create the "day's residues" that preceded the dream: first, Freud's story about the boy who is drawn to move from passivity to activity after going through a medical examination; second, the baby brought to the doctor after crying for hours; and third, a reminiscence that is described in the text in the following words:

> The last two nights Freud has had his chow dog in the room. Two nights ago, as he came out of his hour with Dr. Jackson, he ran through the hall like a boy, expecting the dog to follow. But Dr. Jackson (she was just leaving) spoke to the dog, and the dog remained to speak to her.[1]
> (56)

The dream is given an important place in the text, followed by the residues of the day that preceded it along with the associations that Blanton offers, yet the dream remains rather obscure and its enigmatic nature does not dissolve. Nevertheless, a thread of meaning can be drawn between the dream and Freud's assumption of the essential transformation of the boy from passivity to activity. Blanton's transformation in the dream from passivity to activity is presented not as positive but as a movement whose implications are destruction and death. Bobs, whom Blanton presented earlier as a child substitute for a childless father, is presented in the dream as merciless, and Blanton responds with violence. The act of cutting the dog's throat, even though it is presented as a way to save the helpless porcupine, in fact hurts both the beloved dog and Blanton himself. The images of Freud calling to his dog when the dog prefers to stay with the female patient, and the doctor who does not succeed in finding the reason for the baby's crying while the mother does find it, do not accord with Freud's assumption about the developmental advantage of the boy's transition from passivity to activity, but connect instead with the limitations of such a transition.

The dream and its associations emphasize the significance of the feminine, as suggested by Freud's dog giving precedence to the female patient who "spoke to the dog, and the dog remained to speak to her" and by the baby's mother who has the best insight into the baby's suffering. Blanton continues his associations with the dream both in analysis and in his writing, saying,

> I also remembered that babies were said to come from hollowed stumps, and I thought of the 'fretful porcupine,' a quotation from *Hamlet*. During today's session I recalled another Shakespeare quotation—'untimely ripped from his mother's womb'—which I said was from *Julius Caesar.*
> (56)

The porcupine, who in the dream finds temporary refuge in the hollow tree and soon afterward is caught in the dog's mouth, evokes in Blanton associations from classic poetry and folklore. The second association with Shakespeare is in fact drawn from the play *Macbeth*, where it refers to a maternal presence that had been tragically and prematurely lost. The association with the hollow tree tells of the primary absence of a maternal presence, the lack of the maternal, which is replaced by a dead, hollow stump. Blanton then mistakenly relates the quote "untimely ripped from his mother's womb" to *Julius Caesar*, and Freud corrects him, pointing out that it is actually taken from *Macbeth* (Act 5, Scene 8). This is Macduff's testimony about himself, in which he explains that he is the one who can kill Macbeth, in spite of the three witches' prophecy that "none of woman born/Shall harm Macbeth" (Act 4, Scene 1), because he, Macduff, had actually never been naturally born. Blanton's confusion of the two Shakespearean plays may perhaps arise from their shared motif of the murder of the father. The quote from *Hamlet* about the "fretful porcupine" is an image for the dread involved in the troublesome secret carried by the ghost of the dead king, Hamlet's father (Act 1, Scene 5).

A rich associative texture is presented here in connection with Blanton's dream of the dog and the porcupine. This associative texture, revolving around Shakespearean plays and recent reminiscences, evokes the theme of violence, which first appears as stemming from phallic competition yet on deeper examination is revealed as an aggression stemming from maternal absence, a cruel delivery into a motherless world. Macduff's sin is murder, yet within his archaic history there lies the secret of his traumatic birth. Hamlet is apparently occupied with the competition between the two heirs to the crown, yet his mother's betrayal is soon revealed as a key factor in the tragic chain of events. The reader is also reminded of Oedipus and the tragic chain of events stemming from the archaic secret of the prophecy given to his parents and their subsequent abandonment of him.

The evolving complexity of the associations with Blanton's dream leads the reader into an implicit dialog that the writer creates with Freud and his theory, with respect to the development of the male as a movement from passivity to activity. Blanton, as I will discuss later, is preoccupied with infantile inhibitions and regards Freud as a source of inspiration, yet his dream expresses the value of the feminine and maternal aspects of experience. Blanton's text suggests here that the absence of these aspects can be followed by an overly dominant phallic stance characterized by violence and destruction.

It is also interesting to examine Freud's reaction to Blanton's dream. Although it carries an obscure, implied, criticism, Freud meets the dream not with disapproval but rather with a deep responsiveness. Perhaps the broad narrative space that the dream offers, along with the rich matrix of associations that accompanies it, allow the dream to resonate in Freud's mind in a way that goes beyond his phallocentric theoretical stance. Following the discussion of the dream and its associations, Freud reveals that on his visit to America, approximately two decades earlier, he had wanted to see a porcupine, but eventually got to see only "a dead one." On his return to Europe, "Dr. Ferenczi gave me this little model." After this reminiscence, Freud goes into the other room and brings out "a small model of a porcupine for me to see" (Blanton 1971, 56).

The Hungarian psychiatrist and psychoanalyst Sándor Ferenczi (1873–1933) was Freud's analysand and colleague until theoretical arguments pushed them apart. After receiving praise and recognition as a psychoanalyst, Ferenczi gradually developed his own distinct theoretical views and clinical innovations, but these were rejected by the psychoanalytic community of his time, which may have been a factor in his early death. The reception of his late views was so negative and critical that in Freud's official biography, Jones argues that Ferenczi must have lost his sanity toward the end of his life to propose such views (Jones 1957a, 177–191). This argument is also implied in the eulogy Freud wrote for Ferenczi soon after his untimely death (Freud 1933).

Through the years, following further developments in psychoanalytic thinking, Ferenczi's writings and innovative thoughts have in fact received widespread acknowledgment and have found their position at the center of the psychoanalytic corpus. Today it is commonly acknowledged that, if Freud serves as the father figure of psychoanalysis, Ferenczi is the mother figure, and the return to Ferenczi is therefore understood as the essential retrieval of a lost parent. The distinct thinking of the Freud–Ferenczi pair and the dialectic ties between them have occupied psychoanalytic thinking through the years. This thinking includes the most pivotal issues that occupy psychoanalysis: understanding psychic development in the context of fantasies alongside the effect of the environment and in the context of drives and defenses alongside object relations; the emphasis on interpretation and corrective experience in the psychoanalytic process; and the emphasis on abstinence and the intersubjective encounter in the analytic stance (Berman 1996, 1999).

Freud's presentation of the little porcupine model he had received from Ferenczi may possibly be expressing solidarity with the importance of the receptive/feminine stance, somewhat mistakenly viewed as passive. The act of presenting the statue, with all its meanings, also connects Blanton's discomfort in the foreign realms of Vienna and Viennese culture with Freud's discomfort in the foreign realms of America and American culture. Similarly, the analytic encounter between analyst and analysand, foreigners to each other, an encounter to which each subject brings his own distinct world and culture, also exists as foreignness. In the encounter between Freud and Blanton there were, specifically, the differences between Judaism and Christianity and between Austria and America, and the differences in their knowledge of psychoanalytic language, which was also foreign to Blanton. This foreignness creates a psychic pain drawn from the inevitable gap between self and other, a gap that also possesses great potential for growth and consolation.

Freud's presentation of the porcupine model received from Ferenczi is then given further implications and meaning, as Blanton mentions incidentally that after this session, which took place in April of 1930, he did not meet Freud for a couple of days because he traveled to Budapest to meet Ferenczi. The meeting was initiated by Blanton, who wanted to discuss with Ferenczi "the problem of stuttering" and the possible effectiveness of psychoanalysis as a treatment for this problem (57). Blanton's return from Budapest brought with it subsequent significant changes in the analysis, as we are informed by the editor. Due to his deteriorating health, Freud had to suspend the analysis once again and spend time in a sanatorium in Vienna and then in Berlin.[2]

This pivotal dream of the porcupine and the dog, along with the analytic work done with it on the intrapersonal and interpersonal levels, actually occurs at a dramatic phase in the analysis, although Blanton does not present it as such. This phase can be considered dramatic because the reader soon discovers that a couple of days later, Freud suddenly had to leave his residence for a Viennese sanatorium because of cardiac problems, and then had to move to Berlin to receive a new jaw prosthesis. This brings us closer to the work of mourning embodied in the memoir, which will be discussed later. At this point I want to turn to another pivotal aspect of the work of memory embodied in the memoir of Freud not just as an inspiring analyst, but also as a writer.

Freud as the writer of *The Interpretation of Dreams*

Prior to Blanton's encounter with Freud as analyst, he had been introduced to him as a writer, in particular as the writer of his canonical book *The Interpretation of Dreams*, where he serves as both writer and protagonist. According to Blanton's wife, reading was an integral part of Blanton's life: "From an early age, Smiley had been an inveterate and rapid reader" (Gray Blanton 1971a, 7); "an extremely rapid and even an obsessive reader" (1971b, 121). As a child, he used to read in the attic of the family's house and according to Gray Blanton, "when he was pressed by the surrounding wall of adults, this was his refuge" (1971b, 121). Blanton's memoir gradually reveals the magnitude of affinity that Blanton felt with Freud's persona as the writer of *The Interpretation of Dreams*, an affinity formed in the process of reading.

At the beginning of the analysis, Blanton tells Freud that he has chosen to turn to him for analysis because for him, Freud "was an artist as well as a scientist" (Blanton 1971, 23), and that he "could not be analyzed by someone who did not have wisdom and an appreciation of the nuances of life" (25). In the course of the hour, Blanton speaks of a story he once wrote "about a Negro boy whom the other boys made fun of." Freud asks him whether he "did any artistic writing, meaning stories or other fiction," and Blanton replies that he has tried, but found he "was not good enough. Perhaps that was why I went into psychiatry" (25).

A dramatic break in the writing begins, as we have seen, after the first two weeks of analysis, when Blanton joins Freud in Berlin, where Freud is undergoing medical procedures; they continue together in this setting for many weeks, making a total of about four months in which Blanton does not write in his diary. Perhaps even more striking is the fact that this cessation of writing appears in the text as is, with no explanation or even mention of it. Thus, the analysis commences at the beginning of September 1929, and after two weeks of continuous writing, the narrative suddenly breaks its sequence and continues only at the end of January 1930, with the exception of one single entry in November of 1929. No less interesting than the reasons for this break in writing, reasons that the text leaves obscure, are the conditions that led Blanton to return again to the writing after the many long weeks of silence. The first entry after the break, on January 22, starts with the following sentences:

> I mentioned I was reading *The Interpretation of Dreams* and how thrilled I was by the drama of the thing: A poor Jewish doctor—who was looked upon by his colleagues as a crackpot, who had given up his chances of

advancement for his beliefs, with only the support of his faithful patients—solves the problem of the meaning of dreams, and then, one summer's day, sits down and begins his epoch-making book with "I shall prove..."—not "shall attempt" or "endeavor," but "I shall *prove*."

(37–38, emphasis in original)

In other words, Blanton is thrilled, even more than by the content of the book, by the position that Freud allows himself as narrator, putting himself into the center of the text with no apprehension. This act of textual positioning is, in Blanton's view, "high drama, ranking with the great moments in human thought" (38). The book has left such a significant mark, Blanton goes on to say to Freud, that evidently, even 30 years after it was published, "it seems the best minds of the world have been unable to modify the book in any essential" (38). In spite of Freud's humble response that he "had no idea of being dogmatic or of challenging the world," he admits that he is about to publish the eighth edition, and that "the main structure of the book remains unchanged" (38). The affinity Blanton feels for Freud's book is revealed after their joint stay in Berlin, during which Blanton is exposed to some of Freud's medical problems. It may be that for Blanton, presenting Freud as the young, determined writer serves as a compensation for the possibly fragile features of Freud that have been prematurely revealed to him.

During the second phase of analysis, in the summer of 1935, Blanton reveals his wish to write an autobiography one day and his apprehension about hurting people close to him in the process,

> At sixty-five, I expect to write my autobiography.... I shall want to use material you have said to me and my impressions of you. This is the embarrassing question I have to ask." Freud ... said, "I don't see why the question was embarrassing. You have your personal relations with me, and you are free to write what you like.
>
> (69)

In the next session, Blanton continues to be preoccupied with textual issues, especially with the essential determination required for writing. He returns to *The Interpretation of Dreams*, asking Freud whether it is true that he wrote it in just one summer. After Freud replies that the first draft of the book was indeed written in one summer, Blanton says, "It was a remarkable tour de force," and continues, "The more I read the book, the more remarkable it becomes... you are so sure—that is, your touch is so certain—there is no fiddling about. You do not hesitate to say, 'Dreams are always such or such'" (72). Here, Blanton retrieves the image of Freud as the determined author in order to work through his own apprehension as a writer. Freud the analyst, interestingly, tries to cool down Blanton's admiration toward him by differentiating between the Freud who wrote the book approximately four decades earlier and the present Freud, perhaps also differentiating himself as an analyst from himself as a writer, and says, "Perhaps my sureness was due to the enthusiasm of the young discoverer" (72).

At the last session of the 1935 sequence, Blanton brings his copy of *The Interpretation of Dreams* with him and asks Freud to sign it for him. Freud writes a dedication in German, for which Blanton offers a translation: "To my dear Dr. Smiley Blanton, 17-8-1935—for memory's sake" (80). Perhaps the memory to which Freud refers in his inscription is not only the memory of analysis, but also the memory of himself as the author of the distinguished book. In contrast to Freud's remark during analysis, which positioned his persona as the young writer in the realm of the past, the inscription repositions him again in the present as an author who has created an eternal mark on history and culture. As with the figure of the porcupine that Freud had shown Blanton a couple of years earlier, a figure that carried manifold meanings, both actual and symbolic, Freud's dedication in the book that has been so pivotal for Blanton carries manifold meanings, as the dedication is written by the analyst-writer to the analysand-reader. During the encounter with Blanton as analysand and as reader, Freud is created both as analyst and as author. Just as transference revives past relationship patterns and experiences, reading revives past texts, and in this revival, new meanings are born, relationships and texts are born anew.

Blanton's preoccupation with the persona of Freud as the author of *The Interpretation of Dreams* continues into their third analytic encounter, in the summer of 1937. Blanton writes about a session in which Freud's maid Paula asks him to enter directly into Freud's room without going through the waiting room as usual. He therefore finds himself putting his personal belongings in front of Freud, including his treasured and personally signed book. Freud mentions that he has noticed that Blanton is "never without some printed material" (92). Blanton is surprised by Freud's sharp look, and mentions in the memoir that "I don't know how he knew that I always have a book with me, since I leave it in the hall. The book is always *The Interpretation of Dreams*" (92). Blanton responds emphatically, saying: "Yes, this is my bible. I carry it and reread it every year" (93). For Blanton, the Bible carries deep significant meaning: as a child, he was allowed to read only the Bible and Shakespearean plays on weekends. He concludes the story of this intimate experience with Freud with great enthusiasm: "One gets a feeling of increased power after these visits with the professor. They seem to cause a heightening of one's attention, and to bring to the surface relationships and new concepts that had lain dormant before" (92).

The memoir thus follows Blanton's gradual evolution as a subject on two levels, both as analysand and as writer. In the beginning, his writing tends to closely follow the actual, allegedly objective, sequence of events. As the text progresses, he dares to express his own distinct point of view. Blanton's state of mind at the beginning of analysis involves frustration at not being able to express himself freely, which can be thought of as some form of stuttering or muting. After Freud gives him a set of his *Collected Papers* as a present in February of 1930, Blanton responds with a war dream; in the associations that he makes with the dream he "equate[s] the ammunition with Freud's books" (41). He brings a sketch of a couple of dreams, and one of them is of

> someone asking me to recite, which I do, quoting the passage from Shakespeare about the poet's pen. Which "gives to airy nothing' a 'local habitation and a name.' Here, again, my associations led me to Freud's books and my equating him with Shakespeare.
> (42)

The quote is taken from the play *A Midsummer Night's Dream* (Act 5, Scene 1). The act of giving form and shape to "airy nothing" is presented as the distinct power of creation that the poet possesses. The poet's pen is presented as an image that turns the air, as a sensual and symbolic essence, along with "things unknown," into a written text. In this context, the pen embodies that which is written. Blanton is presented in the dream as the enthusiastic reader who can recite the classical texts but is not able to grasp the enchanted pen. Thus, his evolution as a subject with a distinct voice is presented as only partially fulfilled.

This context sheds light on Blanton's last request of Freud, on the occasion of their final separation in London, in September of 1938. After he speaks of his wish to develop in psychoanalysis and become a training analyst, he also returns to his longtime wish to write an essay about Freud: "I then spoke of the desire I had to write an article about him, showing his character, his courage, his attitude" (109). For Blanton, writing about Freud is an important, even crucial, act, which may be a way to express his deep attachment as well as to claim authorship of his own voice and his distinct perspective on Freud.

Analytic and textual dialog on areas of controversy

Toward the end of the first phase of analysis, in April of 1930, the issue of negative transference is discussed. In response to Blanton's denial of any negative feelings toward his analyst, Freud suggests that "it sometimes happens that a patient makes a mental reservation, which is easy to do, and then the analysis goes on happily and smoothly, with little or no negative transference" (58). Blanton inquires whether Freud has identified "any direct evidence of this in my case," and Freud replies that he hasn't, yet adds, "I only gave it as a possibility. Perhaps the one thing I might mention is the optimistic attitude toward persons and things that you often take" (58). The obscure possibility of negative transference continues to resonate in the sessions and in Blanton's writing. The memoir gives expression to areas of dispute between the writer and Freud and offers possible interpretations for them. Three main areas of dispute, which receive different amounts of working through, are described in the text. The first area of dispute is religious belief, which receives the broadest process of working through and appears in a relatively explicit form. The second is American culture, which receives a partial working through. The third area is the identity of the author of the Shakespearean plays, which is not worked through in analysis and receives only indirect expression in the memoir.

The subject of religious belief develops gradually in the dialog between Blanton and Freud and occupies a pivotal place. During the years of analysis, Blanton went through a process of gradual conversion to Christianity. In his childhood in Nashville, he had received a Protestant education in the Presbyterian Church; as a young man, he pushed away from the church toward secular life; and in middle age he returned to religious life. As already mentioned, he worked as a psychotherapist in a clinic that was attached to a church and developed a psychotherapeutic technique with religious and psychoanalytic foundations.

> At the beginning of his analysis, Blanton dreams a dream of a Methodist preacher who had built a very compact but stupidly designed church. There is only one door, and the two steps leading up to it are so arranged that the lower one, when raised, is a stool for adults, while the higher step, when raised, is a stool for children.... In the rear is a tank for immersion (this despite the church being a Methodist one). The tank has a small cast-iron bathtub, like a coffin, too small for immersion. One end is broken. The preacher shows us around.
>
> (45–46)

The associations with the dream led the analytic pair to an interpretation that "the steps and the stool show my attitude toward analysis in the dream. The church is analysis. The dream is a criticism of analysis. Analysis deals too much with the anal aspects of life, especially with that of the child." Blanton continues this line of interpretation concerning his critical stance toward analysis, writing: "I said that psychoanalysis is a kind of religion but suited only to the very intelligent, for it would be very arid for the average person." Freud concludes the dream work by interpreting Blanton's critical stance toward analysis as a construct that deserves much praise, yet was created by a Jew: "It is really a Jew that has built the house and is showing you about" (46).

In the first session of the third phase of analysis, in the summer of 1937, Blanton speaks of his plan to join his wife in Lourdes, France, after the two weeks scheduled for analysis. Lourdes is a major pilgrimage site that, according to Catholic belief, offers miraculous healing. After his visit to Lourdes, Blanton wrote an article offering an approving look at the curative effect of the place (Blanton 1940). In the session in which they are speaking about it beforehand, Freud does not hide his disbelief in phenomena of this kind, and goes on to inquire whether Blanton is Catholic. Blanton reply is quite striking:

> No, I am nothing. My religion is about like yours, as expressed in *The Future of an Illusion*. But I feel that average people cannot have bleak

religion. Their minds are not well enough furnished. They must have an idealized father to depend on.

(84)

This reply is striking, in my view, because Blanton declares here an almost total identification with Freud's radical antireligious attitude, even though in that period he has been strengthening his religious ties.

Freud, as a loyal adherent of modern thought, was one of religion's most determined critics. In *The Future of an Illusion*, Freud suggests that the main motivation for religious belief is an infantile surrender to the father (1927). Blanton probably wants to avoid a confrontation with Freud and therefore settles on a remark about the limitations of "average people." A few days later, Blanton returns to the subject of religious belief and asks Freud to explain his attitude on the matter. Freud's stance remains sharply determined, and he states, "Of this I am sure: Faith represents a childish relation to the parent." At this point, Blanton is also determined not to remain silent about his religious views, and says that he and his wife have had arguments on the subject and that he thinks that "one could believe what one wished—as, for example, in God or in the Virgin Mary—as long as science did not disprove it." Freud rejects this view and says: "You have no right to believe because of ignorance. Of course, if people believe this or that in their private lives, I would not fine or punish them. But scientifically they have no right" (Blanton 1971, 97).

The dialog on the subject of religion continues to develop in the final phase of analysis, which takes place a year later. This is in the summer of 1938, a short time after Freud's arrival in London. At that time, Blanton explicitly reveals to Freud the therapeutic work he has been doing using Christian principles and expresses his bitterness toward the New York Psychoanalytic Society and Columbia University, by which he feels rejected: "I feel that I don't belong" (110). These experiences, along with his deep affinity for Christianity, have led Blanton to draw closer to Dr. Peale and to develop this distinct method of therapy with him at the Marble Collegiate Church. In 1938, when Blanton finally chooses to tell Freud of the distinct professional path he has taken, he finds Freud fragile and less determined. Thus, Freud limits himself to a simple question, "Do you think you can do it?" and Blanton, in his writing, offers his translation of Freud's question: "He meant whether I could collaborate in a satisfactory way with a minister" (104). Blanton replies with determination, "I see no reason why I should not do this church work without impairing my psychiatric standing and psychoanalytic standards." This time, Freud is the one who seems to be avoiding confrontation, expressing agreement with Blanton's stance. The conversation then moves on to Lourdes and an incident of miraculous healing that Blanton witnessed; "I then gave him our theory of the cure—that it was a transference to the ideal mother which originated the impulse to live" (105). Even though Freud takes an explicitly interested and uncritical stance, Blanton remarks that he "got the impression that Freud was still skeptical, but he said nothing" (104).

The very fact of Blanton's revealing to Freud the fact that he has been doing therapeutic work in connection with a Christian church expresses a transformation from his avoidant stance as an analysand toward a more differentiated and daring stance. The transformation carries with it a turning point in the dialog with Freud, as Blanton does not stop at revealing his religious-therapeutic activity but goes on to express more of to his orthodox Christian background, which includes anti-Semitism. Thus, when the conversation turns to the New York Psychoanalytic Society, in which Blanton feels like an outsider, he points out the majority of Jewish analysts there and then makes the following declaration: "Then it seems to be the custom of Jewish people to destroy, to cast out, to kill their teachers. They stoned the prophets and crucified their great teacher" (117). Blanton is making a striking analogy between Freud and Christ, the two prophets. A question that can be raised in this context is to what extent had this enthusiastic reader, who in his childhood had been allowed to read almost nothing but the Bible, formed a bond between the two holy texts, his two bibles, the holy text encountered in childhood and Freud's text encountered in adulthood. Freud gives Blanton what seems to be a rather avoidant response, saying, "the Americans—meaning the Gentiles—do not seem much better" (117). Even though Freud is positioning himself as being in support of the Jews, in contrast to the Americans or Gentiles, it would seem that Blanton, in his surprisingly zealot words, is trying to differentiate Freud from the Jews, just as Christ became differentiated from them; it is possible that Blanton sees both Freud and Christ as founders of new religions. Yet in this final dialog about religion, it seems that Blanton has gradually expanded his ability to express himself in these matters, while Freud has become weaker and more self-absorbed.

The second area of dispute in Blanton's analysis, which appears in the text in a less developed form, is the dialog concerning America. In the second sequence of sessions, in 1935, Blanton brings up Freud's attitude toward American culture for the first time. As a loyal member of this culture, Blanton feels that Freud tends to disparage it unjustly. He brings up remarks he has heard from Freud during their sessions:

> Freud had been critical of the country, referring to its poor education and culture. I cannot quote him exactly, but as nearly as I can remember, he had said, "You Americans are like this: Garlic's good, chocolate's good—let's put a little garlic on chocolate and eat it."
>
> (78)

Blanton adds that from his point of view, Freud is not being fair to America, for America, in contrast to Europe, is a democracy, and democracy forms a culture of "free idealism." Therefore, he states, "it is my belief that psychoanalysis will find its best soil and growth in the U.S." Freud answers, with determination, "I should die happy if I thought so, but I can see no sign of it now. It is rather being abused in the United States" (78). The session ends with Blanton feeling "somewhat discouraged after my hour, as though I had been childish and had showed off before the professor" (79). It seems that the crucial aspect that has been overlooked in the dialog between them is transference. Reading this dialog makes it clear that Blanton's motivation for bringing up this issue is the complex question of whether Freud's personal attitude toward his American analysand is affected by his resentment toward the analysand's culture.

The subject of Freud's attitude toward American culture is brought into the discussion again during the last phase of the analysis, in 1938, but in this regard Freud remains determinedly negative:

> In the course of the hour, I asked him whether the regard and affection shown him in America made him feel differently toward us. (He has always expressed a certain antagonism against the United States and physicians in general.) He answered, "No." I noted the progress psychoanalysis was making in the U.S. and said, "I think that in the free spirit of a democracy like the United States, analysis could and is making good progress." There was no reply.
>
> (103–104)

As mentioned in the first chapter, Freud's negative attitude toward America was formed on his only visit there, in 1909. He had unpleasant memories of this visit because of the isolation he felt, both socially and culturally. There was an aspect of denial in Freud's negative attitude toward America, and his intense animosity made it somewhat difficult for him to be patient with the patriotism of his American patients.

In addition to the disputes over religion and American culture that appeared in the dialog between Freud and Blanton, there was a third area of dispute that arose between them, yet was expressed much more obscurely. It is interesting to note that whereas the first two issues are discussed in relatively explicit form, this third issue is completely absent from Blanton's text. It is only present in a footnote by the editor. This third issue of dispute was the true identity of an author who was crucially important to both subjects, William Shakespeare. The affinity that both Freud and Blanton felt for the classical author was woven into their dialog from its very beginning. As noted earlier in the discussion about the poet's pen, Shakespeare's plays had been intimate companions for Blanton since childhood, and he quoted from them often, sometimes as a borrowed voice with which to express his deepest emotions.

As I mentioned above, Blanton avoided writing for approximately four months during the first phase of analysis, from September of 1929 to January of 1930. During these months, as we learn from the editor, a crisis occurred in the transference relationship, one that was revealed only many years later by

Blanton in a lecture he gave at Union College. According to Gray Blanton, Blanton spoke of a session in which the subject of Shakespeare's plays came up:

> "Do you think Shakespeare wrote Shakespeare?" Freud said to me. "Do you mean the man born at Stratford-on-Avon—did he write the plays attributed to him?" "Yes," he replied. I told Freud I had specialized in English and in drama for twelve years before I went into medicine, had been on the stage for a year or so, and had memorized a half dozen of Shakespeare's dramas. And I could see no reason to doubt that the Stratford man had written the plays. "Well," said Freud, "here's a book I would like you to read. This man believes someone else wrote the plays." I was very much upset. I thought to myself that if Freud believes Bacon or Ben Jonson or anyone else wrote Shakespeare's plays, I would not have any confidence in his judgement and could not go on with my analysis.
>
> (37n)

Indeed, Freud himself mentioned, in the speech he gave upon receiving the Goethe award for literature (Freud 1930, 211) and in a footnote added to *The Interpretation of Dreams* in 1930 (Freud 1900, 266) that he had come to doubt whether the classic plays attributed to Shakespeare were truly written by him.[3]

As with his stance toward religion, expressed with determination in analysis, here too, in regard to Shakespeare's true identity, Freud again chooses an active position. He expresses his opinion with great confidence and with what seems as no regard for the implications of this position on the transference. By taking this active position, he may have wanted to encourage his analysand to go through a process he had recently gone through himself concerning the same matter. Moreover, Freud possibly wanted to encourage Blanton to work through an ideal father representation in regard to Shakespeare. Nevertheless, the impression from Blanton's narrative is that he was not then in a position for this acknowledgment and his reaction indicates that he experienced it as a challenging intrusion. Perhaps this was the reason he avoided including it in his memoir.

The three areas of dispute mentioned here, then, are presented in the memoir in various levels of working through. Alongside the positive transference, the engagement with these issues suggests that Freud's potent and determined voice was sometimes experienced by Blanton as a personal inspiration and sometimes as a burden. The memoir expresses the writer's conflict between the desire to create his own voice in analysis and his anxiety about the implications that such a creation of his voice could have on the transference relations. This conflict is woven throughout the memoir, especially in regard to these areas of dispute. Blanton continues to return to the issues of religion and American culture with Freud, in what sometimes seems like an effort to represent them in a better way and thereby receive the recognition he yearns for. This is possibly one of the main reasons for which Blanton returns to Freud time after time for further analysis, in what seems like an interminable process. Before he leaves Freud in London, he asks whether he can come "next year for even a longer time," and Freud answers sincerely, "I am afraid I shall not be here" (Blanton 1971, 113).

Blanton's narrative of separation

The constantly repeated return to Freud after the termination of each analytic phase presents the story of an ongoing termination that is repeated, yet whose meaning remains obscure. In this prolonged encounter with Freud, the passing of time, especially Freud's aging, is a conflictual dimension for Blanton. He writes about Freud's increasing weakness and his growing matrix of symptoms, such as deteriorating hearing and sensitive prostate, yet also constantly emphasizes Freud's vitality, which gives the impression of his being much younger than his actual age. Even in their final encounter in 1938, when Freud had just arrived in London, ill and exhausted, Blanton writes, "The overall impression I get of Freud in one of keenness, cheerfulness, alertness, and even gaiety" (102).

Freud himself is described by Blanton as speaking of his aging, by contrast, with a salient and decisive lack of inhibition. For example, Blanton paid in advance for his sessions at the beginning of each phase of analysis. Freud's regular reply, as he took the money, was that Blanton "must promise to ask for a return of this from my family in case of my premature death" (48); "If I should die before the two weeks are over, it can be returned to you!" (61). In addition, when it was time for each separation from Freud, Blanton would express his wish to come and see Freud again in the near future, and Freud's reply tended to be that he was sorry that he was not certain whether he would still "be here" (81, 98, 118). After receiving Blanton's payment for the 1929–1930 analysis, which had begun with the interruption caused by Freud's medical procedures, Freud stated somewhat decisively, "I think about the possibility of death every day. It is good practice" (48). In its determination and vigor, Freud's consistent attitude toward death is consistent with the voice of the much-admired author of *The Interpretation of Dreams*, yet this issue evokes anxiety in Blanton. The memoir obscurely raises the challenge of separation from a potent and vigorous father figure who had given Blanton a voice when he felt mute, and yet this voice was sometimes experienced as foreign, as a borrowed voice. I offer a look into the narrative of separation offered in Blanton's memoir, a narrative constructed of four separations from four phases of analysis.

The first separation from Freud took place at the termination of the initial and main phase of analysis, which lasted for about nine months. The termination occurred in June of 1930, in the Tegel sanatorium to which Freud had been admitted, and after analysis had suddenly stopped two months previously because of Freud's deteriorating health. This amputation of the continuity of analysis served as a repetition of the amputation that occurred at the beginning of the analysis, in September of 1929. Thus, Blanton's main analysis included two periods of significant amputation, one at the beginning of the process and one at its end. In both cases, Blanton was invited to accompany Freud on his travels, with the aim of continuing the analysis. In both cases, the question of the extent to which this aim was able to be fulfilled remains unknown, and in both cases, Blanton completely avoided writing about this period. Gray Blanton adds in a footnote to the first interruption that "although Smiley followed the professor to Berlin, as planned, no diary notes for this period were found, and the next entry appears after they returned to Vienna" (35n). About the second interruption, Gray Blanton remarks that at some point Blanton "went to Berlin to continue his sessions with Freud, but apparently the meetings were very irregular, and there are no diary entries for this period other than the final one in June" (57n).

Gray Blanton apparently felt that these footnote remarks were required as a way to explain Blanton's silence, for in his own writing he only mentions Freud's notification at the beginning of analysis and very briefly describes their final meeting in Tegel. The last meeting involves a brief and formal exchange, quite saliently detached from the analytic story woven by Blanton. The description of this meeting centers on a letter of introduction, addressed to Ernest Jones, with which Freud has supplied Blanton; in addition, Freud replies in the affirmative to Blanton's question about whether Freud judges that Blanton is ready to practice analysis. The possibility of returning to Freud for further analysis is not mentioned (59).

Five years later, Blanton returns to Freud for further analysis, scheduled for two weeks in the summer of 1935, in Vienna. The termination of this phase is given a central position in the text and is presented as a clear negation of the previous termination between them. The 1935 termination takes place at Freud's summer house in Grinzing. The day's entry starts with Blanton's having "a hard time remembering to bring" back an umbrella he had borrowed from Freud's residence the day before, as an expression of the hard time he was having remembering that this was their last session (79). Blanton brings to this session a series of three recent dreams, all of which

> seemed to represent childish wishes for love from the professor—to be passive in relation to him as my leader—and also to express my active heterosexual aspects.... In the analysis of the last dream, I identified myself with the dog: A person was taking me away, but I wished to stay.
> (80–81)

In his dream, Blanton, who appears as a dog, clasps Freud tight in a desperate attempt to avoid a repetition of the premature separation. In the actual moment of separation between them, Freud offers Blanton his hand, and Blanton mentions that he clasped it (81). Afterward, another significant moment of farewell is presented. The final exchange of farewells at Freud's gate, is followed by the writer's great impression of this separation scene:

> I left from the garden at the rear side of the house and came around to the street gate. It was unlatched, so I stepped out and turned to close it. To my surprise, I saw Freud standing at one of the windows of the consultation room that looks on the street. The house is about forty feet from the street. As I looked up, he waved to me good-bye. I waved back and took off my hat. I closed the gate, and when I looked again, he was gone.
> As I walked down the narrow street of the old-time village of Grinzing, the picture was indelibly etched on my mind of the frail, slight man with the fine, high forehead, the gray beard and white hair waving good-bye. I must say my eyes remained misty for a while.
>
> (81–82)

Completely unlike the abrupt termination that took place at the German sanatorium five years earlier, the present termination is presented as a transformative moment. The fragile figure of Freud is presented as a combination of potency and slightness, intimacy and differentiation. In response to Freud's wave, Blanton waves back and takes off his hat. This mature and culturally adaptive gesture stands in contrast to the dog being dragged away from Freud's room in the dream. The possibility of holding two distinct positions toward separation—namely the infantile position in the dream versus the mature and reconciled position in reality—is indicative of an innovative psychic space whose creation is attributed to analysis. The scenery of the old village may represent a reconciliation with the past and the possibility of transformation. Surprisingly, this distinct moment of termination was repeated in the next sequence of sessions, in the summer of 1937. This farewell scene was spontaneously repeated in almost the exact same way, in an indication of the essential significance it held for both participants:

> As I went through the gate to the street and started down the hill, I looked at his sturdy window. Freud was standing by the window, as on a former time, and waved me good-bye. I raised my hat, then went down the hill and to the car.
>
> (98)

The prolonged dialog of separation receives its most intense expression in the final separation, in the summer of 1938, right after Freud has moved to London. The sequence of sessions, which had been planned for two weeks, is abruptly shortened to eight days due to the condition of Freud's health. In addition, as mentioned, the sessions are moved because Freud himself is moving among various hotels; he has not yet relocated to his final home in Hampstead. In one of the sessions, Blanton brings up the professor's frequent remarks on death, and Freud replies, "When you are my age, you think of death naturally. But those who think and speak of death are the ones who are not afraid of it" (111).

In the final session, on September 7, Blanton speaks explicitly about his deep gratitude toward Freud: "I then spoke of the good I had got from him—not simply from what he had said but from his character and attitude" (117). He goes on to speak of the doubt he has about fulfilling "the need of men between 55 and 60 to get a philosophy that will enable them to go on confidently and contentedly." He adds, quoting what he said to Freud,

> "As Shakespeare said, 'Cowards die many times before their deaths,' and when one reaches the age of death, it is easy to die.' And again I quoted Shakespeare: 'Men must endure their going hence, even as their coming hither: Ripeness is all.'"
>
> (118)

The first quotation is from Shakespeare's *Julius Caesar*, Act 2, Scene 2, and the second quotation is from King Lear, Act 5, Scene 2. In the final moment of farewell, "Freud slapped his hand into mine and said, 'I should be glad to see you, if I am able, any time you come ... Good-bye!'" (118, ellipsis in original). The memoir and the narrative of separation it offers end with the following declaration, "How different this scene of parting, at the Esplanade Hotel, from the two partings before in the old wine village of Grinzing! Since I had seen Freud the day before, the whole world had turned over" (118).

After the first separation, in Tegel in 1930, a separation to which Blanton was led submissively and silently, the three subsequent separations express the process of Blanton's becoming an active participant in the creation of his narrative of separation. From 1930, Blanton strives to meet with Freud time and time again and works hard to create meaningful separation moments, enriched with dreams, images, and introspection. His eyes meeting Freud's eyes at the window express Blanton's need for mutuality at the moment of separation, and Freud's response to this need, in quite an intimate way. It may be that it was the two scenes of separation in 1935 and 1937 that made it possible, in their final encounter in 1938, for Blanton to acknowledge Freud's situation as a man approaching death and finding himself violently and abruptly torn from his home and culture. After he had achieved this developmental milestone as analysand, able to recognize the subjectivity of his analyst, the time was then possibly ripe for a final separation.

The search for the fragmented voice

I want to suggest that the amputations in the textual sequence of Blanton's memoir constitute its most obscure aspect. They appear without context or suggested meaning and signify the lack of representation of some very distinct experiences. Blanton's analysis was challenged by a relatively large number of changes and interruptions, due to Freud's fragile physical condition. Salient in their absence are the writer's emotional responses to these changes, which are only represented through the disruptions in the textual sequence. As already noted, it is not only the entries for the sessions when the analyst and analysand were both away from their regular setting that are missing, but also any notes about the general interaction between them at the time. For instance, we might wonder about the extent to which Blanton was exposed to Freud's medical problems and the emotional implications of that exposure. Also emphatically absent are any mentions of the arrangements for their shared travels and their shared return to Vienna afterward.

The first disruption, occurring at the beginning of the analysis, in September of 1929, is followed by a textual silence of approximately four months, which lasts weeks after the analysis returned to Vienna. In a nine-month-long analysis, a silence of about four months cannot be considered a circumstantial one, but constitutes a voice that is present by its very muting. Freud informs Blanton of the change of plans at the end of their initial session. As they approach the door, Blanton asks Freud, somewhat casually, how long he plans to stay there, meaning at his summer residence at Berchtesgaden.

> "I leave on the 15th of September," Freud replied, "but I go to Berlin for a month." With a shrug, he added, "You can either accompany me, or you can wait until I return to Vienna." I assured him that I should accompany him, since I wished to do as much work with him as possible while I was in Europe.
> (21–22)

In the second textual amputation, which begins in April of 1930 and includes the period during which the first and main phase of Blanton's analysis ended, even Freud's announcement of the abrupt disruption is not mentioned.

I suggest that these textual mutings are not simply a circumstantial absence of writing but represent break lines, in which the complete lack of context or meaning provided is the resonance of an experience that has no way to be told apart from silence and no way to be represented apart from absence. To look further into this assumption leads the reader to the writer's history, yet he leaves this aspect of his life largely obscure in his writing. The epilogue, written by Gray Blanton, however, does shed light on Blanton's history. For example, she writes about Blanton's relationship with his father:

> His father was a somewhat shadowy figure to him. They loved each other dearly, and his father did everything he could for his son, but they had practically nothing in common except the past. Their conversation always fell back on reminiscence.
> (Gray Blanton 1971b, 131)

She goes on to describe young Blanton as a lonely child, living on a farm with his family, which consisted solely of adults: "Smiley always felt he had been badly spoiled. People who observed the situation did not think so. They thought that he had been overcontrolled, overmanaged, and overloved" (120–121).

His father is not even mentioned in Blanton's writing. His mother appears in the text, in the second sequence of sessions, in 1935, in his associations with a dream. The dream presents Queen Victoria:

> I related last night's dream, which involved the Prince of Wales, Queen Victoria, and her inability to hear me when I addressed her, either because she is deaf or because my poor speech is at fault. I lean over a balcony rail and cry out to her, "You are still mistress of your realm, and you can still rule it despite your deafness."
>
> (Blanton 1971, 75)

Freud's deteriorating hearing occupied Blanton at that time, and the analogy between Queen Victoria in the dream and Freud is therefore quite explicit and was obvious to Freud when he listened to Blanton's account of the dream. Blanton's uncertainty in the dream with regard to the queen's inability to hear him, namely whether that inability is an indication of her deafness or a result of his "poor speech," represents the uncertainties that Blanton experienced as an analysand coping with Freud's growing difficulty in understanding him, a difficulty that became more pronounced as the years progressed. In the center of the dream there appear two notions in regard to the queen. First is the clear acknowledgment of the queen's growing weakness. The use of the word "deaf" is blunt in comparison to previous articulations in dreams and reality. Second, Freud is represented by a feminine figure. Indeed, in the first session, in 1935, Blanton describes Freud with these two characteristics, writing, "I had to speak loudly and slowly. Apparently Freud is now slightly deaf" (64), and then adding, "His movements, as always, are quick and birdlike—almost feminine" (65). Blanton mentions that "the professor was very amused by the dream. 'Oh,' he said, 'I am a little hard of hearing, but if you speak a little slowly and a little louder—not yell—I can get it all'" (75). Thus, it seems that, in spite of his humorous tone, Freud had some difficulty with his representation as a deaf queen.

At the end of this session, Freud invites Blanton to continue working on the dream, and adds, "There is still some secret which we have not yet reached" (75–76). The following day, Blanton brings Freud another association with the dream, in which he appears as Queen Victoria's grandson, and tells Freud that she could represent his actual grandmother: "My grandmother in reality was my mother as well, for she had reared me from an early age" (76). He continues his associations with his dual maternal representation:

> I then spoke of my mother's strong will and the resolution with which she became a teacher in a society where women were not supposed to work ... of my grandmother and her love, of her old-fashioned, rigid discipline, of her drinking during the final, senile year of her life, although

she had always been a teetotaler. I spoke of her stubbornness—and also of the professor's in not coming to the U.S. for dental treatment.

(77, ellipsis in original)

Blanton thus had two mothers: his brave, determined mother, who died in his infancy, and his loving, rigorous grandmother. The dream suggests that Freud represents this dual maternal figure in the transference, Blanton's mother's determination resonating with Freud's thought and writing and Freud also representing the elderly grandmother's deafness and stubbornness.

I want to draw attention to the ellipsis at this crucial point in the text, the only place where Blanton mentions his mother, whom he lost at an early age. Jacques Derrida discusses the intriguing phenomenon of ellipsis in his *Writing and Difference*. In a chapter devoted to the subject, Derrida refers to ellipsis, or what he calls *elliptic essence*, as a phenomenon in which something is present in its absence, an absent presence that carries the meaning of absence that cannot be expressed in other, more explicit, ways. It is suggested that ellipsis should be understood as a repetition of that which cannot be expressed otherwise, a lack that is "invisible and undeterminable" and yet present as such (2001 [1967], 294–300). Following Derrida's thought, the ellipsis that appears at this dramatic point in the text can be understood as the absent presence of an experience that has no other way to express itself. (Perhaps this grammatical sign can also serve as a key to understanding the two textual amputations in the first phase of analysis, described earlier.) The location of the ellipsis within the first and only appearance of the mother may signify a repetition not only in the text, but also in the writer's psychic sequence.

There is no reminiscence of his mother's early death in Blanton's memoir, but he did write about this painful loss in a short autobiographical text that he wrote as an assignment in 1906, when he was a student at Harvard, approximately two decades before he met Freud:

|My babyhood didn't differ from that of most babies except that I was very frail and was ill most of the time. When I was three years old and my mother died, I remember going into the room where my mother's corpse lay upon the bed, my father sitting on a chair and sobbing bitterly. It seemed strange. I toddled over to father, pinched at his trousers and said, "papa what are you crying about, why don't you come to dinner?" And then my negro mammy came in and carried me away and I remember no more.

(Blanton, in Ginsburg 1999, 379–380)

This is a tight, condensed reminiscence, a capsule of memory, in which the events remained as they were experienced in childhood. The prolonged implications of these events for Blanton's life were so deeply repressed within himself that his impression in retrospect is that his early childhood "didn't differ from that of most babies." Nevertheless, it seems that some of his main psychic dynamics can be traced in this encapsulated story. The fragility that predominantly occupied Blanton in relation to Freud can be understood, given this story, as a form of projection of his mother's fragility as well as his own as a child. The name attached to his nanny, "mammy," was a common name in the South for African-American women who worked as nannies. It seems that in Blanton's early reminiscence, the use of this name serves as a way to express the abrupt exchange between the real mother and her substitute.

After young Blanton has been taken away from his mother, there is a break in the sequence of memory, an amputation. He writes, "I remember no more." This break in the sequence of memory tells the story of a traumatic, life-changing event that is coded in memory in its raw, encapsulated form, as if frozen in time and frozen from time, hence Blanton's conflict over time and the changes that it brings with it, as expressed in the transference. One of the implications of this encapsulation is his muting, for in the absence of ways to express this life-changing reminiscence it remains in the psyche as a meaningless yet unforgettable scar: an event that the subject cannot forget but cannot really remember either, a symptom that tells the story of the psyche but at the same time keeps it silent. Blanton did not forget this event of separating from his mother; he wrote the story of this reminiscence as a young man, yet what has been almost completely repressed is the psychic implications of the event. The language that expresses this early loss in the memoir, which does not report this story at all, is the language of silence and amputations. The amputations in the story of Blanton's analysis, especially at times when dramatic disruptions in the analysis were taking place, tell this story of trauma and its implications. This internal dynamic of early trauma and the scar of amputation did not, apparently, receive an interpretive representation in analysis, but its presence affects the transference in terms of the dominance of feminine or maternal aspects.

The need for love and recognition

The dream of the porcupine and the dog, which appeared toward the premature termination of the 1929–1930 analysis, created the foundation for the importance of feminine and maternal aspects in the next phases of analysis. As noted above, the dream led Blanton to associations of being untimely ripped from the maternal womb and babies being born from hollowed stumps. In contrast to the anxiety that characterized his initial encounter with Freud in 1929, Blanton's return to Freud five years later is represented from its very beginning as a return to a protective womb, something of a haven.

As Blanton enters Freud's summer residence in the village of Grinzing, he encounters two women, "Fraulein Freud" and Paula the housekeeper, who greet him heartily. They direct him to wait for his session in the backyard, and the country garden embraces him with softness, opening his mind to images of femininity and motherhood:

> The garden is about 50 yards wide and 100 deep, with many trees and soft, warm grass. After exploring the garden to its end, I seated myself at a table in a comfortable chair and waited. The birds chirped and sang; there was a soft breeze. The maids occasionally talked loudly in the kitchen in the front of the house, which is of cream-colored stucco.
>
> (Blanton 1971, 60–61)

Notice the soft, warm grass, the soft breeze, the comfortable chair, the chirping of birds; even the occasional loud voices of the maids come from the cream-colored kitchen and can therefore imply oral pleasures. In this encounter with Freud, five years after he had last seen him, Blanton finds Freud in such a frail condition that he is not able to rise from his chair to greet him. Freud apologizes for the short meeting that is taking the place of a regular session, due to his medical condition: "My doctor says my heart is not strong. It's nothing; but he says I had best not work today" (61). Freud enquires about Blanton's doings, and Blanton replies, "Much water has passed under the bridge, and not all of it clear," going on to say that he has been working strenuously and hopes that he is wiser now. He adds, "I am happier since my analysis" (62). The dialog continues in the following way:

> "Did it help you *personally*?" he asked.
> "Yes," I replied, "I think it was the most helpful thing—as far as personal understanding—that ever happened to me."
> He impulsively held out his hand, which I grasped. It was a genuine show of feeling on his part, unusual and spontaneous.
> "I think of you often and with the deepest affection," I continued, "even though you do not hear from me often."
>
> (62, emphasis in the original)

This moving exchange invites us into a realm of informal intimacy. Blanton tells Freud, with positive regard and warmth, of his gratitude for his analysis, and Freud reveals his excitement in response. Freud's spontaneous response in many ways contradicts the way in which we tend to think of his analytic stance, as characterized by abstinence and neutrality. Freud's gesture then leads Blanton to reveal his personal feelings toward Freud even more openly. These gestures of intimacy may suggest that the analytic couple are expressing their translation from their previous encounter, in which they were both in turmoil from disruptions and amputations that they did not have the ability or levels of freedom to express. In many ways, the analytic discourse of the first analysis tended to remain in the abstinent language of interpretation, and the analytic experience at that time may have led them to search for other, less formal, languages. The openness with which Freud lets himself express his emotional response here can be regarded not only as a violation of the setting due to his fragile condition, but as a retranslation of the previous analysis in regard to the conditions one needs for psychic growth.

As a way to express these innovative notions, a new dialog is created in this sequence of sessions. This dialog developed on the subject of dogs and the affinity with them. In the initial encounter in September of 1929, the subject of dogs had come up and their shared love for dogs had been revealed. They both felt that dogs were like children to them. Freud's dogs, who changed over the years, served an important function in the dialog between the two men and in the representation of Freud in Blanton's writing. Through the dialog about man's attachment to his dog, a new opportunity opened up for communicating about issues of attachment, and a new language was created that was less mature and thought through. It is worth mentioning that the day's residues that Blanton recalls as preceding the dream of the porcupine and the dog were of Freud coming out of his consulting room with his chow, and that "he ran through the hall like a boy, expecting the dog to follow" (56). Blanton mentions that he had noticed that Freud had had his chow with him in the room for the previous two nights. Blanton seems to be implying that there is a reason for this change, and that Freud may possibly have needed comfort before heading into another sequence of painful medical procedures. Through the years, Blanton remains well aware of Freud's turmoil over his medical condition and refers to it continually in the text. On their last encounter, in 1938, for example, Freud tells Blanton that in the next couple of days he will be undergoing another operation, the 22nd operation in 15 years (110).

As noted earlier, in their last session, in 1935, Blanton brings in a dream in which he is represented by a dog, presumably Freud's dog, and says, "A person was taking me away, but I wished to stay" (81). At the beginning of the third sequence of sessions, in 1937, Blanton arrives at Freud's residence early and is invited to sit in the yard.

> While I was waiting in the yard, before my hour, the professor came out on the porch and called to his dog, who was in the yard. When the dog came, he petted him on the head. It is not the same dog as two years ago—this one is a half-grown chow. The other dog, the professor told me, had died. I said, "It is hard to lose your dog." "Yes," came the reply, "it is very hard."
>
> (92)

Blanton's increasing attention to Freud's special intimacy with his dogs paves the way for a growing communication on this subject, which opens up new opportunities for talking about the ongoing need for intimacy and comfort. When Blanton comes to meet Freud for the third time, this dialog about Freud's grief for his former dog gives new recognition to Blanton's sorrow over his own separation from Freud. Freud's identification with the challenge that accompanies separation gives validation and recognition to Blanton's struggles in this matter. It seems as though emotions can be thought of and expressed more freely in the framework of a dialog about dogs. In their last session in 1937, Freud's dog appears again and is given a central role: "As I sat on the couch, his dog came in, and I petted his head. 'He knows me and has come to see me,' I remarked. 'Yes,' said the professor, 'he has come to see you'" (98). Notice that at the beginning of this sequence of sessions, Blanton serves solely as a witness who observes Freud calling for his dog and petting him, but at the end of this sequence he plays a much more active role in relation to Freud and his dog.

In the final encounter between Freud and Blanton in London, Blanton notices a new Pekinese dog and that the chow is absent. He asks Freud about the chow and Freud replies, "He—or rather, she—is in quarantine, and will be out in three months… This is a substitute dog" (106, ellipsis in original). Although Freud remarks that the Pekinese is "very shy," she comes up to Blanton's hand and licks his fingers. Almost without words, one can feel their mutual understanding with regard to the pain involved in a coerced separation from a loved one.

The dialog about dogs that develops over the years offers an alternative path, a side road, for working through the transference relationship. Alongside interpretations about resistances and inhibitions, the dialog about dogs represents infantile wishes and attachments that remain relevant throughout the years, especially for someone who has faced early losses and challenging life situations. With the communication about dogs, a new language is created between Freud and Blanton, a language that leans more on the sensual than the verbal and includes silences and amputations, obscurities and ellipses. In many ways, it is Freud who initiated this form of communication when he let Blanton witness him running through the hall like a child while calling to his dog, during their first sequence of sessions, or when he spontaneously clasped Blanton's hand, at the beginning of their second sequence of sessions. It is in this second sequence of sessions that Blanton allows himself to be much more expressive about the traumatic implications that separation had for him. It may be that in his second separation from Freud, Blanton, carrying the burden of his early maternal loss and his reaction to it, allows himself to be expressive about loss for the first time in his life.

A crucial thread of meaning lies in these distinct communications between analyst and analysand, about the importance of expressing infantile needs and seeking recognition for them, sometimes even comfort, while struggling with experiences of loss, illness, and death, both in childhood and in adulthood. Alongside the importance of the analytic interpretative work, there is also the importance of the simple clasp of the hand, petting your dog's head, and approaching the window for a last look.

Blanton's memoir presents us with a condensed textual work of translation for a multi-layered, longitudinal analytic experience. The work of memory presented in the memoir is expressed in the narrative of the writer's gradual development as a subject, analyst, and writer. The work of mourning on which the memoir is centered is one of working through areas of dispute in the transference that were only partly worked through in analysis. Moreover, the most pivotal work of mourning that Blanton's memoir presents is the process of painfully learning to separate without breaking. In his narrative of analysis and of separations from analysis, he allows us to witness the gradual creation of a narrative of separation that offers expression to the unbearable pain, along with a growing acknowledgment of its inevitability. The challenge of separation, which is accompanied by the wish to learn how to separate, requires the analytic couple to search for new languages that will make this process possible, languages that can speak what has not yet been spoken of.

Perhaps it is this condensation of reminiscences of the analytic process that prevented Blanton from bringing this important manuscript to publication. As mentioned by the editor, he had intended to prepare "a rounded historical document" (Gray Blanton 1971a, 6), perhaps a biography of Freud. Yet this supposedly minor text invites the reader into a manifold process of analysis and writing that moves through historical and psychic transformations. Perhaps Margaret Gray Blanton's act of bringing this text to publication can also be looked at as a work of translation of her long and very intimate relationship with Smiley Blanton. Smiley and Margaret Blanton were a couple with no children, and she presents their relationship as the most essential foundation of their lives.

In the epilogue, Gray Blanton describes in detail their life together, their sharing of a significant spectrum of interests, and the way they accompanied each other in various life struggles, in research, psychoanalysis, and writing. Gray Blanton ends the book with the following words of farewell: "I had for many years been Smiley's shadow. For years, indeed I had been known as Smiley's Margaret. I even signed myself so at times. Now indeed I was to take up that role in earnest" (Gray Blanton 1971b, 134–135). Two years later she passed away. Much as Blanton's writing was his work of mourning, in which he learned how to separate, the act of bringing her husband's text to publication was perhaps a work of mourning for Gray Blanton in her separation from him, marrying the pain of this experience with the comfort of telling her story.

Notes

1 Dr. Edith Jackson was an American doctor who followed Blanton, a friend of hers from medical school, to Vienna. Blanton helped her get accepted into analysis with Freud. Her analysis occurred between 1930 and 1936. Recollections from her encounter with Freud appear in Roazen (1995, 89–113).
2 Ferenczi continues to appear in Blanton's analysis and text in the 1935 sessions, which took place after the break in the relationship between Ferenczi and Freud and after Ferenczi's death. When Blanton inquires about Ferenczi's psychoanalytic developments, Freud responds at length and with sharp criticism: "You cannot understand Ferenczi's method without understanding his whole history. He was one of eleven

children. His mother was intelligent and efficient, but naturally she could not give this child much love. He could not be singled out. He was starved for love. That was his secret, which came out when he was being analyzed by me. His 'new method' ... was really a passive surrender to the patient. His idea was to satisfy the infantile wishes of the patient and thus get at the infantile material at an earlier and more plastic stage.... Now, if the father were to surrender to every wish of his young child, it would be impossible to have any adequate training. The father must train the child. The analyst, also, cannot surrender to the infantile wishes of his patient. Ferenczi tried to play the part of an overtender father, to give the love he himself had not received and to get love from his patients. That was his secret. He was ill for several years before his death. And during this illness, this tendency to give and get love, because of his childhood starved condition, came out" (Blanton 1971, 67).

3 A discussion of the change that Freud's thought underwent during these years with respect to the true identity of Shakespeare appears in Peter Gay's *Reading Freud* (1990, 5–53) and also in Trosman (1965). The book that led to this change in Freud's opinion was J. Thomas Looney's *'Shakespeare' Identified in Edward De Vere, 17th Earl of Oxford* (1920).

Chapter 4

My Analysis with Freud: Reminiscences by Abram Kardiner
Memory, mourning, and writing[1]

Introduction to Kardiner's *Reminiscences*

Abram Kardiner's memoir, *My Analysis with Freud: Reminiscences* (1977), offers the narrative of a remarkable psychoanalyst who had a lifelong dialog with Freud that involved deep, intense, and ambivalent emotions, later developed into a clinical and theoretical stance. Kardiner wrote this memoir from the retrospective viewpoint of more than five decades after his analysis and on the verge of death. It was based on a series of interviews conducted by Bluma Swerdloff in the early 1960s for Columbia University's oral history project. The manuscript of the interview series is held in the Rare Books and Manuscripts Library at Columbia University (Kardiner 1965); this chapter is both a reading of the memoir and of the previous interview series. The two texts served Kardiner as an invitation to a work of translation of his life and encounter with Freud.

The memoir unfolds Kardiner's personal story in a generous and revealing way, rich in reminiscences and retrospective insights, while inviting the reader to share an intimate experience. Kardiner was a young psychiatrist and psychoanalyst when he suffered from recurrent bouts of depression and sought analysis. As the years passed, he became a well-known figure in the New York Psychoanalytic Society and the International Psychoanalytic Association. He published many books and articles, taught and supervised psychoanalytic training, and led important research in the field of psychology and anthropology, war distress, and social oppression, at Columbia University (Kardiner 1939, 1941, 1945; Kardiner and Ovesey 1962).

While some of the main aspects of his thought leaned on classical psychoanalysis, he held strong views against Freud's theory of libido and drives. In 1930, Kardiner was one of the founders of the New York Psychoanalytic Institute, but 11 years later he left the institute along with other members (including Sandor Rado, George Daniels, and David Levy), and together they founded the Center for Psychoanalytic Training and Research, housed at Columbia University. This was considered a revolutionary step at the time, because of both the separation from the main institute and the choice to found a psychoanalytic establishment at an academic institution (Atkins 1978; Frosch 1991).

In 1921, two decades before this move, when Kardiner was 30 years old, he went to Vienna for six months in order to be analyzed by Sigmund Freud. At that time, there were only eight practicing psychoanalysts in New York, and Europe was the only place where one could undergo a didactic analysis. American psychiatrists who were interested in the new field had to leave their homes and their work for a number of months, sometimes years, in order to secure an analysis with Freud or one of his students. Kardiner's analysis was arranged by his first analyst, Dr. Horace Frink, who had also been Freud's analysand.

The memoir opens with the letter Kardiner received, in Freud's handwriting, accepting him into analysis for a six-month period; it is presented as the threshold to a new life, a letter that "changed my faith and my world" (Kardiner 1977, 16). Kardiner describes his first impression of Freud, as they greeted each other at the railroad station, "I was disappointed. I expected a taller man, and he had a raucous, cracked voice; but he spoke impeccable English" (16). The next day Kardiner had a meeting with Freud in his office. This meeting created a contrasting impression that showed no traces of the previous disappointment:

> Although we had exchanged only a few words, I had an immediate, implicit trust in Freud. He had an air of authority and strength and I felt completely at ease with him—and myself. I was certain that this man could not only help me personally, but would launch me on a most exciting career.
>
> (17)

In this introductory personal meeting, along with the overall positive impression that he receives from Freud, Kardiner also hears the news that Freud is six hours short of the time he would need every week for his five American patients, and is suggesting that one of them should turn to one of Freud's European colleagues for analysis. None of them agrees to make this sacrifice, however, and therefore they all meet in Freud's consulting room, where he offers that they can each receive five analysis sessions with him every week instead of six. Later, it comes to the American patients' knowledge that the British group of patients had not been asked to make a similar sacrifice. Kardiner adds, bitterly: "Interestingly enough, James Strachey, Alix Strachey, and John Rickman, the English contingent, did not have to sacrifice one hour a week. We mere Americans could be sacrificed" (18).

Kardiner's work of memory

After entering through the "golden gate" of analysis with Freud, Kardiner presents his life story in the first person, following the exact narrative he had told Freud some 55 years previously. Freud's interpretations are represented here as minor, while the historical narrative of Kardiner's childhood and adolescence is placed in the forefront. This narrative is the basis for the significant analytic work that was later carried out on dreams and the construction of the past.

Writing allows Kardiner to recall the encounter, at the outset of analysis, with his psychic life and past events. The story is presented from two points of view, the first belonging to the experiencing subject, telling his major life events in the present tense, and the second belonging to the 30-year-old subject, telling Freud the story of his life from past to present, in retrospect. (The potential third point of view, of the 83-year-old writer and experienced psychoanalyst, is missing from this part of the memoir; it appears only in subsequent chapters.) In this way, the reader is invited to join Kardiner on his analytic adventure with Freud at its very starting point.

The story begins with Kardiner's father as a 30-year-old man (which is Kardiner's own age at the time of analysis) in Russia. The story tells us of a marriage imposed on this young man and the vicissitudes he and his little family went through before Kardiner was born, among them the birth of Kardiner's sister, the gradual immigration to the United States first by the father and later by the mother and baby, the poverty and hunger, and the miscarriages of two pairs of twins (Kardiner 1965, 80–81). Kardiner claims that he has no clear memories of his mother. After her death, the 3-year-old Kardiner was left with an older sister and a father who would stay away from home for long hours, leaving his two children out in the cold. His early childhood is described as the "dark ages," "a ceaseless nightmare, with starvation, neglect, a sense of being of no account, and a bewildering depressive feeling" (Kardiner 1977, 27). Aspects of Kardiner's childhood and himself as a neglected and harassed child were revived and repeated in specific periods in his life as an adult and specifically in the regressive state in which he found himself during analysis with Freud.

Shortly after his mother's death, his father remarried and the two children were presented with a stepmother, whom they were directed to call "Auntie." Kardiner stresses her importance to their family life and to himself as a child, as she saved them from destructive neglect and despair: "She took me out of the chaos of a devastating and unstructured environment and led me into a paradise of an ordered world" (28). He even dedicated the memoir to her (alongside his wife). Nevertheless, Kardiner notes that in contrast to his present gratitude to his stepmother, as a child he "was not then in a position to appreciate what this remarkable woman did for me" (28). He therefore maintained an obedient yet cautious stance toward her. This basic mistrust was probably because she would belittle and humiliate Kardiner and his sister and, moreover, when he was between the ages of 4 and 7, she seduced him into touching her in intimate ways, directing him to suck on her breasts. Kardiner explains this deviant behavior with her pain at never having had children of her own, yet admits that it had devastating implications for him: "This was indeed a strong stimulus to a child of four. For I remained passionately attached to her but not without a bit of mistrust and a constant feeling of being nobody" (28).

One of the main themes of Kardiner's story is that as a result of this sequence of traumatic events in his early childhood, he developed a strong dependence on caretaker figures, especially his father, followed by a split in the self. One aspect of that self was the neglected, abandoned child, humiliated in his quest for love, deprived and depressed, and helpless in his dependence on an absent or abusive caretaker. The other aspect of the self was the compliant and gifted child, responsive to his environment, enjoying a special stance as a favorite son to an admired caretaker (41–44).[2] This split carried with it a complex challenge in the analytic work of memory and mourning. It involved great anxiety about revealing the unconscious and deep dependence on the analytic setting.

The challenge of reminiscence

Kardiner's first analysis was in New York with Dr. Horace Frink (1883–1936). When he began the analysis, Kardiner knew Frink as Freud's analysand, Kardiner's own neurology professor in medical school, and the author of *Morbid Fears and Compulsions* (Frink 1918). Frink's book had affected Kardiner deeply at a difficult stage in his life after his internship in medicine ended. Kardiner set up a meeting with Frink, which in retrospect, began a fateful transition "that decided my future" (Kardiner 1977, 52). Frink suggested that Kardiner start psychiatric training and didactic analysis, offering himself as Kardiner's analyst. About entering analysis for the first time, Kardiner writes:

> At that time, I knew nothing about what went into a therapeutic session. Hence, I went in without any foreboding or fear, but very soon after I began I found myself scared and frightened. I was apparently protecting myself against some unidentifiable danger.
> (52)

The analysis reached a breaking point after Frink offered Kardiner a tantalizing interpretation. It involved the theme of the father and aroused Kardiner's oedipal conflict, both as a reconstruction of the past and as a live experience in the transference. While reminiscing about his childhood in analysis, Kardiner recalled a popular song of that time as "Sweet Isaac Ben Bolt," instead of "Sweet Alice Ben Bolt," and adds, "I had substituted my father's name for the ballad's dead Alice" (52–53). The name of the song is actually "Sweet Alice, Ben Bolt" and is a lamentation for the dead Alice, addressed to a third person named Ben Bolt. Frink replied to this slip of the tongue with the remark, "It's obvious that you wanted your father to die" (53). Kardiner responded with great bewilderment:

> His statement about my wishing my father dead had an immediate and devastating effect on me. My impression was that my father was my rock of ages, my dependence on him inordinately strong, and yet I wanted him to die?... This revelation, that I wanted this man whom I consciously adored dead, devastated me. I did not dispute this interpretation because I felt that I had no authority to do so, but I left the hour in a state of anxiety.
> (53)

Frink's reply offered not only an interpretation of the father as a reconstruction of the past, but also a recreation of the historic relationship in the here-and-now of the transference. Symbolically, but for the anxious Kardiner also realistically, this interpretation turned Frink himself into the authoritarian and dreaded father figure. This dramatic analytic moment was not worked through in analysis, however. Shortly thereafter, the analysis reached a deadlock and ended abruptly.

At that time, Kardiner "had a very dramatic dream," which started a chain of tantalizing psychic events. He vividly remembered the dream and the following sequence of events and later brought them to Freud for interpretation:

> I was in a cellar in which there were a great many old articles of furniture that had been discarded because of age or because they were broken. They were in disorderly array. A balcony overhung the right side of the cellar, and on this balcony were standing three Italians with their penises exposed, and they were urinating on me. I felt very humiliated and downcast. I woke up in a depressed state.
>
> (53–54)

After he woke up, Kardiner rushed to his psychiatrists' staff meeting at Manhattan State Hospital. He was presented with a patient who "had an unusual symptom for a schizophrenic—he had lost his 'memory.' And with this, a chill ran through me. 'By god, the same thing could happen to me!'" (54). Kardiner felt so bewildered at that time, he asked permission to be excused from work and rushed home, where he had another provocative dream, of having intercourse with his stepmother: "but there was something unusual about it. I felt as if I was ripping something up as I inserted" (54). In this context, it should be noted that the memoir describes the author's romantic experiences and disappointments, but does not tell us anything about his sexual experience. The dream of an explicit and somewhat violent sexual act with his stepmother may imply the dread and temptation involved in the return of the repressed, while the maternal womb stands for the unconscious and the rapture stands for the revelation of painful, forgotten memories.

In his first encounter with Freud, Kardiner asked for an interpretation of the disturbing dream of the three Italians, as a request for a new beginning with Freud and to solve the enigma they presented. Freud took the request in earnest and offered Kardiner an intriguing interpretation:

> Three Italians equal one big Italian, your father. You felt small, humiliated, outdone by your father and belittled by him. What the amnestic Negro you saw in staff was, was a projection into the future of what you actually feared in the past. What you feared was therefore not what was going to happen but *what actually had happened*, and which you not only forgot, *but feared to recall*. And what you feared with Frink was that if he knew of your murderous intentions toward your father, he would withdraw his

> love and support, as you once feared your father would. And what you feared was the return of your sense of humiliation which devastated your childhood.
>
> (55, emphasis in original)

In this interpretation, Freud offers insight into the complex relationship between Kardiner and his father in childhood and the repressed feeling of humiliation and deprivation it involved. Freud's interpretation points to the vicissitudes of the work of memory, the hide-and-seek it entails, the conscious wish to recall, alongside the unconscious wish to forget. Freud also makes the connection, obscured until that point, between Kardiner's paternal representation and the unresolved transference toward Frink. This interpretation highlights Kardiner's dread of his phallic representations, his childhood father, and perhaps his psychoanalytic father as well. Alongside these important insights, there is an enigmatic atmosphere surrounding the dream, which is even more present to Kardiner when he recalls it in writing. He concludes the description of the dream by saying that although Freud "made some sense out of it … I am not sure, even now, that I fully understand it" (53). The obscurity of the unconscious, as expressed in dreams and slips of the tongue, provokes anxiety in Kardiner. In a concluding remark on the crisis in his analysis with Frink, he states, "What frightened me most was that I could entertain ideas of which I had no awareness" (53).

The return of the repressed that occurs during the process of reminiscence continues to provoke anxiety in Kardiner's second analysis. After Freud's interpretation of the dream of the three Italians, Kardiner leaves the session "in a very agitated and disturbed frame of mind," and that night, he has another dream:

> In this dream, I was standing on an embankment. Two or three men were digging a trench. I was very exercised over their activities, and I kept importuning them to please stop digging, saying that they would find nothing of any value, that they would find nothing but an old rag. Finally, in the dream, they did come up with a rag, and I said, "You see! There isn't anything there."
>
> (57)

The trench presented in the dream resonates with the old cellar with the broken furniture in the previous dream, and may represent the unconscious and the emotions aroused from the return of the repressed. The shift in the men's position, from men urinating from a balcony in the previous dream to workers digging for an old rag in the current dream, suggests that a world made of old and broken household articles may be preferable to the torment of humiliation.[3] The broken furniture from the first dream and the old rug from the second dream suggest reminiscences; Kardiner can point to their existence, but is unable to give them any meaning. In both dreams, the tantalizing encounter with humiliation creates a wish for the continuation of repression. Indeed, the next day, Freud interprets this dream as a fear of recalling malevolent aspects of the childhood father: "You want the picture to remain as you retouched it... You evidently were terrified of him in your very early childhood" (58). Kardiner's memoir offers a working through of the strong dependence on paternal representations—the father, Frink, and Freud. This dependence is underlined by the absence of the mother.

Kardiner's father appears in the memoir as a complex and ambivalent figure. On the one hand, he is described as "a calm and most entertaining fellow" (36), whom Kardiner admired for his resourcefulness and ability to build himself a new life as an immigrant. This was especially emphasized by Kardiner in his analysis, for he came to Freud at the same age that his father was when he emigrated with his young family from Russia (44). As discussed above, Frink's premature interpretation enabled unconscious materials to gain access to conscious thought, but in ways that were nevertheless obscure. Looking back on the sequence of events that the interpretation triggered, Kardiner understood his anxious reaction to the schizophrenic patient's loss of memory as a reflection of his own loss of memory of his early childhood father. His retrospective insights are expressed in the interview with Swerdloff:

> What I had forgotten was the fact that my father made the impression upon me in childhood of being a very violent man, which I'm sure he was during these years of depression when he couldn't make a living. He was cross and he was irritable and he was mean, and I suspect also, in trouble with my mother, with whom he did not get along very well. All of these things, between 18 months and three years of age, I surely did not understand. So it wasn't any erroneous idea. I was reacting to the fact that somebody has lost his memory; I had forgotten this.
> (Kardiner 1965, 58)

This reminiscence obscurely represents the maternal figure, of whom Kardiner reports having no memory. She appears solely as a blurred victim in the shadow of the violent father, but nevertheless present. In the memoir, Kardiner states: "I started out being afraid—no, terrified—of him. This was undoubtedly because I saw him abuse my mother by beating her. I was probably witness to many brutal scenes between my parents" (Kardiner 1977, 40).

In contrast to this somewhat repressed dreaded father, then, a relatively benevolent father representation was created. This change appeared following "the advent of my stepmother." Thereafter, my father "was no longer the irritable and overwhelmed person of my earliest years" (36). Nevertheless, Kardiner emphasizes that his father and stepmother had demanded absolute obedience from their children, and humiliating ceremonies were conducted daily, even for minor misbehaviors. The stepmother "would write on my forehead 'good' or 'bad' with her index finger, which made it visible for the whole world to see" (41). She would report Kardiner's daily misbehaviors to his father, who would then threaten to send Kardiner away: he "would order my things to be packed into a bundle and tied to a broomstick, and with this suspended over my shoulder, I was marched to the door" (42). Kardiner concludes his account of this form of parental education by saying, "Thus was obedience the guide to my early years. My submission was complete and absolute" (42).

The termination phase of analysis

Freud's dream interpretation, given at the outset of the analysis, involving the little child belittling himself in order to prevent abandonment by his father, is presented as a valuable understanding of Kardiner's relationship with his father and with authority in general. Nevertheless, looking back, Kardiner criticizes Freud for not applying these understandings to the transference relationship he had developed toward Freud himself: "The man who had invented the concept of transference did not recognize it when it occurred here. He overlooked one thing. *Yes, I was afraid of my father in childhood, but the one whom I feared now was Freud himself*" (58, emphasis in the original). At another place in the memoir, Kardiner states, "As with my father, I would repress my self-assertion with Freud in order to maintain his favor and support. The central fact in the transference situation was overlooked by the man who had discovered the very process of transference itself" (100).

In a work of mourning done in retrospect, Kardiner characterizes his relationship with Freud as maintaining the pattern of his childhood relationship with his father, himself serving as a preferred son to an adored yet dreadful father, and by this, the son protects himself against helplessness and neglect:

> I made a silent pact with Freud. "I will continue to be compliant provided that you let me enjoy your protection." If he rejected me, I would lose my chance to enter this magical professional circle. This tacit acceptance on my part sealed off an important part of my character from scrutiny.
> (59)

Kardiner's grief and sense of incompletion after the analysis ended stands in contrast to Freud's expressed satisfaction with the analytic process. This dissonance receives an ironic expression in a letter Freud wrote to Frink, stating that "Kardiner's analysis is complete and perfect. He ought to have a great career" (68).[4]

The story that Kardiner tells of his analysis focuses mainly on his life history up until the encounter with Freud and the dream interpretation that was offered as part of the analytic work. In retrospect, Kardiner criticizes some of Freud's interpretations, but these critiques are made only in retrospect. During the analytic process, he describes himself as having been a patient captured in an admiring and devoted stance, as expressed in the following:

> As I look back upon this part of my adventure in Vienna, I must make the following comments. First, I was too bewildered by the entire experience,

its condensation, its concentration, for it to have given me any kind of perspective whatsoever in the total field.

(93)

The lack of perspective caused Kardiner to let himself be entirely absorbed in the analytic process.

The depth into which he allowed himself to sink with Freud is indicated by his response to the termination of analysis. It had been agreed in advance that Kardiner's analysis would be for a six-month period, and toward the last month Kardiner was informed by Freud that it was time for working through:

> At the end of the fifth month, March, he [Freud] began saying, "Herr Doktor, ein bisschen Durcharbeitung (working through)." Now, this idea caused me a good deal of bewilderment. I had no idea what he meant, and I begged him to elucidate what he meant by *Durcharbeitung*. He said, "Well, why don't you bring your childhood neurotic manifestations into your current life?"
>
> (62)

Freud's words sounded foreign and strange to Kardiner's ears. He failed even to understand the German word for working through, *Durcharbeitung*. It felt to him as though Freud were speaking in a foreign language, and not just because he spoke German. From this point on, the narrative changes from a tightly bound and coherent story into a fragmented and broken recounting, in short and somewhat scattered chapters. The separation thereby becomes the breaking point of the narrative, both in the analysis and in the text, in terms of process and structure. Afterward, the analysand-author has been left with fragmented notions and impressions and the urge to challenge himself with the painful work of mourning. This is one example, from the memoir, of the return to the point of breakage:

> Sometime in early March, Freud told me that my analysis would terminate on April 1. I was very much disturbed by this and protested vehemently, but Freud would not be moved. When he reminded me that he had stipulated a six-month period in his original paper to me, I was even more shocked. I had not forgotten it; I had never really seen it. It had simply not registered with me.
>
> (67)

Even though Kardiner was supposed to have been aware of the time limit, as shown in the letter presented at the outset of the memoir, the announcement about the forthcoming termination hit him like thunder. The bewilderment that struck him is indicative of the depth of attachment with which he had entered the transference relationship. The lack of any internal registration on his part of the time of termination indicates the profound impact the separation from

Freud had on him, as a repetition of early traumatic experiences. Nevertheless, this repetition served as more than a mere re-traumatization, for in this case the obedient Kardiner turned into a desperate fighter who "protested vehemently," which implies an inner change.

In response to Freud's invitation to a *Durcharbeitung*, Kardiner reacts with what seems like dissociation: "However, as for me, at the time his invitation that I should work through this whole thing only left me bewildered. From this point on, the analysis drifted" (63). The dismantling, or falling apart, of the analysis reflects Kardiner's traumatized reaction to Freud's announcement. The description of his feeling as "bewilderment" takes the reader back to the "dark ages" of his early childhood, in which he had a "bewildering depressive feeling" (27). In his writing, Kardiner observes the state he was in as an analysand and concludes that at the time, he was totally absorbed in admiration of and compliance with Freud, adding that he "was much too close to the experience to appraise what had happened" (68).

The retrospective standpoint gives him the opportunity to articulate the state of mind he was in then, "As for my experience with Freud, it was an adventure filled with hypnoidal atmosphere, a charismatic personality of great charm, persuasiveness, and genius, too" (93). The term "hypnoidal atmosphere" emphasizes Kardiner's feeling of enchantment with Freud during analysis. Hypnoidal states appear primarily in *Studies in Hysteria*, describing the hypnotic state of mind into which one enters in response to acute stress (Breuer and Freud 1895, 215–222). In the common type of hysteria, the symptoms relate to the content of the trauma, and the emphasis is put on the social prohibitions that prevented any emotional reaction to the traumatic event when it occurred. In hypnoidal hysteria, however, "conditions are determined, not by the content of the memories but by the psychical states in which the patient received the experiences in question" (11). This unique atmosphere described by Kardiner revived archaic dependence and contributed to the pleasure and intensity of the analytic experience, yet it also had a negative impact on the patient's ability to cope with separation. During termination, Kardiner's repressed memories of hopelessness and neglect were vividly and painfully revived.

In a retrospective work of mourning, Kardiner assumes that his diving naïvely into this intense, condensed experience prevented him from preserving different perspectives on it. As an analysand, Kardiner felt completely wrapped up in the process, and when it ended, he felt he was slipping into complete abandonment:

> I was puffed up with pride, arrogant as a peacock with having been one of the elect, molded fresh by the hand of the great master himself. However, this did not last long, for I soon discovered that my training was inadequate to the practice of psychoanalysis, and that I had embarked on an odyssey without map or compass.
>
> (Kardiner 1977, 93–94)

The tormented feelings he had known as an abandoned and derelict child, suffering from "a constant feeling of being nobody" (28), arose again. His use of the image of an odyssey suggests the image of leaving all precious things behind in response to the demand to embark on an unknown path. Analysis is thus represented as the lost home, while the United States, to which he must return, is the realm of the unknown. In contrast to the heroic odyssey, a mission demanded and guided by the gods, this odyssey is presented as a tragic constraint, set by an authoritative and abandoning god/analyst. The analytic setting thus became a primary container for the possibility of integration, a womb for the repressed experiences and identifications to be reborn as integrative representations. The premature termination left Kardiner feeling like an infant born prematurely, needing to cope with the demands of harsh reality.

Although Freud expects his patient to work through the analytic insights and translate them, Kardiner insists on a different reaction. The previous metaphor of himself after separating from Freud as "embarked on an odyssey without map or compass" (94), which is then woven into the image of the analysis as "drifting" (63), suggests that at that point the analysis had lost its direction and become a shipwreck, of which he found himself the lone survivor, destined to find his own way.

At the time of analysis, Freud was for Kardiner an incredibly potent and abundant figure, but in retrospect as part of a complicated work of mourning, Freud's avoidant stance in relation to his patient's powerful transference toward him is presented as a mystery. Questions troubled Kardiner's mind throughout the years: Why did Freud not interpret his patient's obedient transference? What was his emotional stance toward his patient? How deep into his psyche did he see? And most of all, why did he let him go so soon, leaving him broken and lost? The text tries to decipher these questions using a couple of insights arrived at retroactively.

The first insight is that Freud's avoidance was related to his lack of interest in working through the depth of transferential dynamics. Kardiner mentions that after the analysis ended, Freud remarked to him that "I have no great interest in therapeutic problems" (77). The second insight that the memoir provides into Freud's avoidant stance toward interpretations of transference has to do with Freud's preoccupation with his analysis of Frink and its tragic consequences. Horace Frink, introduced above as Kardiner's first analyst, was an American psychiatrist destined by Freud to be one of the founders of psychoanalysis in the United States. It is now known that Frink's analysis with Freud had devastating consequences. Frink came to Freud for analysis in 1921, already a practicing analyst, married with two children. He confessed to Freud that he was in love with a patient, a wealthy American, whom Freud also met and hoped would contribute financially to the psychoanalytic movement. Freud failed to acknowledge Frink's fragile state, focusing instead solely on the sexual aspect of his life, and encouraged the two lovers to leave their families and get married. This transition led Frink to a severe psychotic breakdown and suicide attempts. During that time, and after Kardiner's analysis ended, Frink returned to Freud for analysis, but he was not able to pursue it and instead was hospitalized. These events led to further tragedies in the lives of the people involved. Both Frink's wife and the female lover's ex-husband died of illnesses shortly after the separation. The relation between Frink and his lover did not last long, and after it ended, she sought analysis with Sándor Ferenczi. Eventually, Frink was expelled from the psychoanalytic society (Breger 2000, 279–281; Gay 1988, 565–566).

The memoir suggests that Frink's analysis had a crucial, yet largely unspoken, influence on Kardiner's analysis with Freud, especially on Freud's countertransference. This influence is given expression especially in a scene that occurred at the termination phase of Kardiner's analysis. Freud chose that moment to make a point about Kardiner's opinion that psychoanalysis "couldn't hurt anyone" (Kardiner 1977, 67). He presented Kardiner with two photographs of Frink, one taken before analysis and the other after a year of analysis. Kardiner writes, "I was shocked at what I saw. In the first photograph, he looked as I had known him. In the second, he was haggard, emaciated, and looked twenty years older" (67). Kardiner's first meeting with Frink had been after Frink's analysis with Freud but before his tragic breakdown, and Kardiner described him as an impressive figure. In the memoir, with the added information about Frink's tragic chain of events after his analysis, Kardiner implicitly examines Freud's analytic stance toward himself. Freud's stance was characterized by intimacy combined with a persistent avoidance of interpreting not only Kardiner's transference but also his failed love life, which was very troubling for Kardiner at the time (101).[5] Through this work of translation, Kardiner is able to shed new light on Freud's presumed preoccupation with the result of Frink's analysis and the dilemmas that that suggested. This is implied in Freud's act of revealing the before-and-after photos, which suggest the harmful potential that lies in the psychoanalytic process and especially in the dependence the analysand develops toward the analyst. The complex matrix of connections among the three psychoanalysts was even more tangled than that, for during the termination phase of Kardiner's analysis, he discovered that "Frink was coming back to Freud for more analysis, and this disturbed me." He had been expecting Frink "to launch me on my new career" (67), after Freud disappointed him in this aspect (17), but instead found himself fatherless both in Vienna and in New York.[6]

The implicit tale of Freud and Frink as a pair of paternal figures created in the analytic setting and the complex interrelations between them, deciphered years later, is offered as a crucial work of translation to Kardiner's unresolved dependence on and admiration for them. In addition, there is the retrospective understanding of their limitations, for reasons outside his control. The powerful, and in many ways desperate, dependence on the father serves as the backbone of Kardiner's memoir on Freud. But this theme cannot be thoroughly understood without another pivotal layer, the absence of the mother.

The absence of the mother

The mother appears in the memoir through her absence, and Kardiner claims that he possesses no memories of her. He presents the information he had managed to collect about her:

> My mother had to go to the East River with a bucket and carry a heavy pail of coal, distributed by some charity or other, and carry it home over a long distance. In the meanwhile, I was a neglected child, living under conditions close to starvation
>
> (25)

An early memory is brought up from "those dark ages;... of being very small and playing on the floor with another little boy. An angry woman slapped my hand and went back to sit on a chair at a table—the only furniture in the room" (25). A crucial aspect of Kardiner's maternal representation was brought to consciousness during the analysis, and its interpretive process was imprinted on Kardiner for the rest of his life as Freud's "masterpiece." This working through starts with a dream interpretation concerning the stepmother. Kardiner had a dream during analysis, about "an enormous cat whom I apparently was not afraid of, but who was unmoving and indifferent" (58). The strongest impression left by the dream was "the enigmatic expression on the cat's face. It seemed immovable, unapproachable, indifferent" (59). Freud offered an interpretation that tied together Kardiner's two mothers, starting with the stepmother: "While it is true she gave you a structured environment, she also overstimulated you sexually and thereby augmented your guilt toward your father... You identified yourself with your helpless mother, for fear of identifying yourself with the enraged, aggressive father" (59–60). Kardiner responded that he "could understand the identification and the female part. As a child, I remember feeling that it was an extraordinary privilege to be one of these remarkable creatures" (60).

Soon after, Kardiner

> had a dream about a mask, from which I awoke with great apprehension.... Freud asked, "What was there about the mask that frightened you so?" My first response was that it was the facial immobility, the lack of expression, the fact that it neither smiled nor laughed, and that the face was immobile.
>
> (61)

Kardiner connects his reaction to the dream to a phobia he suffered from, as a child, of masks and wax figures. From that, "Freud drew the conclusion that the possibility was that, 'the first mask you saw was your dead mother's face'" (61). Kardiner's first reaction was shivers through his body; later, he reconstructed the early repressed memory with help from his sister. According to her, little Kardiner was staying home with their chronically ill mother.

> Apparently, I wanted something and I shook her. She did not respond or answer, and I was frightened. When my sister came home for lunch, she discovered that my mother was dead and that I was alone in the room crying.
> (62)

Another meaningful reminiscence concerning the mother's death involves the day she was buried.

> That evening no one was at home. A dark room lit by a kerosene lamp. Someone was playing the harmonium in a nearby apartment, and I have always hated that instrument ever since. These events took place in the first week of November 1894, and for many years afterward I regularly had depressive reactions every fall.
> (26)

This experience remained strikingly sharp in Kardiner's memory after all the years, a vivid psychic representation that influenced his long-lasting preferences and state of mind. The memory was kept in his consciousness and exhibits the characteristics of a screen memory, which obscures and stands in for traumatic memories.[7] Kardiner's recollection of that evening represents his childhood as a time of solitude and neglect. At the end of that dramatic day, the only human presence he was offered, in the secluded environment available to him, was the music of the harmonium, a pump organ that was considered a poor man's piano. The musical presence was not experienced as comforting, however; it may even have sharpened his pain. Nevertheless, a few years later Kardiner learned to play the piano and became a talented and enthusiastic piano player, implying a certain link to this early memory.

The mother is therefore represented in three memories: the conscious memory of the woman slapping his hand in the empty room, in which her identity remained obscure; the repressed memory that remained only as a neurotic symptom of the mask phobia; and the alleged screen memory of the harmonium tune, attached to her death. The memoir expresses, in hindsight, an understanding that Kardiner's amnesia about his mother served as a defense against a deep identification with her. This denied identification with the mother is interpreted by Freud as part of Kardiner's struggle to identify with the dreadful authoritarian father. To this interpretation, Kardiner replies, "'I have no such recollection, nor do I have any recollection of what she looked like.' I paused for a moment waiting for comment. Freud said nothing, so I continued. 'I remember seeing her shrouded face in the coffin'" (41). The text implies that Kardiner was aware of this reminiscence as a consciously preserved event, but that what was nevertheless split off from consciousness and left unknown was its deep psychic imprint on him. The psychological implications of the mother's death were denied, and with them her presence as a living mother was also denied consciousness. This had been mentioned earlier, when Kardiner recalled his father's violent attacks on his mother. The compassion he had from a young age for horses that were abused and beaten in the street is understood by him, in retrospect, as having to do with an echo of the repressed mother: "No doubt these horses behaved like mother, who permitted herself to be beaten by my father" (33). The repression of the mother also served partly to repress the child's identification with helplessness and neglect.

A repressed childhood reminiscence concerns the events subsequent to the mother's death, when Kardiner was appointed to be her "Kaddish" (mourner), at the age of three and a half:

> I remember the deep snows through which my sister and I had to plow to get to the synagogue and back. I performed this ritual daily from February to November in a hypnoidal state from which I had to be roused by my stepmother
>
> (29)

According to the manuscript of the interviews, the Kaddish memory remained repressed throughout the analysis and was only aroused decades later during these interviews (Kardiner 1965, 474–476). This memory can also be regarded as a screen memory, representing the traumatic loss of the mother, for the Jewish mourning period lasts 12 months rather than the nine months mentioned, and moreover the time of year mentioned is usually not a time of heavy snows in New York.

Kardiner's representation of his mother is characterized by fragments of repressed and screen memories, which were recovered gradually over the course of his life. This fragmented maternal representation was probably influenced by her short and harsh life, her limited presence in her son's life, and the lack of any supportive environment for the mourning process in Kardiner's childhood. The mother's obscure and limited presence stands by contrast to the appearance of the stepmother, as a figure whose presence was overly prominent and ambivalent.

Alongside the gratitude Kardiner expresses, in the memoir, for Freud's understanding of his long-lasting mask phobia, he also gives expression to his dissatisfaction with Freud's interpretation of his identification with his mother. Freud understood Kardiner's life turmoil as an unconscious identification with the mother's weakness due to his unresolved latent homosexuality. Kardiner describes, with irony, that at first this interpretation confused him and "took me aback" (Kardiner 1977, 60), until, "in comparing notes with other students," he soon found out that "unconscious homosexuality was a routine part of everyone's analysis" (Kardiner 1977, 61). In the series of interviews,

Kardiner expressed a sharper critical stance toward Freud, for what he considered to have been a false and harmful line of interpretation: "I think Freud had a need for this, and I think it played a significant role in his ability to dominate over other men. I think this was an important constituent in his life" (Kardiner 1965, 122).

Work of memory and mourning through writing

Alongside Kardiner's explicit criticism of Freud's limited understanding of the repressed mother figure, there is an insight into a strong identification between analyst and patient concerning loss and mourning. The memoir offers that during analysis, Kardiner notices his analyst's depression, and in response, Freud admits his deep pain, as described in the memoir:

> I once remarked to him that at times he seemed depressed. He admitted that this was true, because his daughter Mathilda [sic; see below] had died only a short while before I arrived in Vienna some months before, and he was very much under the influence of her death. He could not get over it.
>
> (Kardiner 1977, 76)

The honest confession made here by Freud is interrupted by a prominent slip in the text, mistakenly rendering the dead daughter's name as the eldest daughter Mathilda instead of the young and beloved Sophie. At the termination phase of analysis, Freud asked Kardiner to "please see his son-in-law and his grandchildren" when he passed through Hamburg. This request met with ambivalence from Kardiner at the time, and as it turned out he "never got the opportunity to do so" (76). By the time of writing, Kardiner was surely aware that the younger grandchild, who had lost his mother and who was Freud's most treasured grandson, Heinele, had died two years after Kardiner was to have visited. This loss plunged Freud into a deep depression (Jones 1957a, 96–97).

Freud's deep sorrow over Sophie's death is given an obscure yet intimate expression in his *Beyond the Pleasure Principle*, written at around the time of that loss. This classic book, to which I now turn, opens with the writer's observation of a child playing with a wooden reel with a piece of string tied around it:

> What he did was to hold the reel by the string and very skillfully throw it over the edge of his curtained cot, so that it disappeared into it, at the same time uttering his expressive "o-o-o." He then pulled the reel out of the cot again by the string and hailed its reappearance with a joyful "da" ["there"]. This, then, was the complete game—disappearance and return. As a rule one only witnessed its first act, which was repeated untiringly as a game in itself, though there is no doubt that the greater pleasure was attached to the second act.
>
> (Freud 1920a, 15)

The conclusion that Freud draws about the childhood game is that it served as a developmental practice for the purpose of learning to accept the separation from the mother. At that time, the child was said to be strongly attached to her:

> It was related to the child's great cultural achievement—the instinctual renunciation (that is, the renunciation of instinctual satisfaction) which he had made in allowing his mother to go away without protesting. He compensated himself for this, as it were, by himself staging the disappearance and return of the objects within his reach.
>
> (15)

The game enables the child to practice an active role in the challenge of separation, instead of a passive one. Freud claims that this game cannot be explained solely by the pleasure principle, for "The child cannot possibly have felt his mother's departure as something agreeable or even indifferent" (15).

In a footnote to this part, Freud offers some crucial information:

> When this child was five and three-quarters, his mother died. Now that she was really "gone" ("o-o-o"), the little boy showed no signs of grief. It is true that in the interval a second child had been born and had roused him to violent jealousy.
>
> (16)

The contrast between the child who shows no signs of grief over his mother's early loss and the painful yet playful cry of "o-o-o," this time without the complementary cry "da" that symbolizes her return, creates a reading experience of vivid loss that has only allegedly been worked through. Although Freud does not give away the identity of the child, and only mentions that he himself had "lived under the same roof as the child and his parents for some weeks" (14), it is known that the child playing the *fort-da* is his grandson Ernst, Sophie's firstborn son, and that Sophie died unexpectedly during the writing of this book.

Some crucial layers of meaning are laid out obscurely in the text. The first layer is the author's ties to his subjects of observation: Ernst and Sophie, son and mother, grandson and daughter. The second layer is the father/author's work of mourning for his daughter, through the observation and analysis of his grandson's game. The third, and deepest layer is the sorrow and guilt over the brother whom the child envied and who died tragically soon afterward. This is an early childhood traumatic experience that Freud the grandfather shared with his grandson. A deep identification is thus woven between the narratives of the boy crying for the lost object that sometimes returns and sometimes doesn't and of the grandfather/writer/father of psychoanalysis. The text gives voice to the expression of incurable grief, embodied in the unanswered cry of "o-o-o" (Derrida 1987 [1980]).

Kardiner's memoir, written at the end of his life, presents vital insights into the author's encounter with Freud and his childhood memories. It offers a work of translation under two aspects. The first aspect is the reconstruction of the past (a work of memory) as created in analysis, in the series of interviews, and in writing, especially the repressed memories of the absent mother having to do with Kardiner's presence at the time of her death and his role as her mourner. The second aspect of the translation offered by the memoir is the interpretation of the conscious residues of the transference (a work of mourning), especially concerning the abrupt termination of the analysis and Freud's complex analytic stance, connected with his preoccupation with the vicissitudes of Horace Frink's analysis.

At the termination phase, Kardiner remembers nothing but two enigmatic dreams, very different in their atmosphere from the dreams that appeared at the beginning of analysis. Freud's response to them was also very different from his response to the first dreams: "Freud made no comments about either dream except to say that snow dreams indicate a depressive mood, which must appertain to my mother's death" (Kardiner 1977, 63). I will focus here on one of the dreams:

> My first dream was an endless plainlike Russian steppe—covered with snow. My association to this was the snow common in early childhood, and my going to and from the synagogue to say kaddish for my mother, when I was three and a half years old. It was always through deep snows.
>
> (63)

The dream image of the steppe suggests the deep ties among early memories, mourning, and writing. Specifying that the steppe is "Russian" may be an allusion to the origins of the Kardiner family and possible intergenerational experiences of loss. As mentioned, the Kaddish memory had been repressed by Kardiner for many years; the associations with the dream therefore probably arose while writing the memoir, rather than during analysis. The dream suggests that although the analysis created a primary connection for Kardiner with his archaic memories, the connection that was formed was only a limited one. The dream also resonates with Freud's writings about Sergei Pankejeff, known as the Wolf Man, whose analysis introduced the controversial act of forced termination (Freud 1918).

Writing enables Kardiner a retrospective look at what is understood in *après coup* as a joint work of mourning for patient and analyst. It offers Kardiner a look back at the encounter with Freud and allows him to perform a work of mourning over current and past losses. Writing allows a playful movement between past and present, self and other.

Notes

1 This chapter is based on the paper "Memory, Mourning, and Writing: Abram Kardiner's Memoir of Freud" published in *The Psychoanalytic Review* (Tzur Mahalel 2018). Copyright Guilford Press. Reprinted with permission of The Guilford Press.

2 Although implicated, Kardiner avoids the psychoanalytic terminology of true and false self (Winnicott 1960); in fact, he consistently avoids the use of diagnostic psychoanalytic language. According to the memoir, "What made Freud such a great analyst was that, at least at that time, he never used theoretical formulations, but made his interpretations in simple language" (Kardiner 1977, 97). Apparently, this was Kardiner's style as an analyst as well (Bieber 1982).
3 Bion's notion that in undeveloped areas of experience, thinking "moves not in a world of dreams, but in a world of objects which are ordinarily the objects of dreams" (Bion 1967, 51) seems to fit here for the old and broken objects as images of the dreamer's untransformed thoughts. These areas of experience, drained of the potential they hold for thinking and memory, are understood as psychotic. This sheds light on Kardiner's identification with the schizophrenic patient mentioned earlier who had lost his memory.
4 Kardiner describes a benevolent and intimate relationship with Freud, which stood out as unique even among Freud's other analysands. The memoir recounts a detailed reminiscence of Kardiner being invited to a meeting with the exclusive group of British analysands, which otherwise tended to remain distant from the American group. James Strachey and John Rickman invited him to join them because they wanted to understand his success in making Freud talk during analysis, in contrast to his avoidant and silent presence in their own analysis. Rickman even confessed that Freud had a tendency to fall asleep during his sessions (Kardiner 1977, 77–78).
5 At the time of analysis, Kardiner was occupied with a broken heart, having been rejected by a girl he had cherished in his early 20s. Kardiner's response to this rejection was a deep and prolonged depression: he attempted suicide; left medical school, where he had been a distinguished student; and compulsively dwelled on his lover and vied for her attention (Kardiner 1977, 45–50). He even regarded himself as married to her, even though their relationship had taken place mainly in his fantasy life (Kardiner 1965, 25–38).
6 In retrospect, Kardiner was of course aware of Frink's tragic chain of events, but he does not mention it in his writing. The only point at which Frink's breakdown is mentioned, interestingly, is in an expression of loyalty to Freud, explaining Frink's deterioration as totally unconnected to analysis: "What neither Freud nor I knew at this time was that the drastic change in Frink was due not to the analysis but to other causes" (Kardiner 1977, 67).
7 Freud elaborates on screen memories: "not only some but all of what is essential from childhood has been retained in these memories. It is simply a question of knowing how to extract it out of them by analysis. They represent the forgotten years of childhood as adequately as the manifest content of a dream represents the dream-thoughts" (Freud 1914a, 148).

Chapter 5

An American Psychiatrist in Vienna, 1935–1937, and His Sigmund Freud by John Dorsey

"My Sigmund Freud"

Introduction to Dorsey's *Sigmund Freud*

John M. Dorsey's memoir of Freud and his analysis with him is the least known among the corpus the present book covers. This memoir was distributed in a limited edition and tends to be overlooked by researchers. Lohser and Newton offer a rare reading of the memoir, with their focus on revealing Freud's technique through the eyes of his patients. They claim that throughout the memoir, Freud appears to be bored with Dorsey as an analysand (Lohser and Newton 1996, 106). Aside from the memoir's limited distribution, the main reason for the small number of references to this volume is the limited attention that the memoir gives to the actual analytic events, as well as its focus on abstract ideas, presented in a vague and rather idiosyncratic way. It should perhaps be said that the text is not very well written: it is rambling, confused and often incoherent. Especially striking in the text is the unusual way in which the author relates to experiences and persons in his life as "his." The assumption behind this narrative idiosyncrasy, which I will discuss in greater detail later, is that a subject can only narrate what he or she sees from his or her own point of view, and not as a general story. Although it makes challenging reading, the importance of this memoir among the collection of texts written by Freud's patients is that it describes an analysis that is distinct for its length at that late period in Freud's life. In addition, the text offers a dual point of view from the author, the first being the diary that he wrote during analysis and the second being his retrospective personal reading of the diary many years thereafter.

Dorsey's analysis took place during his two-year sabbatical at the University of Vienna and the Viennese Psychoanalytic Institute. His analysis with Freud began in October of 1935 and ended in November of 1936. His diary from that period includes his experiences during his internship in Switzerland before the analysis; then the months he spent in Vienna, in analysis and in psychoanalytic and psychiatric studies; and finally, the aftermath of his analysis with Freud and a second short analysis with Heinz Hartmann (1894–1970), which began in November of 1936. Hartmann was an Austrian Jewish psychiatrist and psychoanalyst, Freud's student and analysand at the time that Freud recommended him as a second analyst for Dorsey. Hartmann was later widely known as the founder of ego psychology, a pivotal school in American psychoanalysis during the 1950s and 1960s. In 1938, Hartmann escaped with his family from Europe and built a new home in New York. He was one of the main founders of the New York Psychoanalytic Society. In the preface to his memoir, Dorsey emphasizes that he has reproduced the diary in its original form and avoided making any alterations or edits to it. However, an introduction and postscript have been added to the original text, together with additional notes to the text giving the writer's personal thoughts, associations, and interpretations during his late reading.

John Morris Dorsey (1900–1978) was an American psychiatrist and psychoanalyst from Clinton, Iowa. He earned his academic degrees at the University of Iowa and served as a professor of psychiatry at the University of Michigan from 1928 to 1938. In 1935, he earned a generous two-year scholarship for psychiatric study in Europe. From 1946 to 1961, Dorsey was a professor of psychiatry at Wayne State University, and later he became a university professor giving general courses of a philosophical nature (Dorsey 1980). His professional path was mainly as an academic researcher and lecturer, and he published books and papers on psychiatry. He also claims to have practiced psychoanalysis on a daily basis; what he seems to mean by that is self-analysis and psychoanalytic reading, rather than psychoanalytic practice per se.

Dorsey's memoir opens with an account of his short period as an intern at Burghölzli, an important psychiatric institute in Switzerland. In October of 1935, a month after his arrival there, Dorsey received a letter from Freud inviting him to start analysis immediately. In spite of the discomfort that stopping his internship so soon after it began must have occasioned, Dorsey accepted the offer without any hesitation. Only two days after receiving the letter, Dorsey was in Vienna with his wife and two children.

When he arrives for his first appointment with Freud, Dorsey is disappointed at first:

> After I did arrive at the Professor's home I was a little surprised again when I found the ordinary apartment house he lived in for over forty years, the steep street he walked and the neighborhood he visited, to be unexpectedly unremarkable. There was a butcher shop at the street level, and on the street wall the plain sign: *Professor Dr. Freud.*
>
> (Dorsey 1976, 18)

The encounter with Freud himself, on the other hand, is described as very far from disappointing:

> Professor Freud came out of an adjoining room, receiving me graciously with a friendly wave of his arm. Immediately I was aware of his alert

presence. My reverent father transference began there.... He had already been a revered heroic figure in my mind ... he seemed a very strong minded person of particular refinement.... His attention, interest, and general presence were that [those] of a younger man.

(18–20)

The diary, as well as the retrospective text woven around it, presents Freud in an ideal light, and even on occasions when certain points of dissatisfaction or doubt from Dorsey's side are expressed, even obscurely, he emphasizes these feeling and thoughts as being firmly in the past, as lessons that were waiting for him to learn and internalize them. For example, Freud's advanced age is presented in the diary with the advantages it held for Dorsey, but in hindsight he admits that Freud's advanced age also had negative implications for him as an analysand. In retrospect, Dorsey emphasizes the fact that now that he is an old man himself, it is easier for him to identify with the condition Freud was in at the time of Dorsey's analysis:

When we first met, the Professor's age was not far from my present one (75 years), and knowing what I do now I would then have preferred him as an analyst on account of his years. However, then my imagination did at first tend to invest him with some so-called disadvantages of old age. Thus, I would raise my voice and try to speak distinctly, allow for possible loss of memory, suspect distraction or disinterest, and so on.

(22)

In addition, the memoir presents Dorsey's reservations about the demanding analytic setting only implicitly, while explicitly emphasizing its various advantages. This persistently positive stance occasionally enters the realm of magical thinking. For example, at the beginning of their analysis, Freud suggests the following structure for their daily sessions:

My analytic hour was to occur six days a week, every day but Sunday, without vacation, except Christmas Day. He asked if I would prefer any special hour and I replied, "No." He suggested 6:00 p.m., somewhat to my surprise, and I told him that suited me best because he mentioned it first.

(19)

Thus, Dorsey rejects the opportunity that Freud offers him to give input into the decision about his appointment time; then, when Freud suggests a time, Dorsey is surprised by it, although he does not explain why he is surprised. He expresses a stance toward Freud of complete devotion, gratitude, and admiration; similarly, the time Freud offers him is the perfect time, as if there were no barriers between them, no alienation, and no differentiation. Another example of this unusual stance occurs when, at the end of the first session,

Freud remarks jokingly that he expects Dorsey to have learned German by the following week. Although Dorsey is aware that this was intended as a humorous remark, he opens the next session in German and continues to struggle with the foreign language until Freud offers that he should return to English. As the memoir continues, Dorsey tends to use more and more German phrases, perhaps as compensation for his early "failure."

It should be mentioned that the analysis takes place during an especially demanding time for Dorsey, because this period is officially a sabbatical in which he is expected to be doing psychiatric studies. This requirement clashes with Freud's request that Dorsey invest all his efforts in analysis and not be occupied with any other professional obligations, a request that has complex implications for Dorsey that he then has to negotiate with his American supervisors. Nevertheless, in his writing, this difficulty is expressed only in a simple passing remark, thereby muting the objective and subjective implications of Freud's request (21).

Enchantment and separation in transference

In his preface, Dorsey expresses complete and absolute admiration for Freud. This attitude is established even before his analysis begins and remains unchanged, though perhaps intensified, during and after analysis:

> I was exquisitely aware of considering Sigmund Freud to be undoubtedly one of the mightiest of men in my chosen vocation of medicine generally and peerless in my area of mental health specifically. Being a hero worshiper from earliest childhood helped me to cultivate an extraordinary readiness to take advantage of my exciting chance to work with my most admired one of all. Fearful I was, but bold enough to see what I could make of this ideal mastermind.
>
> (xvi)

Given this admiration, it did indeed require boldness on Dorsey's part to meet Freud and fulfill his wish to become Freud's analysand, and even greater boldness to write the story of his analysis and a memoir about Freud. He admits, "I have been wishing to *present* that stirringly eventful period of my being for a long while now, always feeling unequal to it" (xv, emphasis in original). The creation of this text is thus presented as the fulfillment of a deep wish, as well as being the occasion for great anxiety. It opens with the following declaration:

> Oh, that I might feel able to compose a masterpiece of precise, perceptive, and refined self-examination worthy of my fascinating psychoanalytic experiences that I have grown as my own in my living of my Wien. Never have I felt greater need for both a scientific and literary mind, nobly

planned, than at present when I try to inscribe events in my sentient consciousness as they were processed in my free association with my Professor Freud.

(xv–xvi)

The encounter with Freud is presented in Dorsey's writing in the context of a disciplined obligation to the work. Dorsey is especially intrigued by Freud's determination and vigorous investment in the analytic work while facing personal challenges of various natures:

> The Professor and I worked together six days a week. Throughout more than a year's work with him this schedule was most rarely interrupted. When I learned later of the health hardships he had been undergoing, I marveled at his ability to keep all the difficulties integrated into the conduct of his work.
>
> (x)

While the analytic encounter is presented as strenuous work, however, the encounter with Vienna is presented as a passionate and sensual love story:

> Vienna is beautiful in every season, especially early spring, lilac time! The soft warm Föhn coming over the Alps from the south, relieving both of our mild winters. The swiftly passing summer sun, and long glorious fall! ... Vienna, my Vienna, lived up to my expectation literally as the City of Dreams. Here my dreaming became most meaningful for my growing self-understanding. I tingled with realizations of Vienna as being the cosmopolitan center it was appreciated to be by my foremost scientists, artists, musicians, poets, linguists, medics, men of letters, and, most notable of all, the father of psychoanalysis.
>
> (xii–xiii)

The representation of Freud is much enriched by Dorsey's thrill at Freud's city, to which he composes a love song: "In my Freudian Wien everyone 'lived and breathed' psychoanalysis, never seeming to tire of this love-invested theme. I lived my psychoanalytic community quite as an enlargement of my earliest family and neighbourhood living" (23).

Dorsey's initial meeting with Freud instantly stimulated a paternal transference in Dorsey, "being a hero worshiper from earliest childhood." The history and background of the writer are brought out in benevolent, even admiring, colors. About his mother, he writes, "My mother was a bright, attractive, tender, loving one, furthering my appreciation for life." His "revered" father is presented as "a good-looking, loving, hard-working man... strong and quick." As the youngest of five siblings, Dorsey "was greatly sheltered" About his home and family, he writes: "My home living was unusually peaceful, and my family loyalty very strong.... My religion was a dominating force during my first several years, although it included most notable tolerance" (46–47). The writer's position as the youngest child of the family, and an attentive, somewhat submissive, one, found itself repeated in his transference relationship with Freud, as presented in the memoir: "He [Freud] received a very prompt, workable transference from me, impressing me in a fatherly manner as serious, kindly, and purposeful" (21).

The historic paternal relationship pattern of an authoritative father and submissive son reappears in a dream at the beginning of the analysis:

> The latent thoughts and feelings of one of my first dreams described me accurately as a young and defenceless person being relentlessly pushed about by an inescapable man of great resourcefulness "whom everybody knew," while large quantities of money seemed to be disappearing in the air.
>
> (xv)

While Dorsey's conscious representation of Freud's authority is that it is benevolent and sheltering, in the dream it is given an abusive representation, presented as a kind of harmful wrestling match. The authority figure uses his power to gain more power instead of taking on the role of provider and caretaker. The large quantities of money disappearing into the air offer a concrete, material image of the loss that accompanies participation in this kind of interaction: not only are the young figure's resources depleted and impoverished, but the situation is represented as one in which it is impossible for him to protest or make any kind of alteration.

Early echoes of these themes can be found in a childhood nightmare that Dorsey used to have. "One of my earliest dreams was a nightmare of clinging with my hands to a cliff while a cavalry troop rode over them" (47). Both of these dreams, from two very different periods in Dorsey's life, present him in a helpless and defenseless position, with an intense power potentially or actually harming him. Moreover, in both dreams there is an attempt to minimize the harmful intentions of the agent of harm, thereby also minimizing that agent's responsibility for the harm that is or might be caused. In the childhood dream, the cavalry troop that is about to send Dorsey to his death is doing its deed unintentionally. In the analysis dream, large amounts of money are disappearing into thin air without there being any object represented as responsible for the loss, not even the man of great resourcefulness present at the scene. Yet the presence of the man in the later dream may imply a more developed insight on Dorsey's part into the circumstances, in terms of object relations, that led the dreamer to this fragile state.

One expression of Dorsey's fragile and dependent position in relation to authority in general and Freud specifically is that Dorsey tends to ask Freud direct questions concerning Freud's view of their relationship. These questions usually are not articulated in the text; all we are offered is Freud's partial responses to them or his remarks concerning the inappropriateness of these questions to the analytic work. Thus, after his second session with the professor, Dorsey writes in his diary,

> The Professor was deeply engrossed in his Moses research and writing, but I heard absolutely nothing of that from him. In one of my hours I asked him to express an opinion of me. His only reply was that he found me very personal. At another time in reply to my seeming to myself to be a day late with my latent thoughts associated with my manifest dream, he offered, "It may take a day longer for you." Certainly this comment spurred my conscious effort to attend diligently to my dreaming and its concealed self-revelation.
>
> (59)

Dorsey understands these remarks by Freud as evidence that Freud does not appreciate him. Toward the end of his analysis, he writes in his diary, "Immature people have a need to be 'personal.'" Then he comments on this entry, in a retrospective remark, "I have in mind the Professor's use of this word 'personal,' implying an immoderate need to get too close, I imagine" (114).

One of the main difficulties Dorsey experiences as an analysand is his inhibition with respect to free-associating his thoughts. This inhibition appears in analysis in the form of what Dorsey presents as a scattered and crowded verbalization. Looking back, he sees this redundancy as an expression of his inability at the time to acknowledge his own psychic pain and helplessness. Over the years, alongside the growing empathy toward himself as analysand, his agreement with Freud's criticism also grows. He gradually comes to recognize that he was not truly present in analysis as a continuous experience, especially in the first months:

> For many weeks I was more inclined to hurry and scurry verbally over my hurt-mindedness like a frightened rabbit, not daring to allow myself "time to think" much about what I might be saying by allowing *its* origin, its underlying growth in and of me, to show itself.
>
> (43, emphasis in original)

In the memoir, Freud is presented as an analyst of determined and stubborn reticence and restraint, leaving his analysand deprived and confused. Yet the memoir also depicts a process of conscious transformation that the writer undergoes. Gradually during the analysis, and then after it terminates, he goes through a significant change, a change that is presented as only being possible because of the encounter with Freud's distinct figure. Dorsey is enchanted with Freud, in manifold ways, but most of all, he is enchanted by Freud's inner freedom to think and give expression to his thoughts with relatively little regard for the reactions he receives. The way in which Freud contains himself within himself, subjected only to his own inner world and free to choose the distinct form he uses to express himself on various matters, finds deep echoes in Dorsey's psyche. Dorsey internalizes Freud's voice with such clarity and lucidity that he keeps returning to it throughout the years following the analytic experience, analyzing, translating, and internalizing new possible meanings of the messages communicated to him, both explicitly and implicitly, by Freud.

Freud offers Dorsey a collection of his writings to read, most particularly the 1927 *The Future of an Illusion*. Dorsey writes in retrospect that since that time he has disciplined himself to read Freud's writings on a daily basis and continues to find in them new meanings and insights into his own personal development. Sometimes it seems that this devoted continuance of self-analysis on Dorsey's part, both on a personal basis, as an analysand, and on a theoretical basis, as a reader, is based on the assumption that the process of becoming a subject is completely and utterly dependent for him on the extent of affinity that he establishes with Freud's thought and figure. The stronger the ties he creates with Freud, the deeper the connection he finds with himself.

Alongside the deep admiration that he develops for Freud's independence and lucidity as a person, Dorsey emphasizes that he also gradually comes to recognize the crucial importance of Freud's analytic stance for Dorsey's own self-development. After the first session, Dorsey writes in his diary that it was "truly a soul-stirring experience." This stems from being in the presence of this great man: "Just to think of the father of psychoanalysis, being in the same room listening, correcting, always straightening and progressing" (26). Yet in his late writing about these impressions, Dorsey offers a more complex insight into the transference:

> Certainly that was what I was expecting of my self-analysis at the time. Fortunately it never happened. I profited immeasurably from the non-interfering and conscious self-contained way in which the Professor conducted his work. Those were heedfully self-stirring days. I can still live the aura of purposefully excited self-love pervading them. My psychoanalyst was not partial to comment, and commented so.
>
> (26–27)

This quote reveals Dorsey's distinct writing style, as expressed in the sentences that curl in on themselves in a confusing way.

His characterization of his analysis as "self-analysis" is salient for its deviation from how these terms are generally used. "Self-analysis" is commonly used to refer to the process of analysis that a person goes through with him- or herself, usually in the aftermath of a regular analysis. Dorsey's personal translation of the concept is presented as part of his philosophical view of the inability of the individual subject to generalize from his or her own personal point of view on the world. This point of view is one that develops during his analysis. As an analysand, he has the insight that the subject is the only entity that can tell its own story, and that any expectation of hearing these notions from outside is false. In his later retrospective reading of the impression that the first session made on him, Dorsey suggests the notion that the excitement he experienced was actually not "soul-stirring," but "self-stirring." Over the years, Dorsey comes to regard his fantasy of a dominant yet attentive and devoted father figure as impossible and exchanges it for what he understands to be the model introduced to him by Freud, of an independent, self-contained subjectivity. Looking back on his analysis, Dorsey expresses gratitude for Freud's restraint, in spite of the pain it causes him:

> Fortunately the Professor understood that it was labor that only I could do. He obviously knew that his work was to see me insightfully through my difficult self-confrontation, and my happiness for his comprehension furthered my doing what I could. I benefit indescribably from sensing his *commitment* to his analytic work. He did not, and did not need to, show it as a display. It is surely most effective.
>
> (60, emphasis in original)

Thus, Dorsey's initial fantasy in the transference is to alter his internal conception of his relationship with authority, from an authoritative entity to an attentive and containing one. The fantasy that he will find this affection and devotion in Freud is gradually transformed into a recognition that he should turn these fantasies inwards and try to fulfill them in a self-contained way. "The Professor never encouraged me in the idea or feeling that anything was going on *between* us" (37, emphasis in original); and later, "Certainly the Professor conducted his work as if he were fully aware of the inviolability of individuality, and aware of 'between-ness' as being all within-ness" (70).

This insight is offered in close connection with the initial fantasy:

> My self-analysis based upon my free association must be a soliloquy—not a dialogue. [However, the Professor would often "answer" a question with that understanding reservation in it.] As he good-humoredly put it: "Psychoanalysis is not a game of questions and answers, now, is it?"
>
> (27, the square brackets present retrospective remarks by the writer)

Freud's persistent restraint is experienced during analysis as a complicated and painful challenge. Gradually, however, Dorsey comes to understand Freud's analytic stance as a persistent message to Dorsey to turn his attention inward instead of continuing his constant anxious outward request; a message to seek his own distinct experience, story, and voice. Only toward the end of analysis and, in fact, after it ends, does Dorsey come to fully acknowledge the essential meaning that Freud's stance holds for him. "The one word that characterized his analytic presence was: *commitment*. He practiced the finest tact in the form of ongoing attentiveness to his minding of his own living. From the beginning to the end of each hour there was no loose work, no theorizing, no curing, no criticizing, no acting—just free interest" (36, emphasis in original). The self-attentiveness that characterizes Freud deeply impresses Dorsey, and he regards it as the basis of his creativity and strength: "I might state *he* seemed to be his only technique" (29, emphasis in original).

A key part of the change that Dorsey goes through during analysis involves the innovative insights that he gains into the parent–child relationship and a reconsideration of the child's psychological needs and the ways in which those needs are met by his or her surroundings. This line of thought becomes pivotal in Dorsey's life, and after his return home from Vienna he supervises a child therapy center in Michigan for many years. Dorsey's insights with regard to the psychological development of the child evolve alongside his experience as an analysand. He reveals that at the beginning of analysis, he assumed that its aim would be for him to learn to take a mature position in life while letting go of infantile aspects of his personality. As the analysis progresses, however, Dorsey comes to acknowledge it as a process of revealing and reconnecting to his infantile self. He finds himself redirecting his psychic path toward the infantile experience and state of mind, while pushing aside social demands for adaptation.

This process begins with an event that is presented as a turning point in Dorsey's analysis. At the end of a session at the end of March, he receives a somewhat surprising invitation from Freud.

> After my hour the Professor took me into the room containing shelves of his books. I tried to assist his reaching a book but he preferred to do it alone. He handed me his *The Future of an Illusion*, English translation, smilingly saying, "This will start you on the road to Hades." Earlier I had asked him what psychoanalysis might do to my cherished religious living. He replied that it would be meaningful there, as elsewhere, for offering the possibility of understanding my religious living.
>
> (71)

The Future of an Illusion, also mentioned by Blanton, argues that religious faith is a temptation based on the unbearable helplessness of existence. This challenge to religion alludes to the infantile experience of the oedipal conflict between yearning, anger, and guilt toward the father. What is Freud's message when he invites Dorsey to read this essay with a smile and the warning that it will lead him to Hades? Dorsey's apprehension at the invitation is an expression of his resistance to facing changes in the values in which he was raised and the authoritative object relations that he has internalized. As always, Freud does not flinch from challenging his analysands' beliefs and values, nor does he hesitate to present himself as the representative of Satan. For what is to Dorsey, the believer, a forbidden path is to Freud the path to the modern salvation of secularism.

The Future of an Illusion offers a Socratic dialogue of sorts between the secular voice of Freud and a friend who resists that secularism. This format allows Freud to bring up and address the great challenges faced by those who choose secularism. Using the rhetorical means of the dialogue, Freud lays out his views on abandoning the temptation of religion for the enlightenment of secularism. The essay is an explicit call to make this brave choice, not in order to escape psychic pain but in spite of psychic pain. For Freud, facing psychic pain is the most pivotal means of growth. He describes religious faith as an elusive temptation, which he calls "the sweet—or bitter-sweet—poison" (Freud 1927, 49) as in Sappho's image of Eros. Abandoning religion is presented as a difficult challenge, for this poison has been "instilled" from childhood. People who choose secularism

> will have to admit to themselves the full extent of their helplessness and their insignificance in the machinery of the universe; they can no longer be the centre of creation, no longer the object of tender care on the part of a beneficent Providence. They will be in the same position as a child who has left the parental house where he was so warm and comfortable. But surely infantilism is destined to be surmounted. Men cannot remain children for ever; they must in the end go out into "hostile life." We may call this *"education to reality."* Need I confess to you that the sole purpose of my book is to point out the necessity for this forward step?
>
> (Freud 1927, 49, emphasis in original)

Freud ends his essay with praise for science as an answer to religion. It ends with the conclusion that science provides answers about ourselves and the world around us humbly and responsibly, instead of the illusions that religion gives us: "No, our science is no illusion. But an illusion it would be to suppose that what science cannot give us we can get elsewhere" (56).

In his memoir, Dorsey writes a praise poem of his own to science. Dorsey's poem is called "The Fool's Prayer," possibly in tribute to the well-known poem with the same title by the American poet Edward Rowland Sill (1841–1887). Dorsey's poem is given a central place in the memoir and besides the poem itself, a whole chapter is given that name. The poem, presenting science as the center of human thought and creation, is a reworking of The Lord's Prayer, or Pater Noster:

> Oh science, challenging heavens and earth, Free interest be thy claim. The laws come, thy consciousness be brought on, wherever our senses reach. Improve our uninstructed reasoning and accept each day our courage, honesty, and facts; support our failures, as we support our own ignorance and uncertainties; and lead us not into unreality but deliver us from all error. *Amen.*
>
> (Dorsey 1976, 158)

Sill's "The Fool's Prayer" presents the king's jester as a speaker at the royal feast, in front of the king's guests. His role is to entertain, presumably by presenting a mocking version of a prayer. Yet instead the jester presents a personal prayer to God, asking for forgiveness for human follies and errs. Dorsey's use of the same title for his poem implies that Dorsey might be presenting himself as the king's jester, offering his own humble words to the royal guests of the psychoanalytic community. He is expected to mock religion, and yet perhaps Dorsey wants the king, aka Freud, in whose honor Dorsey has written this poem to science, to find within himself his denied religious faith. Dorsey's poem is addressed to science as a sublime force, holding up and maintaining humanity's wisdom, yet presenting religious language, possibly in an impossible effort at integration. The poem tries to express an integration between two positions with which Dorsey identifies, namely the religious position that was central in his upbringing and the secular position that centers on the creation and development of subjectivity.

Freud consistently affirms humanity's crucial need to free itself from the illusions offered by religion and to face existence in its authentic form, despite the hardship. The view that Dorsey presents is explicitly the same as Freud's, as expressed for instance in Dorsey's call to rely solely on self-consciousness: "How can one be a daring thinker who has been brought up on the philosophy of fear. How can one see all that there is to see (or sense) who does not dare to think with absolute freedom!" (Dorsey 1976, 89). Nevertheless, in Dorsey's "Fool's Prayer," as well as in other places in his text, one can track obscure voices that hold onto an affinity with religion and, as with the transformation that Sill's king undergoes under the influence of the jester, Dorsey also seeks some solidarity in this, even if just a hint of it, with Freud. His retrospective comments on the poem further express a wish for an integration between Freud and religion, "I am beginning to see the identity in the religious 'Thy will be done' and the scientific, 'When all the data are present to bring about an event, it occurs'" (158).

The representation of a muted termination

As already noted, Dorsey's narrative of the analytic process is characterized by its vagueness and incoherence. Yet the termination phase of analysis is presented with impressive clarity, especially in the writing that Dorsey added in retrospect. At the beginning of November 1936, after approximately a year of analytic process, Dorsey has to separate from Freud. As a somewhat late fulfillment of the dream from the beginning of his analysis, Dorsey's economic funds have all gone. In the last month of analysis, he even has to take a loan from Freud's son Martin, offered to Dorsey through Freud (a procedure that would be impossible nowadays for ethical reasons).

During the termination process, Dorsey apparently gathers from Freud that his analytic process is not yet over and that he should seek further analysis before he can be recommended for analytic training. Freud recommends his pupil and analysand Heinz Hartmann. Dorsey mentions that the analysis with Hartmann is possible because it requires considerably less funds than do the sessions with Freud. Hartmann impresses him as a professional analyst and a person who evaluates manifold aspects of life. On various levels, Dorsey sees his second analysis as a direct continuation of his analysis with Freud, for the sessions with Hartmann begin, presumably, immediately after the end of the sessions with Freud. Moreover, Dorsey experiences Hartmann's technique as being very similar to Freud's, namely a restraint that relies almost entirely on the analysand's associations. He concludes his account of his encounter with Hartmann by saying, in retrospect,

> From the start I valued this development as a natural continuation of my privileged work with Professor Freud. Dr. Hartmann honored as I did the Professor's completing of his analytic work exactly as he did, and I have always appreciated the extraordinary smoothness of my difficult transition.
> (135)

Interestingly, the separation from Freud is almost absent from the diary, perhaps because it was not thoroughly worked through at the time. The possibility of a second analysis with a different analyst is discussed, yet the transition itself, which Dorsey describes in his late notes as "smooth," is not given any representation at the time. Dorsey's late reading in the diary does, however, give the experience of separation from Freud a central place. While the diary presents a smooth and inevitable transition from Freud to Hartmann, the retrospective text written by Dorsey is immersed in "mourning" and "gloom":

> The time all too rapidly arrived that was set for termination of my free association with the Professor. A definite date was necessary from my standpoint on account of my lack of funds. The actual stopping came hard. Although I recognized a specific completion in my appreciation for my work I felt strongly the need for furthering that appreciation. I found the idea of being thrown back upon myself without my Professor,—a heavy burden involving painful self rejection including an intensive sense of failure.
> (131)

The forced termination due to lack of funds is made even more difficult to bear because of the pain involved in Freud's recommendation of further analysis before Dorsey can turn to analytic training. Dorsey writes in retrospect about this deep disappointment,

> I had been hoping desperately all along to attain my personal development as a fully disciplined psychoanalyst as soon as possible. I felt sure that

Professor Freud could make me do it. The insurmountable truth remained: I seemed unable to do it, without growing further helpfulness for that doing.

(131–132)

In the narrative of the following weeks, the difference between the contemporary representation and the retroactive representation of the separation from Freud gradually widens. While the diary entries discuss lectures and meetings with colleagues with ease, the retrospective text tells a story of painful crisis. In his late reading, Dorsey finds himself thinking about a matter-of-fact remark in the diary about "cloudy days with little sun." Looking back, he understands this remark as presenting an image of his sad inner state at the time, about which he was in denial:

> Despite my sincere feeling that my Heinz Hartmann was the most worthy successor of my Professor I naturally mourned the seeming loss of the Professor, and the 'cloudy days with little sun' undoubtedly referred to the gloom from my unresolved transference
>
> (136)

Dorsey understands in retrospect that in the weeks after his separation from Freud, his pain at the premature termination was his core experience and inner occupation. At the time the termination took place, the experience is presumably too intense to reach the level of consciousness. The pain involved in that experience is therefore worked through in his retrospective writing, as a late work of mourning:

> I continue to nurse my hurt. During the first week I find Dr. Hartmann all that I could hope for as the one with whom to extend my self-analysis. I had already grown him as an independent, courageous, self-contained, freedom-loving, quiet man. Nevertheless I continued to suffer from my transferred dependence upon my Sigmund Freud, now aggravated by the discontinuation of my daily Stunde with him.
>
> (137)

One factor that contributes to making the separation from Freud such a challenge for Dorsey is his inhibition about mourning. At the beginning of his analysis, he writes in a diary entry of the uneasiness he feels in response to what he perceives as Freud's tendency to focus on painful experiences and invest effort into seeking their roots and possible meaning. Therein lies a conflict for Dorsey, because he is apprehensive and tempted at the same time. He was filled with admiration for Freud's courage, yet ambivalent about the supposed implications of extended self-consciousness. About Freud's technique, he writes:

> He taught himself the hard discipline of psychic responsibility.... Understanding the transformation of self unconsciousness to self-consciousness occurs by becoming aware of how the mind is constantly growing itself by living its own discovered roots. For him, self-analysis was interminable. Everyone must understand his own growing self from his own growth of experience only.
>
> (37)

In a retrospective comment on these notions, Dorsey admits: "Most difficult for me to accept fully was the pure helpfulness of suffering, the welcoming of unhappy associations as being equally valuable to happy ones, the seeking rather than avoiding of the motivating force of sorrowing" (37–38).

This ambivalence toward revealing his unconscious, especially experiences of loss and grief, continues. A couple of weeks into analysis, Dorsey writes in his diary that some time earlier he told his friends that "psychoanalysis involved one's being willing to have all that one holds nearest and dearest die (To be re-born in true-er relationship). I added that for a person about to suicide psychoanalysis would probably be a pleasant experience" (64). It seems that Dorsey understands the potential of revealing painful experiences by raising them from the unconscious in analysis, yet subjectively, the intense anxiety he feels, turns here into a kind of sarcasm, which is not typical for him. As we already noted above with regard to religion and Dorsey's response to Freud's secularism, here Dorsey again responds to the possibility of differentiation from his roots and education with ambivalence.

Another factor that contributes to the complexity of Dorsey's separation process from Freud, and which was mentioned earlier, is Dorsey's lack of sufficient working through in that area. His experience as an analysand at the time of separation resonates with the child in Freud's "Future of an Illusion," "who has left the parental house where he was so warm and comfortable." He concludes, "Men cannot remain children for ever; they must in the end go out into 'hostile life'" (Freud 1927, 49).

During these challenging days, Dorsey's has the idea of writing a play. In his late writing, he understands his turn toward dramatic writing as a way to express and work through his pain. The play is meant to revolve around a lifeboat crowded with passengers from a drowning boat; as the play goes on, the passengers gradually slip to their death in the deadly water. "A flier at fiction: opening with [a] few preliminary general philosophic remarks: setting—capsized lifeboat at sea; plot—suicidal motive in each successive person's slipping from the side of [the] boat under the water" (Dorsey 1976, 140). The psychoanalytic aspect of the play is the intertwinement of conscious and unconscious, for beneath the conscious fear of death there lies, for each character, an unconscious death wish, for different reasons in each case. Perhaps this morbid plot resonates with Freud's invitation to Hades and its implications in terms of Dorsey's reexamination of his historical roots, of the values and beliefs with which he was raised. This reexamination gives him innovative insights, but presents him with complex conflicts of loyalty.

Looking back, Dorsey reveals an affinity between his idea for the play and a well-known play by the American author and playwright Thornton Wilder (1897–1975). It occurs to Dorsey that Freud had once told him that he saw a great deal of resemblance between Dorsey's thought and Wilder's (31). Dorsey is probably referring to the 1927 play *The Bridge of San Luis Rey*, which presents the story of five people who find their death in the collapse of a central bridge in Peru and is told in retrospect by a Franciscan friar (Wilder 1927). The play written by Dorsey can be seen as a personal work of mourning of the premature separation. It is connected with Freud's remark about the connection between Wilder and Dorsey, and it gives expression to Dorsey's complex relationship with psychoanalysis. Psychoanalysis holds for him the temptation of wisdom and mental freedom, yet is also intertwined with anxiety and guilt over questioning the values with which he was raised.

In the months after the termination of his analysis with Freud, Dorsey occasionally mentions efforts he has made to connect and meet with Freud. He tells of a greeting card he sends Freud, in which he emphasizes the deep gratitude he feels toward Freud for the process he helped him go through (152). The memoir also mentions, in an offhand way, that Freud twice turns down invitations from Dorsey to meet (186). Toward the end of Dorsey's sabbatical in Vienna, in May of 1937, the two finally manage to arrange a meeting, a friendly gathering that also includes family members of both of the men. This meeting takes place at Freud's summer house in Grinzing. The village is well-known to Dorsey's family from their stay there during the summer months of analysis. A cheerful encounter is described in the diary. They all eat together and chat, and Dorsey's two young boys draw much attention. Freud speaks German and remarks that the children are "*Mutter ähnlich*." He then turns to one of the boys and suggests that he not eat the cherry stems, yet the child feels free enough to respond laughingly that they are good to eat. In regard to Dorsey's feelings during that event, he writes, "Although he remained completely my self-contained Sigmund Freud, I felt that there was hope for me, for my becoming whatever I wanted to become in terms of my developing myself psychoanalytically" (190). These words in one diary entry are the only expression of any turmoil felt by Dorsey at the actual time of separation, as opposed to in *après coup*. It is probably not a coincidence that it is only after the final encounter with Freud, an encounter characterized by warmth and familiarity, that Dorsey is able to give expression to his pain over their separation.

Telling a story in psychoanalysis and in writing

One of the most precious gifts Dorsey describes himself as having received from Freud is the importance of the story in the process of constructing and broadening psychic space and in freeing oneself from moments of inner and interpersonal impasse. In Dorsey's analysis, the literary sphere is presented as holding the potential for an innovative point of view, as an invitation to imagination, which frees the individual from mental and emotional restraints.

For example, Dorsey writes about his tendency to ask Freud questions about his analytic stance, which is characterized by restraint:

> I also wanted to know more clearly why the Professor did not begin to take a more active role in my psychoanalysis. Again he told a story. "The Japanese gardener who was reproached, after being hired, for sitting for several days and doing no work, rejoined that he *was* working; the first step in building the garden being to take in the landscape"
>
> (53, emphasis in original)

The space that Freud opens with his story of the Japanese gardener, challenges the authoritative relations as they are perceived in the transference. Within the framework of the story, Freud is represented by the gardener asking for patience, while Dorsey is represented as his reproachful employer. In addition, Freud is represented as a foreigner in the story, adding to the encounter between Dorsey and Freud a dimension of intercultural exchange, which requires patience and endurance yet offers the potential for enrichment. The Japanese gardener presents the meditative aspects of psychoanalysis, which require the investment of time in order to put aside the haste of reality, and turn his impression of the landscape inwards. One can be reminded in this context of Freud's words to the analysand at the beginning of analysis: "Before I can say anything to you I must know a great deal about you" (Freud 1913a, 134).

Later in Dorsey's analysis, he turns to Freud and inquires how to free his associations.

> Once I spoke of the difficulty in free association. The Professor recalled complaining of an attack of dysentery he suffered during an American camping trip with Dr. James Putnam. The most help Dr. Putnam had to offer was, "That's too bad," observing that such an intestinal upset occurred often in foreigners. Professor Freud added genially that he had no more help to offer me than that.
>
> (Dorsey 1976, 69)

This miserable incident, the attack of dysentery, which took place during Freud's single trip to the United States, contributed to Freud's negative attitude toward American culture. James Jackson Putnam (1846–1918), the eminent American professor of neurology, was hosting Freud at his Adirondack camp; Freud experienced Dr. Putnam's response to his illness as detached and cold, thereby contributing to his suffering at the time (Breger 2000, 189–190; Gay 1988, 206–213).[1] With this reminiscence of the attack of dysentery, Freud offers Dorsey a somatic image for the difficulty in free-associating. The psychic inhibition of the mind resembles an illness of the digestive system. With this significant personal story, perhaps Freud is also trying to communicate the comforting message that he himself also suffers from human inhibitions of the mind and body. Nevertheless, this memory of a very negative experience that Freud had in Dorsey's homeland is yet another reminder of the intercultural challenge with which Dorsey and Freud struggle, a challenge that holds not only potential for enrichment, as in the previous story, but also frustration and pain.

Another example of the use of the literary sphere is Freud's use of parables. In response to Dorsey's repeated question about the estimated duration of the analysis, Freud

> responded by relating the tale of the wayfarer in Aesop's fable, a tale which suddenly came alive for me: When the traveler came upon Aesop who was laboring on the road—breaking up stone—and asked him how long it was to the next town, say to Megara, Aesop responded, "Go." Angrily the traveler turned away and resumed his going. "Three quarters of an hour," called Aesop after him. The wayfarer asked, "Why didn't you say so in the first place?" Aesop explained, "I wanted to see just how you went, so that I could decide upon it."
>
> (66)

With this story, Freud offers an interpretation of his restraint not as avoidance but as a generous examination of the analysand's distinct steps and pace. The story suddenly "came to life" for Dorsey at the time of analysis. His retrospective examination of this moment intriguingly raises the question of the extent to which he has understood Freud's message. Perhaps the examination that Freud offers of the analysand's pace does not fit Dorsey's needs, as an apprehended analysand. Years after analysis, Dorsey grows to recognize this moment as one of the transformative moments in which, as he reveals, "finding myself thrown back upon myself for help, so to speak, I grew further in the direction of acknowledging fully that all help must be self-help" (66).

A less successful use of the literary sphere in the analysis occurs on one occasion when Dorsey expresses his repeated impatience at the duration of the analysis. Freud meets this with less patience, offering a story with a markedly sarcastic tone toward American culture:

> Again my free associations bring out my concern about the length of my analysis. The Professor speaks good naturedly of the American who boasted of making the complete tour of the Louvre in one hour and three-quarters, and who then added, "And if I'd had my roller-skates on I could have made it in an hour and a half." I imagine I do present myself as a would-be Charlie Paddock in psychoanalysis.
>
> (68)

In this story Freud expresses sharp and explicit criticism, yet Dorsey remarks that it is told "good naturedly," perhaps as a way to soften its bluntness somewhat, and hence he also expresses identification with Freud's criticism on a personal level, presenting himself in quite a ludicrous light.

The literary space offered in Dorsey's analysis is presented in the memoir as possessing an integrating potential: the potential to gather complex and painful experiences and transform them into a structure, a construct that can be thought of, elaborated, translated, and revived. The continuity of the story enables the reader of Dorsey's memoir to reread the stories that Dorsey, as analysand, has "read" from Freud's "oral text," and they come to life in a way that is similar to the way in which they came to life in analysis. Their presence enables the reader to revive and retranslate them in ways that are offered by the literary space.

The connection between the literary and the psychoanalytic is expressed in the memoir when Dorsey returns to Freud's 1920 essay, "A Note on the Prehistory of the Technique of Analysis" (Freud 1920b). There, Dorsey says, Freud writes about how he invented the method of free association. At the age of 14, Freud received a text entitled "The Art of Becoming an Original Writer in Three Days." Dorsey explains that "the method consisted of writing down without censorship the mind-revealing content of the uninhibited stream of consciousness" (43). Writing is therefore given the meaning of being a profound way to continue Freud's legacy and ideas. Yet a memoir that centers on a "mastermind," as Dorsey calls Freud, demands to be a "masterpiece." This expectation fills Dorsey with ambivalence and apprehension. On the one hand, he is eager to give expression to the transformative process that he underwent in analysis. On the other hand, the act of writing can be interpreted as an act of competition with his admired paternal figure.

In his writing, Dorsey is interested not only in repeating the analytic relationship in a work of memory, but, moreover, in offering a subjective translation of that relationship:

> As might be understandable, whenever my fellowman discovers that his Dorsey 'worked with Professor Freud' he expects him to be able to talk or write about *the* Professor himself. Only *the* Professor is capable of any or every observation regarding his own mental development, including all conduct of his life.
>
> (30, emphasis in original)

The question of how to write the story of analysis from the point of view of the analysand was a challenging question for all the writers presented in this book. One of the pivotal challenges that Dorsey struggles within this context is the vagueness of Freud's stance toward him. Freud sometimes impresses Dorsey as being open and generous in offering himself as a model of a self-contained subject, relying solely on his own mental and psychic resources. Yet Freud is also presented as being impatient and critical. The abrupt termination of Dorsey's analysis with Freud does not allow him any thorough working through of these transference issues, and they remain over the years as residues, waiting for retranslation and integration. Dorsey's longitudinal self-analysis is occupied with the challenge of retranslating Freud's analytic stance to make it gradually more and more suitable for his needs. The retranslation that Dorsey offers of his analyst's stance emphasizes the benevolent aspects of Freud's restraint and ambiguity that Dorsey has grown to appreciate:

> I enjoy living over and over the fact that his, so-to-say, giving me my head completely (that is, his not trying to teach me anything) was the most helpful learning experience I ever had. I needed specifically just that, —his knowing clearly his own self and how it had been necessary for him to grow to know his own self.
> (41)

Over the years, Freud becomes an extremely dominant model for Dorsey, and he invests great effort in trying to understand Freud's thoughts, preoccupations, and analytic stance. It can be said that Dorsey does indeed create "his Freud," a private representation that relies partly on actual reminiscences, but more than that relies on Dorsey's changing needs throughout his life. In the preface, Dorsey states,

> My most difficult language lesson teaches: My every word can be nothing but my own linguistic growth, despite the fact that I can and do enjoy its functioning as if it is not referring to me at all. Therefore, I carefully record: All I can mean by describing Sigmund Freud must really refer to *my* image of my Sigmund Freud.
> (xvi, emphasis in original)

Writing about Freud represents the actualization of this creation, for the writer recreates his own Sigmund Freud, a creation that connects to actual memories, but in obscure and nonbinding ways. The links between Freud as a literary protagonist in Dorsey's writing and Freud as an actual person preserved in the writer's memories are not clear, and it does not seem as though Dorsey is particularly interested in investing effort in this question. The textual creation stands at the center of his writing and represents the highlight of the writer's growing subjectivity. Through the memoir, Dorsey completes a process wherein "all language is idiolect, all talk is soliloquy, all writing is autobiographical" (87). Therefore, according to Dorsey, a person can only aim to speak his own mind and write his own story.

There are three processes that are presented as being responsible for bringing Dorsey to his level of self-consciousness, and they are his analysis with Freud, the self-analysis in which he was engaged afterward, and, inseparable from the first two, his writing (xii). Dorsey's various writings belong mostly to the scientific literature, yet they are understood and presented by him in retrospect as autobiographical. He represents his inspiration as a writer as relying heavily on Freud as a writer, analyst, and man. Dorsey emphasizes Freud's distinctive use of language as an analyst, the respect and accuracy with which he chose each word that he articulated: "My Sigmund Freud was keenly conscious [of] the power of the word as a vehicle for his technique and he seemed to use each word with care" (35). This same respect for language also characterizes Freud as a writer. Dorsey's return to Freud's essay about how he invented the method of free association, mentioned earlier, reveals the notion that writing frees the mind in similar ways to psychoanalysis, allowing the subject to explore and create his or her singular voice. The literary sphere that is opened to Dorsey in his analysis is a further source of inspiration to him, as he finds enriching potential in writing as a way of continuing his encounter with Freud.

Toward the end of the memoir, Dorsey expresses his astonishment at the value of writing that has been revealed to him. Writing is presented as a maternal womb in which new life is conceived and developed. The ever-developing bond with Freud as an analyst, writer, and man becomes a nest in which Dorsey can conceive his singular voice:

> I am continuing to try to unravel some of the tangle I have made of my magnificent life, renewing previous efforts I exerted to make the best I could of its overwhelming vicissitudes. How understandable to me becomes the self helpfulness of the author in his (her) literary creativity.
>
> (170)

The memoir opens with a declaration: "My literal awakening to myself as being the inviolable individual I am, occurred with my accurate appraisal of the lifesaving nature of my self-consciousness" (1). As discussed previously, the awakening embodied in the memoir is the most profound expression of Dorsey's manifold processes of revealing his unconscious.

The solution that Dorsey finds to this challenge is to create a detachment between the text and its actual referent or addressee, as Dorsey emphasizes at the beginning:

> In the following account of my self-analysis with the psychoanalyst of my choice, Sigmund Freud, I am absolutely certain of one fact, namely, that it is all and only about myself.... Only my Sigmund Freud is able to record anything whatsoever about his self, and this he has done magnificently.
>
> (2)

The disconnection between the narrative and its referent gives the writer a freedom, allegedly without constraint, to create his own partly fictive, partly autobiographical story about his analysis with Freud. Nevertheless, I want to stress that the weakness of Dorsey's memoir is that this ambition does not prove to be successful. Dorsey's text does not succeed in creating a fictive literary creation, for it remains tightly tied to the actual referent, to Freud, and in many ways to the actual encounter with him. The effort invested by Dorsey in his attempt not to focus on the analytic events turns the narrative into a mixture of contents and ideas that do not finally cohere into an integrated and communicative text.

The distinctive title of the memoir exemplifies, to my mind, the failure of Dorsey's attempt to free the text from its historical context. The fictive aspect of the memoir finds expression in the concept of "my Sigmund Freud." This concept is an attempt to express the way in which the figure of Freud will be reborn through Dorsey's writing. Yet the rest of the title of the memoir is completely situated in a particular historical context: "An American Psychiatrist in Vienna, 1935–1937." The creation of Freud through the act of writing is mainly meant to allow the creation of the writer himself as an independent subject and to describe this transformational process. Nevertheless, the figure of the writer is represented solely as "an American psychiatrist," one out of many. His figure is redeemed from its anonymity only by its reliance on the figure of Freud, which is presented as his. Although the writer aspires to create an independent narrative, it is his affinity with the distinguished figure that is presented as the only way for him to make his distinctive voice heard and to become a subject.

The only place in which Dorsey's text distinguishes itself from its reliance on the other and situates itself as an independent text is in the separation narrative from Freud that it offers. Dorsey's diary from the time of analysis expresses a complete and absolute identification with Freud's narrative of separation, a narrative that suggests that the analysand moves from one analyst to another with no significant inhibitions or turmoil. The text that Dorsey writes years later, however, moves beyond this conformity and succeeds in creating a new story that gives representation to the deep pains that are involved in the abrupt termination of the profound dependence that the analysand has developed, a termination that is not thoroughly worked through in analysis. The new story of the termination stands in opposition to the previous story, which suggests that the termination process only occurs as an actual event, allegedly without evidence of psychic turmoil. Yet in obscure psychic layers, a crisis has happened or possibly been repeated, and it demands long years of affinity with Freud and self-analysis to enable it to return as a live and significant experience.

Note

1 The negative impression this event left on Freud is presented in Grinker's reminiscences: "'That's too bad' still rang in his ears twenty-five years later, for this expression and nothing more was all he received while suffering from intestinal cramps at Putnam's Adirondack camp" (Grinker 1973, 183).

Chapter 6

The Wolf Man and Sigmund Freud by Sergei Pankejeff
Between a case study and a memoir[1]

Introduction to Pankejeff's *The Wolf Man and Sigmund Freud*

In *Goethe's Elective Affinities*, Walter Benjamin offers a distinction between life's biographical events, which he calls "material content," and life's essence, which he calls "truth content."

> Only the material content of the life lies open, however, and its truth content is hidden. Certainly the particular trait and the particular relation can be illuminated, but not the totality—unless it, too, is grasped as a merely finite relation. For, in itself, it is infinite.
>
> (1997 [1925], 325)

Whereas life's biographical events tend to lie open before us, life's finite essence and meaning remain in the shadows of obscurity.

This chapter offers a comparative reading of Freud's canonical case study "From the History of Infantile Neurosis" (1918) and of the memoir written by the protagonist of that case study, Sergei Pankejeff, known as the Wolf Man (Gardiner 1971a). This reading centers on the complex matrix of meanings embodied in the act of lifting the veil. The neurotic symptom of a veil seemingly in front of the analysand's eyes is interpreted by Freud as a repetition of his birth in a *Glückshaube* (German for "caul," literally a "lucky hood"). The veil is represented as an ambivalent object both for Freud and for Pankejeff, who are enticed by the sense of a final truth behind the veil yet constantly doubt the possibility of grasping it. For Freud, psychoanalysis is the very process of lifting the veil, yet his analysand remained for him an unsolved riddle. Pankejeff, in a volume dedicated to the story of the Wolf Man, created an autobiographical text that deliberately avoids telling the story of the analysand, thus drawing a veil over his story. The paradox embodied in lifting the veil is discussed in relation to Walter Benjamin's distinction between materiality and truth and his notion of the inherent unity of the veil and the veiled.

The Wolf Man's case occupied Freud his entire writing life and continued to occupy psychoanalytic literature throughout the years to an unprecedented degree. *From the History of an Infantile Neurosis* was the last case study Freud wrote and one of the most detailed. Not only the case study but also the patient himself who was known as the Wolf Man occupied the psychoanalytic community throughout the years (Abraham and Torok 1986 [1976]; Brooks 1984; Loughman 1984; Mahony 1984; Offenkrantz 1973; Werbert 1998). Ongoing interest in the Wolf Man has produced new examinations of his pathology and the analytic work with Freud, as well as new interpretations of works about him. This continuous interest can be explained by the obscurities and contradictions surrounding his character. In the concluding remarks of the case study, Freud discusses the Wolf Man's complexity and resistance to interpretation as a riddle as-yet-unsolved: "Personal peculiarities in the patient and a national character that was foreign to ours made the task of feeling one's way into his mind a laborious one" (Freud 1918, 104).

A bond was forged between Freud's text and the subject who was given a pseudonym in that text, a person who became a persona and lived his adult life with the dual identity of Russian émigré and the subject of Freud's famous case. Approximately five decades after Freud's case study appeared, the patient at its center published a memoir telling his life story and a separate essay offering recollections of his analytic encounter with Freud. The two pieces (Pankejeff 1971a, 1971b) were first published in English and German in 1971 in a volume edited by the American psychoanalyst Muriel Gardiner. In addition to the texts written by the Wolf Man, the volume also reprints Freud's famous case study about him; an additional case study written by the analyst Ruth Mack Brunswick, originally published in 1928 (Mack Brunswick 1928); the editor's own recollections of the Wolf Man, based on their long relationship; a selection of Pankejeff's letters to her; and her diagnostic impression of his personality. Thus, the texts collected in this volume were written by four different authors at various times. Freud first published his case study after World War I, approximately five years after the analysis ended. Mack Brunswick published her paper about a year after the Wolf Man's second analysis ended. Gardiner published her own recollections of the famous patient in various journals from the 1950 until the book was published.

I want to propose the Wolf Man's memoir not only as a reference point for the canonical case study, but as its own distinctive literary creation. The texts offered by Pankejeff naturally allude to Freud's case study and various other texts about the case and its famous subject. They also express his stance toward himself as a psychoanalytic persona or construct. With Freud's case study, Pankejeff became a literary creation, his analyst's protagonist. Thus, Freud served not only as his analyst but also as his biographer (Hadar 2012). This dual function in Pankejeff's life was made even more influential by the canonical position the case study attained in the psychoanalytic literature and beyond. This position made Pankejeff an exemplary figure, a prototype of the neurotic and the analysand. A comparative reading of the texts—Freud's and Pankejeff's—reveals a dialog between two literary voices, the canonical and powerful voice of the analyst and the marginal and mute voice of the analysand. The reading I offer of these texts will include Freud's rendering of the analytic encounter with Pankejeff and Pankejeff's rendering both of the analytic encounter and of his reading of the case study written about him. The comparative reading of the texts suggests the theme of lifting the veil (der Schleier) as a pivotal image that carries various meanings.

One book, four authors

The diverse cast of contributors Gardiner's *The Wolf Man and Sigmund Freud* (1971a) allows us to view the complex web of relationships among them. As noted, the Wolf Man was first Freud's analysand and then Mack Brunswick's, and he kept up a friendly and somewhat therapeutic relationship with Gardiner throughout the years. Ruth Mack Brunswick (1897–1946) was an American doctor who came to Vienna in 1922 for an analysis and psychoanalytic training with Freud. During her analysis with Freud, the Wolf Man returned to him for help at a time of deep psychic turmoil. Freud offered him Mack Brunswick as a psychoanalyst and guided that analysis from a distance (Appignanesi and Forrester 1992, 373–376; Mahony 1984, 140). Muriel Gardiner (1901–1985) was an American psychiatrist and psychoanalyst who came to Vienna in 1926 to study medicine and seek analysis with Freud. Eventually, she ended up in analysis not with Freud but with Mack Brunswick. The analysis lasted a couple of years, during which she completed psychoanalytic training (Appignanesi and Forrester 1992, 376–378). During that time and up until the Nazi occupation, Gardiner took an active role in the socialist underground in Vienna and in arranging visas for Jews to find safe refuge outside Nazi territory.[2] Thus, in the late 1920s, the Wolf Man and Gardiner were in analysis with Mack Brunswick in Vienna at the same time. In fact, Gardiner first encountered the Wolf Man when Mack Brunswick recommended him to her as a good Russian language teacher.

The real identity of the famous yet anonymous Wolf Man was revealed only after his death in 1979. Though his biography is now quite well-known, I will briefly summarize it before turning to the comparative reading of the texts concerning his life. His name was Sergei Constantinovich Pankejeff. Born in 1887 to an aristocratic Russian family, he was raised in great wealth. In his childhood, his parents would travel abroad for long periods, and the figures closest to him were his older sister Anna and their nanny, Nanya, a loyal and caring mother figure to the young Pankejeff. Anna's life ended tragically in her youth, when she committed suicide while traveling abroad. Grief-stricken, Pankejeff dropped his legal studies and was thrown into a deep depression. (Freud's case study cites a gonorrheal infection occurring some months before Anna's death as the primary trigger for Pankejeff's depression; Pankejeff's memoir does not mention the infection.) During the years that followed, Pankejeff traveled through Europe with a private doctor and committed himself to various sanatoriums. In one of them, he fell passionately in love with a nurse, Therese, who worked there. The vicissitudes of his relationship with her, alongside his depression, led him to seek further psychiatric help.

In February 1910 he arrived in Vienna to meet Freud and immediately began a six-session-a-week analysis that lasted four and a half years. This analysis ended in July 1914, at the outset of World War I, when Pankejeff returned to Russia and fulfilled his longtime goal of marrying Therese, a plan he deferred until the end of the analysis. In 1919, at the end of the war, Pankejeff traveled westward again and came to visit Freud, who gave him a copy of the case study he had written about him. When Pankejeff told him about the return of the digestive symptoms he had suffered in the past, Freud suggested further analysis. Pankejeff agreed, but the course of analysis was interrupted by the aftermath of the Russian revolution, which brought about a dramatic change of circumstances for Pankejeff: a descendant of aristocrats, he found himself destitute and his homeland dangerous. Overnight, he went from being a wealthy aristocrat to being an impoverished émigré. In the years that followed, he received financial support from Freud, and gradually built a life as an insurance agent. He ended up spending most of his life in Vienna, and is buried there. Thus, the symbolic homeland he had been offered by psychoanalysis became his actual home.

In the mid-1920s, Pankejeff suffered another severe crisis, which included hypochondriacal symptoms with delusional characteristics. He naturally turned to his former analyst, but Freud, as we have seen, referred him to Mack Brunswick. His analysis with her lasted a couple of months and did not, according to Pankejeff, leave any significant mark on him (Obholzer 1982 [1980], 55–57, 131–132). The year 1938 was another fateful period in his life, as his beloved Therese committed suicide. Pankejeff, who had not foreseen this, was stricken with grief and despair.

As noted, Pankejeff drew attention from the psychoanalytic community for decades. Psychoanalysts, psychotherapists, and journalists initiated meetings with him for various purposes: personality evaluations, psychotherapy, and short-term psychoanalysis and interviews. At some point in his life, the Freud archive in New York decided to give Pankejeff a monthly pension. For a time, the head of the archive, Kurt Eissler (1908–1999), would come to Vienna for a month every year to offer Pankejeff tape-recorded psychoanalytic sessions. These records have been archived at the Library of Congress and recently made accessible to the public. Eissler also sent reproductions of Pankejeff's paintings of the famous wolf dream, presented in Freud's case study, to psychoanalytic conferences for sale, and two of these paintings are now located in the Freud Museum in Hampstead. It was Gardiner who suggested that he write his memoirs as the Wolf Man. In addition, a series of interviews by the journalist Karin Obholzer with Pankejeff in the last years of his life was published after his death (Obholzer 1982 [1980]). These interviews, which were recorded, followed his gradual physical, mental, and psychological deterioration until his death at the age of 92 in a psychiatric institution. In these recorded interviews, Pankejeff directly criticizes psychoanalysis and his entanglements with it. To some degree, the book promises (as did Gardiner's book, in different ways), to tell Pankejeff's real story, to clear up confusions and inconsistencies. Nevertheless, a reading of Obholzer's text leaves one with the impression that Pankejeff developed patterns of transference toward the interviewer that were similar to those he had developed toward his analysts and editors, thus still leaving his "true" voice hidden behind a veil.

Lifting the veil

An essential component of Freud's case study is the dramatic construction of the primal scene the patient allegedly experienced when he was an infant of 18 months. The construction of the scene was enabled by the interpretation of the wolf dream Pankejeff reported having when he was 4, a dream that Freud believed gave insight in *Nachträglichkeit* into the sexual content of the primal scene. In this construction, the act of lifting the veil is given pivotal importance. First, the dream is distinctly static, and it is notable that the only event is the sudden and mysterious movement of the veil, represented by the window. As Pankejeff described it,

> The only piece of action in the dream was the opening of the window; for the wolves sat quite still and without making any movement on the branches of the tree, to the right and left of the trunk, and looked at me. It seemed as though they had riveted their whole attention upon me.
> (Freud 1918, 18)

The dominant gaze of the wolves toward the child dreamer strikes his attention, and he responds with an observant gaze of his own, "the strained attention with which they all looked at him. The lasting sense of reality." Freud concludes, "It can naturally only be a question of the reality of something unknown" (21).

Before the window opened, by some mysterious force, the child was lying in his bed at night, submitting passively to his unconscious. At some point, according to Freud, the patient is intrigued by this movement of the window and declares, "My eyes suddenly opened" (34). The child's gaze in the dream is an inevitable consequence of the veil's being removed and is understood as a repetition of the infantile gaze at the primal scene, which is recaptured in the dream with its traumatic and vivid quality. The child finds himself looking, and thereby against his will becomes an active witness and interpreter of these erotically charged scenes, in a complex scopophilia. At the same time, the fantasy of returning to a protected sphere is created.

A pivotal expression of the veil in Pankejeff's adult life appears toward the end of the case study, where Freud reveals a symptom of which Pankejeff always complained. The symptom was that of constantly seeing or feeling a veil before his eyes: "The world, he said, was hidden from him by a veil; and our psycho-analytic training forbids our assuming that these words can have been without significance or have been chosen at haphazard" (99). The prolonged quest for the meaning of this rather peculiar symptom in analysis was fruitless until, toward the termination of the treatment, its possible meaning was suddenly revealed:

> It was not until the end just before taking leave of the treatment that he remembered having been told that he was born in a caul [*Glückshaube*]. He had for that reason always looked on himself as a special child of fortune whom no ill could befall.
>
> (99)

Freud offers the following interpretation:

> Thus the caul was the veil which hid him from the world and hid the world from him. The complaint that he made was in reality a fulfilled wishful phantasy: it exhibited him as back once more in the womb, and was, in fact, a wishful phantasy of flight from the world. It can be translated as follows: "Life makes me so unhappy! I must get back into the womb!"[3]
>
> (100)

I want to further develop the interpretation offered by Freud of the *Glückshaube*, the promise it holds, and the traumatic experience of being delivered prematurely into reality. Embryonic life in the caul serves as a metaphor for a timeless form of being intact within an internal world, while delivery ushers the infant into the external realm of time and the senses. The caesura of birth carries with it an ambivalent experience, on the one hand a desire for the sensual arousal of the external world and on the other a craving to regress into the protected realm of the caul. The veil, as Blum (1974) and Greenacre (1973) observe, presents the conflict between the wish to see and the temptation of blinding denial. Pankejeff's borderline personality, as Blum suggests, implies a continuous threat that he experienced beginning in early childhood with regard to his sense of reality and intolerance for frustration, accompanied by an intense symbiotic fantasy of "intrauterine escape to the safety of fusion with his mother" (Blum 1974, 730). The dialectic between the internal and the external turned, in Pankejeff's case, into a neurotic symptom of feeling caught behind a veil, as a repetition of the conflict evolving around the experience of being prematurely torn from the quiet serenity of the womb.

Pankejeff's passive longings for care and nurturance and his experience of unmet dependency needs are expressed not only through the neurotic symptom of the veil in front of his eyes but also in his immediate attachment to analysis and Freud's consulting room. Pankejeff had a strong transference to the physicality of Freud's office setting, which he apparently experienced as a concretization of care and attention. Later on, he felt barred from this place of balm and refuge in a way that repeated earlier traumatic losses. By contrast with this immediate attachment to analysis that Pankejeff presents, Freud, in the case study, emphasizes his patient's rigid resistances, which led Freud to the harsh decision of forced termination: "The patient with whom I am here concerned remained for a long time unassailably entrenched behind an attitude of obliging apathy. He listened, understood, and remained unapproachable" (Freud 1918, 11). In Pankejeff's reminiscences, by contrast, an immediate and potent attachment to the analytic setting is described:

> After the first few hours with Freud, I felt that I had at last found what I had so long been seeking. It was a revelation to me to hear the fundamental concepts of a completely new science of the human psyche, from the mouth of its founder.... I perceived at once that Freud had succeeded in discovering an unexplored region of the human soul, and that if I could follow him along this path, a new world would open to me.
> (Pankejeff 1971b, 138)

Pankejeff's vivid reminiscences of Freud's consulting room emphasize this place as a protected sphere, which implicitly relates to embryonic experience:

> I can remember, as though I saw them today, his two adjoining studies, with the door open between them and with their windows opening on a little courtyard. There was always a feeling of sacred peace and quiet there.... Everything here contributed to one's feeling of leaving the haste of modern life behind, of being sheltered from one's daily cares.
> (139)

Further investigation into the meaning of the veil led me to the idea of the truth in the veil, which appears in Walter Benjamin's work. In *Goethe's Elective Affinities*, Benjamin raises essential questions about literature and literary criticism. Beyond his investigation into the plot and characters of the literary text, Benjamin stresses the reader should be continuously aware that truth appears solely beyond the veil of concealment and disguise, in the spectrum of semblance,

> Beauty is not a semblance, not a veil covering something else. It itself is not appearance but purely essence—one which, of course, remains essentially identical to itself only when veiled. Therefore, even if everywhere else semblance is deception, the beautiful semblance is the veil thrown over that which is necessarily most veiled. For the beautiful is neither the

veil nor the veiled object but rather the object in its veil ... Thus, in the face of everything beautiful, the idea of unveiling becomes that of the impossibility of unveiling.

(1997 [1925], 351)

The truth or beauty that lies in the text can never be revealed in its wholeness but only through obscurity, through the veil of semblance. Moreover, truth cannot be revealed by itself, and thus the process of unveiling remains a fantasy of grasping truth as an absolute. Truth can be grasped only through a veil, for it is merely embodied in the mysterious unity of the veil and the veiled.

Pankejeff alludes to the obscurity of truth as a unity of the veiled and the veil, in a complex dialectic of revealing and concealing. The heart of his memoir consists not of recollections from his analysis but of a broad account of his life story, an independent autobiographical narrative that holds but little resemblance to the narrative offered by Freud in the case study. This difference is indeed striking and stands as a central aspect of Pankejeff's veiling process. Gardiner's edited volume was promoted as the Wolf Man's memoir, thereby disclaiming it as psychoanalytic literature. Yet a reading of Pankejeff's autobiographical essay (1971a) reveals the surprising fact that his psychoanalysis and his relationship with Freud are omitted from the text. The analysis is briefly mentioned, but only as the reason for his long stay in Vienna before his marriage, and Freud's case study is given no more than a single dry remark. Pankejeff (1971b) did write a separate essay dedicated to his recollections of Freud, two decades before Gardiner's volume was published, and the chapter is included in the volume, but even this chapter, dedicated to his analysis, in many ways omits more than it reveals. In this text, Pankejeff focuses on his impressions of Freud the man and the analytic setting he offered but completely omits any view of his own of the process or the line of interpretation so emphasized by Freud in the case study. Although Pankejeff wrote his memoir as a continuation of his reminiscences of Freud, and was aware that the two texts would be published alongside the case study, this omission creates an odd reading experience, as if we were reading the memoir of some anonymous Russian émigré with artistic aspirations. The omission of psychoanalysis from the memoir is especially striking given that Pankejeff lived his adult life in the light (and shadow) of the famous persona of Freud's analysand.

But it is not only the analysis and Freud's case study that are absent from the memoir. Pankejeff's early development and infantile sexuality, the very core of Freud's text, are completely absent also. The memoir gives no attention to the author's sexual life, neither in childhood nor in adulthood. It also ignores the complex matrix of symptoms that accompanied Pankejeff from childhood to old age, and which are described in detail in Freud's and Mack Brunswick's case studies (Mahony 1984, 11–12). Another important difference between the texts lies in the contrast between which life stages each of the texts foregrounds. In the case study, Freud declares his intention to focus almost solely on the patient's psychic development in childhood, as constructed and interpreted in analysis. The subject that is brought out most saliently is the impact of the patient's infantile sexuality. By contrast, Pankejeff's memoir focuses on the theme of mourning, offered as a lifelong thread that begins with his sister's suicide as he is on the verge of adult life, represented as "unconscious mourning," and repeated traumatically in his wife's suicide many years later (Buirski and Haglund 1998). Pankejeff wrote of his childhood only after strong persuasion by Gardiner (Gardiner 1971b, 345–357). He refused to write a more detailed recollection of his long analysis before and after the war. He also makes no mention of the severe crisis he suffered in the 1920s or of the vicissitudes of his relationship with Freud, including Freud's financial support, his refusal to take him on for another analysis, the referral to Mack Brunswick, and the later disconnection from him. Pankejeff's memoir does not explicitly mention Freud's immigration to London or his death, even though it is known that Pankejeff took great pains to get to London during the Nazi occupation of Austria and to meet Mack Brunswick there. He surely knew that Mack Brunswick had gone to London to see Freud for further analytic sessions. And yet, even though Freud's death in September 1939 is not mentioned, the memoir symbolically and somewhat mysteriously ends there (Pankejeff 1971a, 129).[4] Mack Brunswick reports that the two men drifted apart and provides her explanation that Pankejeff found it difficult to witness Freud's illness, and that he was hurt by the rejection he experienced (Mack Brunswick 1971, 283, 304).

The complexity of the unveiling of truth finds further expression in Mack Brunswick's case study. This rather neglected text is remarkable for the complex matrix of transference–countertransference ties it reveals, for Freud was the analyst of both analysand and analyst, of both Mack Brunswick and Pankejeff. Mack Brunswick finds herself in a complex situation at the very outset of the analysis: she discovers that her patient has been financially dishonest with his former analyst and dishonest with her, his current analyst, regarding his symptoms (Mack Brunswick 1971, 279–280). Mack Brunswick's text expresses her struggle, as an analyst, with two complex transference relationships, her countertransference as analyst toward her patient and her transference toward their mutual analyst, Freud. Most of all, Mack Brunswick resists understanding the patient's "peculiarities" as part of his obscure nature, which is how Freud had characterized them, and insists instead that they are conscious dishonesties. She finds herself troubled by her analysand's ambivalent stance toward Freud, which "contained an astounding mixture of fantasy and fact," and decides to stimulate a negative transference by "a concentrated attempt to undermine the patient's idea of himself as the favorite son" (284). Explicitly, Mack Brunswick's text reflects a determined stance of unveiling the truth, yet bearing in mind the truth behind the veil, we may well ask whether her emphasis on her patient's dishonesties prevented her from seeing other aspects of his personality and of the distinct analytic triad formed in this case.

It cannot simply be overlooked that in a volume dedicated to his identity as the famous Wolf Man, Pankejeff created a memoir so distinct from Freud's canonical case study. I suggest that his creating an autobiographical text that deliberately avoids telling his story as Freud's analysand, as might have been expected, should be regarded as a submerged statement, meant to raise questions in the reader. The author-analysand is thus drawing a veil over his story.

A retranslation of the case study

The case study written by Freud opens with a literary decision: "Only this infantile neurosis will be the subject of my communication." The case study focuses almost solely on the patient's childhood and, even more specifically, on his infantile neurosis. Freud made this choice "in spite of the patient's direct request," which was to give expression to "a complete history of his illness, of his treatment, and of his recovery." Freud justifies his decision with the claim that "I recognized that such a task was technically impracticable and socially impermissible" (Freud 1918, 8). Moreover, Freud states that he is telling the story of a difficult analysis, which "is characterized by a number of peculiarities," the analysis of a complex patient, "a young man whose health had broken down in his eighteenth year after a gonorrheal infection, and who was entirely incapacitated and completely dependent upon other people" (7). Freud reports that the patient was classified "in the most authoritative quarters as a case of 'manic-depressive insanity'" (8). Freud, however, disagrees with these authorities and constructs an alternative diagnosis, one that centers on the archaic history of the individual:

> I have formed the opinion that this case, like many others which clinical psychiatry has labelled with the most multifarious and shifting diagnoses, is to be regarded as a condition following on an obsessional neurosis which has come to an end spontaneously, but has left a defect behind it after recovery.
>
> (8)

This neurosis is the infantile neurosis, and Freud's text expresses the quest for this lost narrative of this illness and its roots and implications. The desired effect Freud wants to create in his text is of psychoanalysis mainly as a process of lifting the veil, unraveling repressed memories that continue to trouble the analysand's psyche.

The narrative offered by Freud is brought to a climax in the famous reconstruction of the primal scene the patient had allegedly witnessed in infancy. This is the first time Freud discusses the psychic meaning of the primal scene as an actual experience and as a phylogenetic construct. The problem in this case was that the dramatic and intensely passionate construct of the primal scene had never been transformed into a live recollection in the analysand's consciousness. Freud here proposes the idea of the past receiving a new translation in *Nachträglichkeit*; the connection between past and present is by no means a simple one. Vast rhetorical efforts are made in the case study to present the construct of the primal scene as an inevitable interpretation of an actual or symbolic event, in which the present is not only transformed deterministically by the past, but the past is transformed and translated hermeneutically by the present. This dynamic translation is offered as an ongoing process of transformation and enrichment of meaning (Laplanche and Pontalis 1973 [1967], 111–114).

Freud continued to be troubled by the inability of psychoanalysis to transform psychoanalytic constructs into live recollections, presenting this as a crucial problem at the outset of "Beyond the Pleasure Principle" (1920a). He explains the necessity for new theoretical constructs:

> At first the analyzing physician could do no more than discover the unconscious material that was concealed from the patient, put it together, and, at the right moment, communicate it to him. Psychoanalysis was then first and foremost an art of interpreting.

This kind of work did not bring the expected therapeutic results, for the analyst found himself trying "to oblige the patient to confirm the analyst's construction from his own memory. In that endeavor the chief emphasis lay upon the patient's resistances ... this was where suggestion operating as 'transference' played its part" (18). The case study of the Wolf Man is based on this initial phase in the analytic work, where the primal scene is constructed from a dream interpretation and the analyst tries to encourage the patient to form a live connection to this construct by linking it to his personal narrative.

Pankejeff's memoir both connects to the case study through intertextual allusions and pushes away from its dominance and conclusiveness; the question of its ability to reveal the truth thereby continues. The childhood dream and the reconstruction of the primal scene are of course not mentioned in the memoir. In a communication late in his life, he admitted never having been able to identify with the narrative of infantile sexuality or accept it as part of his personal narrative. This was especially true for the memory of the primal scene and its reconstruction on the basis of the wolf dream. He saw Freud's dream interpretation as "terribly farfetched" and continued by saying, "That scene in the dream where the windows open and so on and the wolves are sitting there, and his interpretation, I don't know, those things are miles apart" (Obholzer 1982 [1980], 35). He concludes this bitter commentary by saying "that primal scene is no more than a construct" (36).

In contrast to the narrative of the Wolf Man's childhood presented by Freud, centering on the wolf dream at the age of 4, Pankejeff presents an alternative transformative event at that age, which is the revelation of his love of music and the destruction of that love. The 4-year-old Pankejeff received a little accordion and found himself "literally in love with it." He describes the intense desire for music that he experienced:

> It was winter, and when darkness fell I sometimes went to a room where I would be undisturbed and where I thought nobody would hear me, and began to improvise. I imagined a lonely winter landscape with a sleigh drawn by a horse toiling through the snow. I tried to produce the sounds on my accordion which would match the mood of this fantasy.
> (Pankejeff 1971a, 10)

Thus, an alternative possibility of psychic development is created here in the potential space between reality and imagination, and between sensuality and the protected sphere. Even though that growth was soon afterward disturbed and exploited by adult impingement, expressed by the father's insistence that the boy present his talent, music had been revealed as an experience of being immersed in beauty constructed of the veil and veiled rather than grasping a finite truth. Pankejeff never returned to playing music after this early experience, yet his affinity with art continued. In his childhood recollections, he describes becoming an eager reader at adolescence, and later an eager painter (Pankejeff 1971a, 20; Weissberg 2012, 175–181).

The avoidance of any explicit reference to Freud's case study continues with Pankejeff's decision to offer a different life story in his memoir and to give central meaning to entirely different events. In the essay dedicated to his recollections of Freud, Pankejeff opens with a description of "the desolate situation in which a neurotic found himself at that period before psychoanalysis." For him, the center of neurotic psychic pain is the melancholic search for an unknown internal object. He states that the neurotic "has come into conflict with his environment and then lost contact with it…. His goal is not a real known object, but rather some other object, hidden in his unconscious, unknown to himself" (Pankejeff 1971b, 135). Whereas the case study centers on childhood history and the development of infantile sexuality, Pankejeff's memoir forms a narrative of loss and of a person for whom the experience of loss gradually became his only certainty. On the sociocultural level, it tells a story of the absolute and complete loss of homeland and culture. The aristocratic Russian society in which Pankejeff was raised is described early in the memoir, only to be ruined and vanish as the memoir continues. On the personal level, the memoir centers on the death of those closest to Pankejeff, most of all the tragic death of his sister Anna in his youth and his wife Therese in his adulthood. Pankejeff draws a thread of grief between these two losses and with it he forms his life narrative. All other events are presented as minor shadows in the light of these deep and intensely melancholic experiences.

In retrospect, Pankejeff situates his sister's suicidal act as a turning point in his life sequence, for it is presented in *après coup* as a prefiguration of his wife's suicide some three decades later. The resemblance between the two events hints at a fateful connection between them. Both involve the sudden death of a beloved woman who tragically takes her life, leaving him shocked, bewildered, and detached. On the early loss of his sister, Pankejeff writes,

> After the death of Anna, with whom I had had a very deep, personal, inner relationship, and whom I had always considered as my only comrade, I fell into a state of deepest depression. The mental agony I now suffered would often increase to the intensity of physical pain.... I had fallen into such a state of melancholy after Anna's death that there seemed to be no sense or purpose in living, and nothing in the world seemed worth striving for.
>
> (1971a, 25–26)

This retrospective point of view on his state of mind after the death of his sister and the emphasis on his despair implicitly alludes to Freud's case study, where Freud emphasizes his patient's lack of any emotion at the loss:

> When the news of his sister's death arrived, so the patient told me, he felt hardly a trace of grief. He had to force himself to show signs of sorrow, and was able quite coolly to rejoice at having now become the sole heir to the property.
>
> (Freud 1918, 23)

This sharp distinction between the two narratives of Pankejeff's response to Anna's death serves as another expression of the unity of the veil and the veiled. The distinction cannot be resolved simply by choosing one narrative over the other, as the correct representation of a finite truth. The truth lies between various emotional responses, expressions of these responses, interpretations and translations of these responses in *après coup*, and narratives the authors choose to present. Freud saw Pankejeff's response to his sexual illness (the gonorrheal infection) as being more profound than his grief over the loss of his sister. Freud's failure to recognize his patient's sorrow stems from the psychoanalytic claim that Pankejeff's pathology was profoundly influenced by his early psychosexual development. Pankejeff's emphasis on his mourning is, among other things, his way of offering an alternative to the famous narrative offered by Freud. Thus, the obscure theme of mutual exploitation is so deeply entangled in the two narratives that Pankejeff's mourning remains a veiled mystery.

The description in Pankejeff's memoir of the loss of his wife three decades after the loss of his sister is intense and fragmented:

> I lived this day and the following ones as though in a state of delirium in which one does not know whether what happens is reality or a dreadful dream.... The question kept hammering away in my mind: how could

Therese do this to me? And as she was the only stable structure in my changeable life, how could I, now suddenly deprived of her, live on? It seemed to me impossible.

(Pankejeff 1971a, 121–122)

Pankejeff's text reveals a certain recovery after each of his losses with the exception of Therese's death, in 1938, which left him in a desolate and fragile condition. His reading of the letters Therese left before taking her life stresses the agonizing guilt he felt for not having noticed her despair (122–124).

Their suicidal acts and sudden and tragic deaths are not the only links that tie together the two women in Pankejeff's life. But the erotic aspect of his relationship with Anna, which is accorded a central place in the case study, is entirely absent from Pankejeff's memoir. During analysis, Pankejeff had a group of dreams that

> were concerned with aggressive actions on the boy's part against his sister or against the governess and with energetic reproofs and punishments on account of them. It was as though ... after her bath ... he had tried ... to undress his sister ... to tear off her coverings ... or veils—and so on.
>
> (Freud 1918, 19, ellipses in original)

Subsequently, the case study reveals that the patient gradually recalled childhood memories of his sister:

> His sister had seduced him into sexual practices. First came a recollection that in the lavatory, which the children used frequently to visit together, she had made this proposal: "Let's show our bottoms," and had proceeded from words to deeds.... His sister had taken hold of his penis and played with it, at the same time telling him incomprehensible stories about the Nanya, as though by way of explanation. His Nanya, she said, used to do the same thing with all kinds of people.

The fantasies that appeared in the dreams during analysis were therefore understood by Freud as a compensation for the sister's active sexual role, which "seemed offensive to the patient's masculine self-esteem" (20).[5] For Freud, this childhood seduction was pivotal in understanding Pankejeff's childhood and adulthood neurosis. Pankejeff's memoir, by contrast, while it gives Anna's tragedy a central place in his life, emphatically omits the sexual aspects of their relationship.[6]

Yet this pivotal theme is not actually absent from the memoir, but rather is presented as truth as the veiled and the veil. In the dream brought to analysis, Pankejeff's infantile desire for Anna pushes him to tear off her veils, but in the memoir this desire is given a melancholic translation through the moment of separation from her. The separation from Anna reveals the image of her coffin being lowered into the family tomb in the Old Cemetery in Odessa: "Just as the coffin was being lowered into the grave, the sun, already low on the horizon, sank, its last rays piercing the foliage and flooding the shining metal casket" (Pankejeff 1971a, 24). The sun on his sister's casket might have a blinding, veiling effect, implying a question about what cannot be seen directly, but only through a veil. Three decades later, by contrast, in a Viennese cemetery chapel after the death of his beloved Therese, the author does not settle for a glance at the coffin from a distance. His sister's body must remain hidden, yet he responds positively to the suggestion given to him to open his wife's coffin. He approaches the casket and looks at his dead wife: "The gas had had the effect of giving Therese's face an unusual freshness; her cheeks were a delicate rose. In her coffin she looked like a very young woman who had peacefully fallen asleep" (122).

In contrast to the untimely deaths of his sister and his wife, Pankejeff's mother died of old age. After Therese's death, she had come to live with her son in Vienna. In a letter addressed to Muriel Gardiner, Pankejeff writes:

> Although my mother's condition caused so many real difficult problems, and although her life was no longer anything but suffering, still her passing has left great emptiness in me.... I believe that my mother, at the last moment, experienced death as a deliverance, for I looked at her in her coffin and could scarcely believe that death could make a human face so beautiful. For I have never before seen my mother looking so sublimely quiet and peaceful, yes, almost of classic beauty.
> (Pankejeff, May 12, 1953, in Gardiner 1971b, 340)

I suggest that the obscure image of Anna's dead body lying inside the closed coffin serves as a prefiguration of the explicit image of the dead Therese and the dead mother. Pankejeff's implied gaze on Anna alludes to the erotic aspect of their relationship. It is given metonymic expression through the sun's last rays, setting on the coffin before it reaches its final destination. The dead Therese's image is emphasized, almost ironically, by her liveliness and freshness, although in reality she was already in middle age. These characteristics, along with the name "Therese" and the location of the scene in the chapel, present the figure of the lover as a saint, for she fulfills her beauty spiritually and symbolically, more than in an erotic way. Pankejeff's mother died about 15 years after his wife, and four and a half decades after his sister. Her beauty, as revealed in her dead body represent the return of the repressed in the most classic form; hence her image as being of "classical beauty" alludes to the passionate love for the mother in the oedipal stage and its intensity based on the archaic longing for her in infancy (Freud 1914b, 87–88). Death endows the mother with the gift of beauty, and her face is described as glowing. Pankejeff's longing and admiring gaze on her body restores to her a lost liveliness and beauty, as he himself, by this same gaze, restores his lost innocence and vitality. The son's late gaze on his mother is also, dialectically, that of an old and desperate son on his tired mother. The beauty of the three dead women appears not as semblance but as truth through a veil, what Benjamin says is the only way that truth can be grasped. For, as Benjamin writes, beauty involves the inseparable unity of the object in its veil. "For the sake of that unity, which veil and veiled compose in it, beauty can essentially be valid only where the duality of nakedness and veiling does not yet obtain: in art and in the appearances of mere nature" (Benjamin 1997 [1925], 351). About one of his depressions, Pankejeff writes, "Like crashing waves, then, come fits of despair, in which life seems horribly ugly, and redeeming death seems beautiful" (Pankejeff, September 21, 1950, in Gardiner 1971b, 339).

Each of the three losses occurs at the outset of a new period in the author's life and serves as a prefiguration of losses yet to come. The death of the sister occurs at the outset of youth, the death of the wife at the outset of middle age, and the death of the mother at the outset of old age. Death is presented as a persistent companion, an intimate and vital presence. Through the images of feminine death, crossing the threshold from living to dying is presented not as a final separation but as a way to revive the past. This idea obscurely alludes to Freud's discussion, in "The Theme of the Three Caskets" (1913b), of the connection between passion for a woman and death. Weaving the sister, the wife, and the mother together in Pankejeff's writing reveals the oedipal thread that is otherwise omitted. The powerful images of the dead women imply forbidden passion and the early seduction by the sister, all of which are omitted from the memoir. Although he loved Therese, his marriage was characterized by continuous infidelities on his part, usually with prostitutes. Her suffering over his misbehavior was an additional source of guilt for him after her death.

Sexuality is linked from its very beginning to guilt and loss for Pankejeff. First of all, his mother is described mainly as absent, primarily because her hypochondria did not leave her much time for her family. Only her children's illness drew her to them, as "an exemplary nurse.... I can remember that as a child I sometimes wished I could get sick, to be able to enjoy my mother's being with me and looking after me" (Pankejeff 1971a, 9). The absent mother was replaced by another devoted maternal figure, Nanya. But he recalls that he understood that the latter's dedication to the child Pankejeff was deeply related to mourning:

> My Nanya was a peasant woman from the period when there was still serfdom. She was a completely honest and devoted soul, with a heart of gold. In her youth she had been married, but her son had died as an infant. So she had apparently transferred all her mother love from this dead son to me.
> (8)

The substitute for the absent mother finds her way to a substitute for the dead son. The relationship received a further libidinal cathexis from the sister's fantasies about Nanya's sexual encounters, mentioned in the case study.

Separation from Freud as an analyst and as a biographer

Pankejeff's termination phase was complicated because he was given a fixed date for it, as a technical decision made by his analyst. In his case study, Freud explained this decision as the solution to a complex impasse in which the analysis had landed,

> The patient with whom I am here concerned remained for a long time unassailably entrenched behind an attitude of obliging apathy. He listened, understood, and remained unapproachable.... His shrinking from a self-sufficient existence was so great as to outweigh all the vexations of his illness.
>
> (Freud 1918, 11)

Freud describes how he made up his mind to set a fixed date for ending the analytic process: "I was resolved to keep to the date; and eventually the patient came to see that I was in earnest" (11). He presents this dramatic act as having had important positive implications for the analysis:

> Under the inexorable pressure of this fixed limit his resistance and his fixation to the illness gave way, and now in a disproportionately short time the analysis produced all the material which made it possible to clear up his inhibitions and remove his symptoms. All the information, too, which enabled me to understand his infantile neurosis, is derived from this last period of the work, during which resistance temporarily disappeared and the patient gave an impression of lucidity which is usually attainable only in hypnosis.
>
> (11)

On the visible level, Pankejeff's story about the termination phase conforms to Freud's, as seen in the following quote from Pankejeff's memoir,

> In the weeks before the end of my analysis, we often spoke of the danger of the patient's feeling too close a tie to the therapist. If the patient remains "stuck" in the transference, the success of the treatment is not a lasting one, as it soon becomes evident that the original neurosis has been replaced by another.
>
> (Pankejeff 1971b, 149)

On a more obscure level, however, the memoir supplies an alternative narrative of the meaning of the separation from Freud. The narrator takes us to a sunny morning a few days before the separation. While taking a stroll on the Prater, Vienna's center, Pankejeff is filled with satisfaction regarding the meaningful process he has experienced with Freud over the previous four and a half years and his returning home to Russia a healthy man, prepared to marry. He has even introduced his fiancée to Freud and received "his full approval" (Pankejeff 1971a, 90) to marry her. Pankejeff had been anxiously awaiting this approval, for during the analysis Freud had advised him not to proceed with the marriage yet. This peaceful stroll ends in a shocking way,

> As everything seemed to be in the best possible order I returned from my stroll in the Prater in a very hopeful mood. Scarcely had I entered my apartment when the maid handed me the extra edition of the newspaper reporting the assassination of the archducal couple.
> (90)

Intrigued by these events, Pankejeff decides on a change of plans. Instead of leaving Vienna immediately after the separation from Freud, he stays on for a few more days in order to witness the burial ceremony of the royal couple:

> From the newspapers I learned that the two coffins would pass through Mariahilferstrasse at eleven at night on the way to the West Railroad Station.... It was raining. Finally in the light of the flickering torches I saw two hearses, one following the other with a considerable distance between them.... The hearses with the coffins moved rapidly, which created the impression of haste and of a conspicuous lack of ceremony. Only the unusual late hour of the night and the fact that the hearses were followed by the military attachés of foreign powers indicated that these were not ordinary mortals who were setting out on their last journey.
> (91)

The quick death ceremony is represented as a mirror reflection of the quick separation from Freud. There is a sharp contrast between the sunny stroll in the pleasant Prater before the separation from the analysis and the dark and secluded death ceremony afterward. There is also a sharp and prominent contrast between the optimistic mood that characterized the stroll and the anguish Pankejeff feels about the wretched burial ceremony for the royal couple who met their deaths as victims of a violent act.[7]

There is of course a metonymic relationship between the two separation ceremonies—the separation from the analysis and the separation from life—which appear side by side in Pankejeff's text. In this way, the separation from analysis is not just represented on a pragmatic level and given a positive meaning, as presented in the analytic discourse with Freud, but it is depicted instead as separation from a world full of life. It should be borne in mind that Pankejeff had come to Freud in a state of prolonged psychic breakdown, and that he had devoted these years to nothing but analysis.

The rushed terror that characterizes the burial ceremony of the Austrian archduke and his wife makes a gradual separation process from them impossible, and the separation from Freud is represented as having had a similar emotional impact on Pankejeff. Even though Freud had announced the date he had set for the termination a year prior to the actual event, the fact that it was determined by the analyst, and that it was given a one-sided positive interpretation by him, made it impossible for the patient to work through the negative feelings involved. The dark and gloomy night on which the burial ceremony takes place suggests the violence involved in the demand to repress the negative meaning of the separation that has been forced on the patient/author. Freud's stance toward the termination is presented by Pankejeff as confident, authoritative, and somewhat lacking in sensitivity, as he is firmly leading his submissive patient toward a vulnerable state. This representation of Freud as emphatically authoritative in their relationship stands in sharp contrast to Pankejeff's description of the relationship in another place in the memoir, where he states that in analysis he felt "less as a patient than as a co-worker" (1971b, 140).[8]

It is interesting to note that it was not only Pankejeff's thoughts that were occupied over the years by the fixed termination date. Freud continued to doubt this particular analytic technique in his writing for many years thereafter. In "Analysis Terminable and Interminable," Freud returns to the question of the fixed termination date, specifically as it was used in the Wolf Man's case:

> There can be only one verdict about the value of this blackmailing device: it is effective provided that one hits the right time for it. But it cannot guarantee to accomplish the task completely. On the contrary, we may be sure that, while part of the material will become accessible under the pressure of the threat, another part will be kept back and thus become buried, as it were, and lost to our therapeutic efforts.
>
> (Freud 1937, 218)

The change from seeing the fixed separation as "inexorable" but crucial, to seeing it as a "blackmailing device," is a significant one. It moves this choice to a less secure and legitimate area. Moreover, Freud suggests here a much more complex implication to this therapeutic decision than was suggested in the early text. His late essay implies that although it may seem that the predetermined separation opens the psychological path to the unconscious, other significant parts of the psyche may by the same token be buried and access to them lost forever.[9]

Nor is it only in his late work that Freud shows the complexity of setting a date for the termination of the analysis. Even in his 1918 essay on the Wolf Man, where he takes pains to legitimize his analytic decision, we can see cracks in his outward determination. He expresses the troubling conflict between his rush to develop and prove his theory and an awareness of the deep and prolonged processes that psychoanalysis requires. For example, directly following an explanation for the crucial quality of the set termination date, we find the following remark in the text:

Of the physician's point of view I can only declare that in a case of this kind he must behave as "time-lessly" as the unconscious itself, if he wishes to learn anything or to achieve anything. And in the end he will succeed in doing so, if he has the strength to renounce any short-sighted therapeutic ambition.

(Freud 1918, 10)

These thoughts about the complexity of the psychoanalytic processes stand in contrast to the idea of the set termination date. The meaning this act receives both in Freud's writing and in Pankejeff's memoir demonstrates the distinguished value of the textual space as a new area of meeting for the analytic couple. In the points of view offered in these texts written by analyst and patient, respectively, on the experience of separation from analysis, writing emerges as a possible way of reinterpreting the analytic experience in a divergent intertextual matrix, of reliving the past in a new way. This new way holds the potential to construct a new analytic experience, which also serves as a literary creation.

Termination from an interminable analysis

In the wolf dream, as a consequence of the veil's being lifted, the subject's eyes are opened to an active gaze. In addition, the wolves' eyes are suddenly and dominantly fixed upon him. Freud, in his construction of the primal scene through the dream, offers an interpretation of the image of the gaze on the dreamer: "They were looking at him with strained attention. This feature comes entirely from the primal scene, and has got into the dream at the price of being turned completely round" (Freud 1918, 42n). Freud concludes that the image in the dream of the gaze of the other is an expression of the defense mechanism of reversal. But this line of interpretation may also protect Freud from acknowledging the effect his own gaze and expectations as analyst had on his patient. By this, I am referring mainly to the fixed termination that Freud imposed on Pankejeff's analysis, and the vicissitudes of that termination.

In the chapter dedicated to his analysis with Freud, Pankejeff presents it as a transformative experience and Freud as having opened the door to a magical world. The forced termination that Freud set to the analysis, however, and the analysand's cooperation with that, prevented Pankejeff from undergoing the necessary mourning process. Though Freud had announced a year in advance the date he had set for the termination, the fact that the date was determined by the analyst, and that the analyst gave it a unilaterally positive interpretation, made it impossible for the patient to work through his negative feelings about it. Those feelings were given a metonymic expression in the memoir through the burial ceremony of the Austrian archduke and his wife (Tzur Mahalel 2017).

Freud continued to doubt the analytic technique of forced termination for many years thereafter, suggesting that this therapeutic decision had much more complex implications than he had suggested in the case study. In "Analysis Terminable and Interminable," Freud (1937) offers thoughts on the Wolf Man's troubles in later years in relation to the assumptions Freud had had about him as a patient. This examination of the changes in his patient's state through the years draws parallels with the changes in his analytic stance: "When he left me in the midsummer of 1914, with as little suspicion as the rest of us of what lay so shortly ahead, I believed that his cure was radical and permanent" (217). Concerning the case study, Freud writes in retrospect about the ambiguity that remains surrounding the question of the Wolf Man's analysis and psychic cure, concluding that "I have found the history of this patient's recovery scarcely less interesting than that of his illness" (218).

Any discussion of Pankejeff's recovery should indeed be challenged by the great losses and psychic pain he experienced over the course of his life. His birth in a caul gave him the promise of good luck and prosperity, and psychoanalysis gave him the promise of psychic cure and fame as a literary protagonist. The memoir that he wrote suggests, in retrospect, a narrative of having had the protective veil prematurely lifted in multiple contexts: the womb at birth, innocence in childhood, the family's wealth, the psychoanalytic setting, and marriage. As the veil was removed, he was forced to suddenly open his eyes and face death, incest, abandonment, guilt, penury, and loss. The other's gaze at him is questioned with respect to its potential for nourishment and growth alongside destruction and abuse. Pankejeff debates the value psychoanalysis had for him, invoking the theme of free will:

> Freud said that even when the repressed becomes conscious, and when an analysis could be regarded as successful, this does not automatically brings out the patient's recovery. After such an analysis, the patient has been placed in a position in which he can get well; before analysis this was not possible. But whether or not he really will get well depends on his wish to recover, on his will. Freud compared this situation with the purchase of a travel ticket. This ticket only makes the journey possible; it does not take its place. But what is this will to recover, really? And what determines it?
>
> (1971b, 148)

The image of the train ticket continued to occupy Pankejeff, and he later expressed his protest more bluntly: "If it is true that everything originates in childhood and that, when everything is remembered, the illness disappears, it must disappear. And one cannot say that the patient is then free to choose. There's a certain contradiction here" (quoted in Obholzer 1982 [1980], 43). Psychoanalysis gave him a home, but only a temporary home, perhaps as ephemeral as every home, veil, or womb offered to him.[10]

Pankejeff's text can be seen as playing the *fort-da* game with Freud's case study (Tzur Mahalel 2018). The memoir connects to the case study both through obscure intertextual allusions and, mainly, through its implicit promise to tell the story not of Pankejeff the man but of Freud's famous analysand. The Wolf Man's intention of claiming authorial subjectivity, in the face of his feeling dispossessed by Freud and his text, is understood in the context of what was in fact interminable analysis. Freud's text is a deliberate effort to lift the veil, both for the analysand and for a universe of readers Freud hoped to persuade. Yet this psychoanalytic and literary tour-de-force is successful only in part, for the truth, as a finite entity, partakes of a constant dynamic of appearance and disappearance in Freud's text, as it is woven into and untethered from the narrative (Laplanche 1999a, 147–157; Mahony 1984). Pankejeff's text is also engaged in a game of *fort-da* with Freud and Freud's text. Freud is implicitly depicted as a wolf, intently staring at the analysand, fixing the analysand's narrative through his interpretations and his writing. The analysand's memoir, by contrast, lifts and then replaces the veil, bringing forth the intriguing notion that truth is better apprehended from beyond the veil. Within the memoir, which was written and published because of the vast contribution that psychoanalysis had made to Pankejeff's life and because of his debt to it, there are troubling implications of exploitation and impossible mourning. These themes are re-created in the way the author turns to the reader with the explicit promise of telling the analysand's (true) story, yet actually plays a game with the reader, repeating his archaic entanglement of temptation and abuse. The author does not explicitly articulate this complexity, yet this obscure dynamic finds its way into the melancholic narrative offered in the memoir and is intertwined with the theme of the veil and the question of truth.

Freud's and Pankejeff's texts can be understood as a mutual attempt to decipher each other's hidden truth, albeit within the context of their differing degrees of power and authority. In the case study, Freud confronts the patient's powerful resistance and exerts authorial mastery by appropriating the patient's truth and constructing the momentous theory of primal fantasies to be translated in *après coup*. In the memoir, Pankejeff presents his alienation from the psychoanalytic persona attributed to him and, in the process of reclaiming authorial subjectivity, finds himself exhibiting only partial aspects of his story, with a continuous denial of his sexual life and symptomatology.[11]

Freud concludes the case of the Wolf Man by describing it as "the case which put the severest obstacles in the way of any description of it" (1918, 104). The Wolf Man's text is thereby offered to psychoanalysis as a mysterious riddle, and the psychoanalytic community follows his curiosity and "instinct for knowledge" (Freud 1905b, 194) by continuous research. Perhaps Pankejeff's inability to renounce psychoanalysis affected Freud and the psychoanalytic community, who, in this entanglement of impossible mourning, could not renounce Pankejeff either. The theme of the veil gives literary expression to the movement from the fantasy of an embryo in a timeless and everlasting womb, "a special child of fortune whom no ill could befall" (Freud 1918, 99), to the premature delivery, forcing the eyes to open wide and exposing the subject to the wild stare of the wolves, a new experience of looking and being looked at. Thus, the reader is presented with a narrative of continuous melancholy and suffering, corrupted sexuality and love relations, and the erotization of guilt.

The traumatic suicides of Pankejeff's sister and wife were marked by the distinct characteristics of the relationship Pankejeff had with each of them. These relations were conflictual because of disavowed, sadomasochistically tinged sexual urges that had to be kept veiled. Pankejeff's determined attempts to corrupt his relationship with his nurse Therese can be considered a reversal of his sister's seduction of him. Therese likely suffered considerably in her marriage to this troubled man, but Pankejeff appears to have little awareness of how this might have affected her. Similar dynamics were also enacted by Freud and Pankejeff, and to a lesser degree by Mack Brunswick and Gardiner, for the texts written by analyst and analysand suggest the ways in which relationships of helping can become erotized and corrupted, and how care can become entangled with use, misuse, and exploitation. We can conclude from the texts written by Pankejeff and by Freud, Mack Brunswick, and Gardiner that they all eventually came to feel a sense of exploitation in connection to what was kept veiled: the veil and the veiled of the analysand's unconscious dynamics.

These complex entanglements of transference relations found their path into the politics of the case study and the memoir; they are also connected with the association of Freud with the gazing wolf. The vicissitudes of the transference relations between Freud and Pankejeff and the manifold variations of veiled truth presented by the literature about this man and his analysis demonstrate the complexity of the analytic process and the riddles it entails. In *Goethe's Elective Affinities*, Benjamin discusses the essence of materiality, which he calls the beautiful. Within the context of the unity of veil and veiled, he articulates it as the secret:

> The task of art criticism is not to lift the veil but rather, through the most precise knowledge of it as a veil, to raise itself for the first time to the true view of the beautiful. To the view that will never open itself to so-called empathy and will only imperfectly open itself to a purer contemplation of the naïve: to the view of the beautiful as that which is secret.... Since only the beautiful and outside it nothing—veiling or being veiled—can be essential, the divine ground of the being of beauty lies in the secret. So then the semblance in it is just this: not the superfluous veiling of things in themselves but rather the necessary veiling of things for us.
> (Benjamin 1997 [1925], 351)

What gives our lives meaning, what cures the tortured psyche, and what gives comfort: these are infinite riddles. These existential riddles are constructed from the unity of the veil and the veiled, from life and its vicissitudes, and from the secret that makes them beautiful.

Notes

1 This chapter is based on the paper "The Wolf Man's Glückshaube: Rereading Sergei Pankejeff's Memoir" published in *Journal of the American Psychoanalytic Association* (Tzur Mahalel 2019). Copyright SAGE. Reprinted with permission of SAGE.
2 Gardiner's activity at that time is described in Lillian Hellman's 1973 memoir (adapted for the 1977 film *Julia*) and in Gardiner's own 1983 autobiography. In the latter, Gardiner describes her dramatic encounter with the Wolf Man in 1938. He was then in severe crisis after his wife's tragic death. Gardiner helped him get a visa to London to meet Mack Brunswick, who was there for further analysis with Freud (Gardiner 1983, 120–122). She emphasized that although she faced an ethical dilemma in arranging a visa for the Wolf Man, who was "Aryan" and therefore not in mortal danger from the Nazis in Vienna, her impression was that the flight to London to meet his psychoanalyst was nonetheless a life-and-death matter for him (Gardiner 1971b, 311–333).
3 It is interesting to note that Freud, too, was born in a caul, which, according to his official biography, was "an event which he believed to ensure him future happiness and fame" (Jones 1953, 4).
4 In a late interview, Pankejeff states that in the 1920s, he came to Freud to ask for money and Freud went into an adjoining room. Pankejeff followed him, but Freud shouted at him, warning him not to enter. Pankejeff's reaction was fear and he never returned to Freud's residence after that. After Therese's suicide, when Pankejeff came to London to meet Mack Brunswick, he asked to visit Freud, but Freud refused to see him (Obholzer 1982 [1980], 61–62).
5 Dimock (1995), in her research on the Wolf Man's historical background in Russia, stresses Anna's importance in Pankejeff's psychic development and suggests a pre-oedipal triangle of Pankejeff, Anna, and Nanya.
6 When asked directly about the subject, in a late interview, Pankejeff confirmed the sexual abuse he had experienced, as described in Freud's case study. He added that when he was 10, the two siblings were looking at pictures of naked women and that he recalls he "felt like expressing something sexual and moved closer to my sister. In any event, she got up and left." He felt rejected then, but in retrospect understands that "she couldn't have done anything else, otherwise it would really have been incest." He concludes this intense experience by saying, "Well, this sister complex is really the thing that ruined my entire life" (Obholzer 1982 [1980], 36–37). Only in this late interview does Pankejeff admit the tremendous effect the erotic aspect of his relationship with Anna had on his psychosexual development and adult erotic life. Abraham and Torok (1986 [1976]) suggest, in a thorough psychoanalytic-linguistic study, that the seduction of Pankejeff by his sister alludes to a primary forbidden abuse of the sister by the father, which is cryptically echoed in Pankejeff's story.
7 The book *Cries of the Wolf Man* suggests understanding the burial ceremony as a metonymic primal scene for the known primal scene described in Freud's case study of the Wolf Man (Mahony 1984, 67–68).
8 The authoritative representation of the analytic relationship, as expressed in Pankejeff's narrative of separation, accords with Ruth Mack Brunswick's impression of Pankejeff in her report on his second analysis, which she conducted. She describes him as a person lacking any sense of empathy and whose attitude towards Freud was based on greed and dishonesty (1971, 267, 279–280).
9 It is interesting to note that Sándor Ferenczi (1873–1933) went through a similar process to Freud's concerning the fixed termination date, but eventually became one of its vigorous critics (Berman 1999).
10 Along with giving Pankejeff a home, psychoanalysis also took his story and used it for the field's own purposes. His odd pseudonym, bestowed on him by psychoanalysis,

carried with it an identity transformation and created him as a persona, a psychoanalytic construct. According to myth, the metamorphosis of the werewolf was due to a curse by Zeus, father of the gods, for the sin of serving him human flesh to eat. To a certain extent, psychoanalysis similarly cursed the subject called the Wolf Man, stripping him of his human qualities and turning him into an isolated mutant.

11 This unresolved conflict between constructing his own voice and de-subjectivation finds expression at the outset of Pankejeff's memoir. There, he presents himself as possessing a dual identity: "I, who am now a Russian émigré, eighty-three years of age, and who was one of Freud's early psychoanalytic patients, known as 'The Wolf-Man,' am sitting down to write my recollections of my childhood" (Pankejeff 1971a, 4).

Chapter 7

Tribute to Freud by Hilda Doolittle (H. D.)

Between the analytic and the poetic

Introduction to H. D.'s *Tribute to Freud*

The book *Tribute to Freud*, by the author and poet Hilda Doolittle, known as H. D. (1886–1961), is a unique memoir. The book first appeared in 1956; an expanded edition appeared in 1974, after H. D.'s death. The memoir is constructed in two parts. The first part, *Writing on the Wall*, was written approximately a decade after H. D.'s separation from Freud and half a decade after his death. This text was written over a period of six weeks (the author mentions the dates of the writing's beginning and ending), during the height of the Second World War in London, during the heavy bombing there (Guest 1984, 253–279). Before the book appeared, the text was published in fragments in the literary journal *Life & Letters Today* in the mid-1940s.

In the years before the war, H. D. suffered from an ongoing writing block, which was one of the main reasons why she sought analysis. Surprisingly, then, the war period led her to innovative and enriched writing, which included experiments in new genres such as memoir and autobiography. During the time when she wrote *Writing on the Wall*, she was also writing another autobiographical text, titled *The Gift* (1998), which offered a portrait of her childhood, and three collections of poems, later gathered into one volume titled *Trilogy* (1973). Alongside the burst of creativity that characterized those years, however, H. D. also experienced psychic turmoil, which led to a severe psychotic break in the winter of 1945. *Writing on the Wall*, then, which centers on Freud and offers a new translation of H. D.'s analysis, was written during a period of crisis in her life. Soon after it was written, she was rushed to the mental health institute *Küsnacht* in Zurich in a severe psychotic state (Guest 1984, 253–279).

After approximately a year of hospitalization, in December of 1946, H. D. was released and chose to continue living in Switzerland (though in Lausanne, rather than Zurich) so as not to be too far from the institute. The breakdown left her visibly changed; after her hospitalization, this tall and impressive woman seemed as if her vitality had been taken from her (Guest 1984, 283). During this period, she re-edited the diary entries she had written during her analysis with Freud; this edited diary makes up the second part of the memoir, titled *Advent*. In 1953, H. D. returned to *Küsnacht* to be treated for medical problems, and she remained there until her death eight years later. Writing continued to be the center of her life (Guest 1984, 305–333). The memoir *Tribute to Freud* is the pivotal text she wrote about her experience in analysis and her relationship with Freud. In addition, she also wrote a poem named *The Master*, but refused to publish it. The poem was published 20 years after her death (H. D. 1981), along with letters she had written to her friends at that time (Friedman 2002).

H. D. was a bold and multitalented artist. She was born in Pennsylvania, in 1886, in the small town of Bethlehem, where her family belonged to the Moravian church. This was a small, secluded community established in America by German-speaking immigrants who had come from Moravia. The community was characterized by piety and devoutness as well as faith in prophecy, immortality, and the occult (Guest 1984, 9–21; Augustine 1998). It was H. D.'s mother who originally came from this community; her father was a professor of astronomy and mathematics, a widower with two sons when he met and married H. D.'s mother. Together, the couple had four more children who reached adulthood; H. D. was the second of these and the only surviving daughter in the family. Two other daughters died in early childhood.

In her youth, H. D. met the poet Ezra Pound, and the two of them developed a strong bond, which included a short-lived love affair. Pound (1885–1972), who was already an established poet at that time and had founded the Imagist movement, had a profound effect on H. D. He read her early poems and ensured their publication. It was Pound who constructed her literary name H. D., from the initials of her name.

During the First World War, H. D.'s brother Gilbert was killed in battle. Shortly thereafter her father died, and H. D. was convinced he had died of heartbreak, writing, "the news of the death in action of my brother in France brought on a stroke. My father died, literally, from the shock" (H. D. 1974, 31). With her husband at the time, the poet Richard Aldington (1892–1962), H. D. had had a pregnancy that ended with a stillbirth. Shortly thereafter, the two separated. She then had an affair that resulted in the birth of her only daughter, Perdita. In the 1920s, H. D. met Annie Winfred Ellerman, known as Bryher (1894–1983), and the two became close friends and life companions. Bryher was an author and artist who came from great wealth. At the time, she was interested in psychoanalysis and had connections with the psychoanalytic community and with Freud. H. D. and Bryher continued to support each other closely throughout the years, and for some period of time the two were also lovers. Bryher supported H. D. financially and promoted her literary publications, and Bryher and her husband even adopted H. D.'s daughter (Friedman 2002, 549–551). The two women lived together and apart in various places in Europe.

In the early 1930s, because of the troubling writing block that H. D. was experiencing, Bryher suggested that H. D. turn to analysis with Freud; Bryher made all the necessary arrangements. The analysis commenced in March 1933, in Vienna, and was prematurely terminated, approximately three months after it started, due to the troubled situation in Vienna after the Nazi occupation. A year later, H. D. returned to Vienna for further analysis, which lasted a couple of weeks.

Tribute to Freud, like H. D.'s late autobiographical writing (such as *The Gift*, mentioned earlier, and the memoir *End to Torment*, about Ezra Pound), is characterized by a distinctive writing style that can be described as a stream of consciousness, written in the language of dreams and associations, enriched by symbolism and intertextual references, a text that invites the reader to a deciphering reading. The text is built, from fragments that vary in length and style, into a textual quilt or narrative of dream associations. The manifold layers of the text invite the reader to multiple different interpretations, but its complexity can also be misleading, for it calls for a fragmentary reading. Feminist readings of H. D.'s text have emphasized the distinct and independent stance that the author establishes in response to Freud's phallic dominance (Duplessis and Friedman 1981; Friedman 1981; Friedman 1990; Tolpin 1991; Taylor 2001; Gonzalez 2002). The psychoanalytic readings of the text that have been proposed treat it similarly to other texts written by Freud's patients: as a personal testimony to, or better still, documentation of how Freud worked (Jones 1957b; Holland 1973; Lohser and Newton 1996). In general, the relatively rich literary and psychoanalytic readings that H. D. offers in her memoir of Freud have been overly identified with her impressions of the analytic encounter; they have tended to be treated as reminiscences and even as documentation. Yet the writer emphasizes her desire to free herself from historical sequence and create a narrative that is not attached to actual events. In my reading of H. D.'s memoir, I want to offer *Mignons's Song*, by Goethe, from his canonical bildungsroman *Wilhelm Meisters Lehrjahre*, as a pivotal motif. I will emphasize the retranslation of the analytic relationship between the author and Freud as a poetic relationship between a lost child and her adoptive father and between the poet and her creation.

The notion of reliving the analytic encounter through the medium of writing stands at the center of the memoir written by H. D., because the termination of her analysis does not present itself in the text as an actual event. Instead, her writing represents a quest for a new poetic encounter with Freud. *Tribute to Freud* offers a unique insight into the ties between literature and psychoanalysis by a patient who is also a poet. She structures the text with her impressions from the time of analysis and from her early childhood. In the process, she recalls a long-forgotten poem that she had known as a child, Goethe's *Mignon's Song*, which offers her a platform for psychic transformation.

H. D. declares the importance of following the distinct sequence that the memoir offers at the very beginning of the book: "I do not want to become involved in the strictly historical sequence. I wish to recall the impressions, or rather I wish the impressions to recall me. Let the impressions come in their own way, make their own sequence" (H. D. 1974, 14). She repeats the notion of freeing herself from the restraints of the actual, with variations, throughout the text.

In one of these variations, H. D. writes of her interest in general impressions and her unwillingness to follow either the historical or the political sequence: "I could verify the actual date of their appearance by referring to my notebooks, but it is the general impression that concerns us, rather than the historical or political sequence" (59). In another variation, she emphasizes the dominant power of the impressions, a power that leads her narrative, her work of reminiscence: "I have said that these impressions must take me, rather than I take them" (95). It has been suggested that writing serves H. D. as a self-analysis, in continuation of the analytic process that she went through with Freud (Friedman 1986; Holland 2000, 133). Yet the author tries not only to weaken critical thought and free her associations; she also aims in her writing to give these impressions independent power, as emphasized by her repeated use of the word "their." She draws a distinction between conscious thought and reminiscence and emphasizes her desire to release memory from its restraints and express its full potential. There is also an implied premise here that memory is an internal reservoir that has the power to lead to innovative insights. H. D.'s attitude toward referential reality is complex, for while the impressions are linked to actual events, H. D. insists nevertheless that their essential meaning does not lie in the events themselves but in something obscure she challenges herself to substantiate and articulate.

Psychoanalysis and the figure of Freud are central sources of inspiration for H. D., yet she does not wish to create a relationship of obedience to them. She wishes instead to write something new. The memoir presents a dialog between herself and her late analyst Walter Schmideberg. In their actual encounter, she told him of her wish to write a memoir about Freud, and he replied, "There will be plenty of memoirs about the Professor. I expect Sachs and the Princess have already done theirs" (H. D. 1974, 14). In *après coup*, she finds words to express her stance, words that were ungraspable to her back then:

> It is easy to be caught, like Schmideberg, in the noose of self-criticism, it is easy to say, "Everybody will be scribbling memoirs," but the answer to that is, "Indeed yes, but neither the Princess George of Greece nor Dr. Hans Sachs aforetime of Vienna and Berlin, later of Boston, Massachusetts, can scribble exactly *my* impressions of the Professor."
>
> (15, emphasis in original)

For her to be able to fulfill her desire to write something new about Freud, H. D. needs to overcome the doubts planted by her present analyst and believe that her own impressions are indeed significant and unique. This dialog also positions her as a representative of minor literature, facing the canon of psychoanalytic literature: an individual outsider facing the community and demanding that her voice be listened to.

Perhaps it is this starting point that causes H. D. to construct the text as a quest or a search; at times, she presents her writing as research, a mutual process into which she invites Freud. For instance, she writes toward the end of the text, "We have only just begun our researches, our 'studies,' the old Professor and I" (100). At other times, she presents the writing as a lonely quest that she can only undertake on her own, as a writer as well as an analysand:

> But when the Professor said, "Perhaps you are not happy," I had no words with which to explain. It is difficult to explain this to myself or to find words to scribble in my note-book. It is not a question of happiness, in the usual sense of the word. It is happiness of the quest.
>
> (145)

Her turning to Freud is presented as part of the same quest,

> We had come together to substantiate something. I did not know what. There was something that was beating in my brain; I do not say my heart— my brain. I wanted it to be let out. I wanted to free myself from repetitive thoughts and experiences.
>
> (13)

One of the challenges H. D. faces is the need or demand to substantiate that "something" that is beating in her brain, violently demanding as it is. Toward the end of the text, she calls it "the wordless challenge" (99), the impossible mission of giving words to a wordless something. There is an inherent paradox in this kind of writing, for the language of experience preserves the impressions in their rawness, intensity, and, sometimes, accuracy, yet this language tends to be intrapersonal and is difficult to communicate. H. D.'s textual journey aims for a reunion with Freud and seeks innovative communications with him, because innovative communications with Freud are innovative communications with herself. This challenge is further complicated by the fact that substantiating something in relation to her analysis also means giving words to areas of disagreement and dispute between Freud and herself. Expressing the disputes and preserving the love: this is perhaps the biggest challenge of all for her. The process of recreating or retranslating her impressions of Freud is for H. D. a quest for her inner voice as a subject and a poet. During this transformative process, she reminds herself time and time again that "The Professor was not always right." These words are repeated in different versions and woven through the text as a kind of mantra; they serve as a wake-up call for her to write her story, to create her own distinct voice.

The memoir as a call to memory

The opening scene of the memoir serves as a call to memory, and the impressions recorded there "take" H. D. to an enigmatic story that begins with the death of one of Freud's patients. The text opens with H. D.'s return to Freud in 1934, a year after the premature termination of her analysis. This re-encounter is presented in the text more as a symbolic event drawn from her associations and fantasies than as an actual event. H. D. emphasizes that her re-encounter with Freud had not been planned in advance; after her separation from him in 1933 she had not planned to return to Vienna. But then she did in fact abruptly return to Freud a year later, after hearing of the plane accident in which his analysand had tragically died.

During her first analysis, H. D. hardly knew this analysand, although they were in analysis during the same period of time and occasionally passed each other between sessions. Yet when she hears the news of his death, she rushes to Freud and immediately gives him a mysterious message:

> I always had a feeling of satisfaction, of security when I passed Dr. van der Leeuw on the stairs or saw him in the hall. He seemed so self-sufficient, so poised—and you had told me about his work. I felt all the time that he was the person who would apply, carry on the torch—carry on your ideas, but not in a stereotyped way.... Dr. van der Leeuw was different. I know that you have felt this very deeply. I came back to tell you how sorry I am.
>
> (6)

These words she says to Freud on their re-encounter indeed raise many questions: How did this analysand whom H. D. admits she hardly knew become so important to her? How does she know so many pivotal things about him, his relationship with Freud, and his crucial role in the future of psychoanalysis? What gives her the confidence that Freud knew all that and "felt this very deeply"? And, perhaps the most puzzling question of all: why was it so important for her to return to Vienna and tell Freud how sorry she was? Freud's response adds to the mystery, as he replies, "You have come to take his place" (6).

The enigma of the opening scene continues with the evocation of two childhood memories. In both memories, the writer appears with her brother Gilbert, who was two years older than she and was later killed in battle. She emphasizes the fact that as a child she was under the intense impression of him being taller than her, physically imposing, and grand and heroic in many aspects. As a child, H. D. felt small and dependent, her brother's passive follower. The first reminiscence revolves around the brother, sister, and father, while the second reminiscence involves the brother, sister, and mother. In the first reminiscence, the brother takes a magnifying glass from the father's desk and shows his little sister how to start a fire with it, using the rays of the sun. The father comes bursting in, firmly saying, "But you know, you children are never to play with matches" (24). As a child, she was frightened of violating her father's prohibition. In *après coup*, this scene receives a new translation, unknown to the three participants back then:

I do not know, he does not know that this, besides being the magnifying glass from our father's table, is a sacred symbol.... This is the sacred *ankh*, the symbol of life in Egypt, but we do not know this—or perhaps our father does know this.

(25)

The enigmatic messages obscurely communicated between the father and his children intrigue her. She finds new links between past and present, between her childhood, analysis, and time of writing: "It is only now that I write this that I see how my father possessed sacred symbols, how he, like the Professor, had old, old sacred symbols on his study table" (25).

In the second reminiscence, the mother is laughing in the street after the brother "has defied her.... He has told her that he is going away to live by himself, and he has moreover told her that his sister is coming with him" (28). In contrast to the brother's determination, "His sister waits anxiously, excited yet motionless, on the curb beside him" (28). The mother stops laughing and walks away, and the two children experience this change differently, "*He* knows that she will come back because he is older and is admittedly his mother's favourite. But *she* does not know this" (29, emphasis in original). In *après coup*, she deciphers this reminiscence, "They make a group, a constellation, they make a groove or a pattern into which or upon which other patterns fit, or are placed unfitted and are cut by circumstance to fit" (29). In this constellation, she was destined to follow her brother, "One is sometimes the shadow of the other; often one is lost and the one seeks the other" (29).

H. D. does not remember to what extent these reminiscences were given significance in her analysis. She is not able to recall whether she even told them to Freud at the time. Yet, in the memoir, they are given a pivotal position: "These pictures are so clear. They are like transparencies, set before candles in a dark room. I may or may not have mentioned these incidents to the Professor. But they were there" (29). Later on, she returns to these two reminiscences and their significance in her retranslation of the past, of her childhood roots, of her encounter with Freud, and of her evolution as a subject and a poet, in order to find answers for herself in a time of turmoil:

> We travel far in thought, in imagination or in the realm of memory. Events happened *as* they happened, not all of them, of course, but here and there a memory or a fragment of a dream-picture is actual, is real, is like a work of art or is a work of art. I have spoken of the two scenes with my brother as remaining set apart, like transparencies in a dark room, set before lighted candles. Those memories, visions, dreams, reveries—or what you will—are different. Their texture is different, the effect they have on mind and body is different. They are healing. They are real.... But we cannot prove that they are real.
>
> (35, emphasis in the original)

These reminiscences seem real because, like transparencies set before candles in a dark room, they let the light penetrate through them and fight the predominant darkness. Nevertheless, in this image the flame of the candle does not appear as is, but through a transparency, a screen, similar to the mechanism of the psychoanalytic screen memories that stand near the early traumatic memories and serve the double function of a reminder and a buffer. With them, the subject can experience a reminiscence, a fragment of the memory's light or essence, yet only through a protective screen, a metonymy of sorts.

With these memories, H. D. creates a triangular space of relationships within her family, yet in an alternative to the classical triangular space offered by the oedipal complex, her triad is made up of a brother, a sister, and a parental figure. The brother receives a pivotal position, which in hindsight refers to his position in her inner world as an object of passion. He is presented as "glowing and gold" in both his personality and appearance, charming and wise, whereas H. D. is "wispy and mousy," passive and mute. She even refers to herself as a child as "it": "it was a girl," compared to her older brother, who (like her younger brother) is described as a distinct subject (107). Both the father and the mother in these memories speak only to the brother: he is the sole carrier of responsibility, their mother's favorite, while the sister is presented as his shadow. In this context, H. D. raises an innovative possibility in regard to the second childhood memory, a new perspective on the situation with her brother and mother, opening to her in *après coup*,

> But though her brain is in a turmoil of anxiety and pride and terror, it has not even occurred to her that she might throw her small weight into the balance of conventional behavior by following her mother and leaving her brother to his fate.
>
> (29)

The two memories offer in retrospect a translation of the enigmatic opening scene of the memoir, in which H. D. rushes to Freud to tell him how sorry she is about the death of his former analysand. This scene opens yet another triangular space involving a brother, sister, and paternal figure. The dead analysand represents the golden, glowing brother; H. D. is the little sister leaning on her brother's presence; and Freud, like the parental figures in the familial memories, sees in the brother the chosen son. H. D. rushes to Freud to comfort him in his sorrow and let him know that she understands his grief; perhaps, in fact, she is the only one who understands. Freud's response leaves unresolved the prominent question of whether he sees H. D. as her brother's shadow, in a repetition of her infantile stance, or whether he is now giving her the power to take the brother's place and become his heir. This scene echoes the family crisis that H. D. experienced after her brother's battleground death approximately two decades earlier and her father's death from heartbreak soon after. H. D.'s abrupt return to Freud can be interpreted as a wish to correct these past losses: this time, perhaps, she can save her father figure from heartbreak and death.

The act of H. D. replacing her dead brother figure as the chosen heir also possesses erotic meanings. In the first childhood memory, the brother seduces the sister into witnessing how he creates fire, and this deed is presented as "one of the unforgivable sins" (24). The father appears and creates the Law of the Father, as Lacan calls it, establishing prohibitions and restrictions on where and how the children are allowed to play. The father declares his desk and matches to be out of bounds to the children, thereby implying that these are adult spaces and activities. In the second memory, the brother declares his sister to be his new feminine figure, thereby dethroning his mother. The mother reacts with laughter and turns away, apparently allowing them their desired freedom. H. D.'s text emphasizes that while the brother interprets the mother's response playfully, the sister takes it at face value and reacts with anxiety.

Erotic aspects are also revealed in H. D.'s interest in Freud's mysterious analysand. His figure is presented with an emphasis on his appearance, his body, the distinct confidence that emanated from him, and the special way his clothes fit his body. H. D. explicitly admits that she envied him

> his apparently uncomplicated personality…. You would have said that his body fitted him as perfectly and as suavely as the grey or blue cloth that covered it; his soul fitted his body, you would have said, and his mind fitted his brain or his head; the forehead was high, unfurrowed; his eyes looked perceptive with a mariner's blue gaze, the eyes were a shade off or a shade above blue-grey yet with that grey North Sea in them. Yes—cool, cold, perceptive yet untroubled, you would have said.
>
> (6–7)

At one moment it occurs to her that he had been the analysand in the session immediately preceding hers and that he had therefore lain on the couch just before her (17–18). Another aspect of the erotic tie between H. D. and that analysand is the name that she and Freud created for him during analysis. The analysand was of Dutch origin and a pilot, so she and Freud called him "the Flying Dutchman" (*Der fliegende Holländer*). This name is associated with Richard Wagner's 1914 opera of the same name, which tells the mythical tale of a legendary phantom ship, occupied by a crew of ghostly pirates, doomed to sail forever without reaching shore. Once every seven years, the ship's captain is cast ashore with the aim of finding a woman who will fall in love with him. If he succeeds, the ship will be released from its curse and the crew will be able to rest in peace. In Wagner's version of the mythical story, on one of the coasts where he goes ashore the ghost captain meets a man who, not knowing of the curse, agrees to give him his daughter Senta. The captain and Senta fall in love. Later, in the tangle of events, the curse is revealed. Senta, despairing of her lost love, throws herself into the ocean while declaring her everlasting love to him. With this, the Flying Dutchman ship is released from the curse and the two lovers are seen ascending to heaven.

In this story, Senta represents the romantic ideal of feminine devotion. In entering into her love, she is destined to lose her life. In the intertextual context, Freud's analysand represents the Flying Dutchman's captain, while H. D. represents Senta. The writer wants to separate herself from the familiar role of the fearful little sister and seeks new possibilities of self-expression, which revolve mysteriously around death and resurrection. In the myth of the Flying Dutchman, Senta reunites with her lover after passing the threshold of death; in her memoir, H. D. returns to Freud, wishing to connect with his dead analysand. Moreover, the act of writing the memoir reveals a wish to cross the threshold of death and reunite with Freud, to bring him back to life.

H. D. ends her words devoted to the analysand named the Flying Dutchman by saying that "he was a stranger" to her; "I did not really know him," she adds. The two had only ever had one direct encounter with each other. It was at the entrance to Freud's summer house in Döbling, on the outskirts of Vienna. H. D. was not familiar with the identity of the handsome young patient; she did not even know his name. Suddenly, he approached her:

> Dr. van der Leeuw bowed, he addressed me in polite, distinguished German, would the *gnädige Frau* object to altering her hour for one day, tomorrow? I answered him in English, I would not mind at all, I would come at four, he at five. He thanked me pleasantly in friendly English, without a trace of accent. That was the first and last time I spoke to the Flying Dutchman. We had exchanged "hours."
>
> (8)

This act of exchange between the Flying Dutchman and herself, which took place with Freud's approval, has a symbolic aspect. The exchange of "hours" in the analytic context represents another exchange between the two, the exchange of enthronement after Dr. van der Leeuw's death. Dr. van der Leeuw's address to H. D. in German possibly prefigures the significance that Goethe's poetry will receive later on.

The gift of the memoir

The sequence of associations then leads H. D. to the memory of Freud's 77th birthday, which took place while she was his analysand. Upon entering Freud's room, H. D. notices that the whole room is filled with flowers. She, in contrast, has not brought a birthday gift.

> I had nothing for the Professor. I said, "I am sorry, I haven't brought you anything because I couldn't find what I wanted." I said, "Anyway, I wanted to give you something different." My remark might have seemed

a shade careless, a shade arrogant. It might have seemed either of these things, or both. I do not know how the Professor translated it. He waved me to the couch, satisfied or unsatisfied with my apparently casual regard for his birthday.

(9)

Like the Flying Dutchman, who was to continue Freud's path but not in a stereotyped way, H. D. wants to bring Freud "something different." She is left to wonder, and still wonders, "how the Professor translated it," in other words, to what extent he followed her obscure intentions.

Though she fails to bring Freud a birthday present during her analysis, on one of his later birthdays she succeeds better, though after at least one more failed attempt. While everyone else thinks that Freud's favorite flower is the orchid, and Freud therefore regularly receives dozens of orchids for his birthday, H. D. is one of the few people to whom Freud has revealed his secret love for the gardenia. After her analysis has terminated, H. D. is living in London, and on Freud's birthday she asks a Viennese friend to "make a special effort to find a cluster of gardenias for the Professor's birthday." But the friend later writes to H. D., "I looked everywhere for the gardenias. But the florist told me that Professor Freud liked orchids and that people always ordered orchids for his birthday; they thought you would like to know. I sent the orchids for you" (9). This try, then, does not succeed, but H. D. continues to be determined.

In November of 1938, after Freud arrives in London, "an exile," as H. D. calls him, H. D. is finally given the opportunity to "continue a quest, a search" to find the desired flower. She sends them to Freud with a card, on which she writes, "To greet the return of the Gods"—but she does not sign her name (11). Thus, H. D. welcomes Freud to London with a reference to the gods whose images he cherished and surrounded himself with. From their initial encounter, H. D. had become deeply attached to Freud's unique "mysterious lion's den or Aladdin's cave of treasures" (132). The picture of the ancient temple of Delphi and the statues of the gods greeted her as she entered the room and gave her solace in difficult moments: "Sometimes the Professor knew actually my terrain, sometimes it was implicit in a statue or a picture, like that old-fashioned steel engraving of the Temple at Karnack that hung above the couch" (9). Freud recognized her attachment to his room and their shared affinity for the ancient. "The Professor said that we two met in our love of antiquity. He said his little statues and images helped stabilize the evanescent idea, or keep it from escaping altogether" (175).

Alongside their shared love for the ancient, the two also shared a love of journeys to faraway places. During analysis, they traveled together metaphorically.

> In one of our talks in the old room at Berggasse, we had gone off on one of our journeys … this time it was Italy, we were together in Rome.… "Ah, the Spanish steps," said the Professor. "It was those branches of

almond," I said; "of all the flowers and the flower baskets, I remember those best." "But," said the Professor, "the gardenias! In Rome, even *I* could afford to wear a gardenia."

(9, emphasis in original)

When, after his arrival in London, H. D. fulfills her wish to send Freud gardenias for his birthday, and accompanies them with an unsigned card, she is sending him a gift that is different from what others have sent, accompanied by a riddle and an invitation to Freud to decipher it. Later in the memoir, referring to a different occasion, she returns in her thoughts to the gift of gardenias, "I did not want to murmur conventional words; plenty of people had done that.... I did find what I wanted, that cluster of gardenias, somewhat later" (63).

H. D.'s choice of flowers that were different from what everyone else sent, along with the mysterious card, are references to affinities and cherished notions shared with Freud that go beyond the conventional therapeutic setting, perhaps beyond conventional thought. In these contexts, H. D. presents her relationship with Freud not only under its analytic aspect but as a mutual and fruitful exchange of love. H. D.'s desire to free herself from conventions in general, and specifically in the analytic context, expresses itself in manifold ways. For instance, she is reminded of Freud's invitations during analysis for her to join him in "the other room," attached to the room in which he received patients. In *après coup*, trying to decipher the meaning of these invitations, to translate the messages they hold, she writes, "I did not always know if the Professor's excursions with me into the other room were by way of distraction, actual social occasions, or part of his plan." She dwells on the various possibilities (to which I will return later) and concludes, "Whatever his idea, I wanted then, as at other times, to meet him half-way; I wanted to return, in as unobtrusive a way as possible, the courtesy that was so subtly offered to me" (68). The ambiguity of his invitations is like the riddle of her greeting card. The letter he writes to her in response, which she quotes in full in the memoir, speaks the same mysterious language:

> Dear H. D.,
> I got today some flowers. By chance or intention they are my favorite flowers, those I most admire. Some words, "to greet the return of the Gods" (other people read: Goods). No name. I suspect you to be responsible for the gift. If I have guessed right don't answer but accept my hearty thanks for so charming a gesture. In any case,
>
> Affectionately yours,
Sigm. Freud
(11)

Freud is thus up to the challenge presented to him, writing back with a solution to the riddle she has sent him. Interestingly, he asks that her confirmation of his solution be silent: "if I have guessed right don't answer." This request revolves around the foundation that the analytic couple shared, of an allusive language, of riddles and aesthetic gestures, of intuitive understanding and mutuality, an unconscious meeting an unconscious.

Freud's letter is presented in full in the memoir as evidence of the existence of this shared foundation and mutual spheres. Starting from this shared foundation, H. D. continues her quest to wonder at, translate, and work through her relationship with Freud. For Freud's letter does not stop at alluding to what they both share, but also implicitly refers to their areas of controversy. This finds expression in Freud's remark on the "Gods," which "other people read: Goods." The playful and somewhat humorous substitution of "Goods" for "Gods" alludes to the notion that the objects she greets are not the gods themselves, but an artistic representation of the abstract idea of the gods. Yet earlier, in analysis, Freud does actually admit the symbolic significance of the images and statues themselves, when he tells her that their presence "helped stabilize the evanescent idea, or keep it from escaping altogether" (175). The tension between the view of the ancient statues and images as material goods and the view of them as holding a divine essence remains in H. D.'s mind as a confusing riddle, an enigma to which she returns time after time. The memoir actually revolves around this riddle, as H. D. expresses, for example, in writing about the "excursions into the other room" mentioned earlier, about which she raises the following questions:

> Did he want to find out how I would react to certain ideas embodied in these little statues, or how deeply I felt the dynamic *idea* still implicit in spite of the fact that ages or aeons of time had flown over many of them? Or did he mean simply to imply that he wanted to share his treasures with me, those tangible shapes before us that yet suggested the intangible and vastly more fascinating treasures of his own mind?
>
> (68, emphasis in original)

For H. D., the presence of the ancient gods and temples is real, as real as the childhood memories she raises earlier, and she wonders to what extent Freud understood her beliefs, and perhaps joined in with some of them, but in a different form, as representations of abstract ideas and thoughts, or whether indeed he saw them as mere material objects that only serve a function, as goods.

The inspirational sources that assist H. D. in investigating various phenomena are imagination, intuition, and fantasy. She believes in transcendence, life after death, finding ways to communicate with divine forces, as part of her roots and education in the Moravian church and her deep affinity with the mythical world. Freud represents to her a complex matrix of both affinity with the ancient world of mythology and the occult, on the one hand, and strong belief in modern science and the possibilities it opens up for investigating phenomena objectively, rationally, and materially, on the other. This unusual combination expressed in Freud's thought fascinates and confuses H. D. She is keen for his understanding and recognition, which fill her with hope and a sense of security. Without his understanding, she feels lonely and frightened.

Analysis as home

The most integrative representation that H. D. offers of analysis, Freud, and her attachment to him is as home, a familiar place where the subject is gathered in, accepted, and fully loved,

> With the Professor, I did feel that I had reached the high-water mark of achievement; I mean, I felt that to meet him at forty-seven, … seemed to crown all my other personal contacts and relationships, justify all the spiral-like meandering of my mind and body. I had come home, in fact.
>
> (43–44)

The image of analysis as home is expressed in the analytic setting in the following words, "I do not want to talk today. I am drifting out to sea. But I know I am safe, can return at any moment to *terra firma*" (133, emphasis in original). H. D.'s inability to talk embodies her inability to transform her inner language into communicative language. The image that she suggests of Freud as a stable ground holds both the stability that is not accessible to her and the understanding of her need to fly. Analysis is here presented as a home base from which one can fly, drift, and create and to which one can then return.

H. D.'s image of Freud as *terra firma* is exemplified in her description of Freud's reactions to her as he senses that she is closing in within herself.

> He, sensing some almost unbearable anxiety and tension in me, would break the spell with some kindly old-world courtesy, some questions: What had I been reading? Did I find the books I wanted in the library his wife's sister had recommended? Of course—if I wanted any of his books at any time—Had I heard again from Bryher, from my daughter? Had I heard lately from America?
>
> (73)

This example shows how Freud sensed that H. D. was locked in her inner world and overwhelmed with anxiety and that he knew how to delicately bring her back from there with seemingly small, everyday questions. The articulation of the questions, which seem both tender and direct, helps to gradually soften the inner walls behind which she has locked herself, and to build bridges to the outside world.

Another example in the memoir of Freud's consoling and unmediated presence can be found when H. D. tells him of her bell jar experience. In 1920, H. D. traveled to Greece with Bryher, who had invited her on this journey after the manifold pain and losses the war had brought for H. D. At one point,

H. D. felt herself being enclosed within a globe or bell jar: "I felt I was safe but seeing things as through water" (130). This experience of being protected against a dreadful world by a kind of transparent protective shield echoes the image of her childhood memories as transparencies set in front of candles in a dark room. Both images reflect a dark world, confusing and frightening. The frightened and tortured H. D. is desperately looking for places of solace, protection, security. She seeks anchors that will tie her down to a stable home base. Yet in contrast to the image of the candles, in the image of the bell jar H. D. implies an actual experience, a hallucination of sorts. During that experience, she was aware of the limitations of this protective shield that her psyche had created, for while being closed in, she also found herself trapped. Freud does not rush to interpret this experience, and H. D. feels that he "understood perfectly." At the end of that session, "As I was leaving, the Professor asked me, 'Are you lonely?' I said, 'Oh—no'" (131). H. D. answers in the negative, yet his question stays with her as a transparency in front of light in a dark room, for it carries the notion that solace and security are difficult to achieve when one feels lonely or trapped within oneself. This question, along with the previous questions discussed, is presented as an act of Freud offering his presence against darkness and dread, as a home.

Alongside her feeling that she was understood and safe in Freud's presence, H. D. is also tortured with doubts about the extent to which he really did understand her views and beliefs. In *Advent*, the second part of the memoir, she presents the experiences that she went through on the first nights of her analysis, "No wonder I am frightened. I let death in at the window. If I do not let ice-thin window-glass intellect protect my soul or my emotion. I let death in" (117). On these long, dreadful nights, H. D. was challenged with odd, morbid images that haunted her and led her to repeated, anxious questions. The questions revolved around her confusion over whether she was experiencing these images in fantasy and dreams or in actual reality. From then on, she seems tortured by these questions and also by the question of whether, assuming that these images are fantasmatic, they are fantasies that were created in the past and are being revived from memory or fantasies that are being created anew as alleged past events. "I don't know if I dreamed this or if I just imagined it, or if later I imagined that I dreamed it" (123); "Did I make it all up? Did I dream it? And if I dreamt it, did I dream it forty years ago, or did I dream it last night?" (128). She is not able to settle the question and gradually drowns herself in repetitive thoughts and doubts that only increase her confusion and dread.

As H. D.'s morbid, perhaps psychotic, anxieties increase in intensity, especially with regard to certain childhood memories, real or imagined, she desperately seeks anchors to reality. "I will have to switch on the light soon, for my eyes, staring into darkness, wonder if again I crossed the threshold" (127). The eyes, separated from the experiencing self as one of the sensing organs, are presented as responsible for anchoring the subject to solid ground, while the self has this dangerous tendency to cross the threshold. This condition requires a concrete act of turning on the light and thereby making a literal and symbolic distinction between light and dark. H. D. emphasizes that she wants to bring these intense night experiences to Freud but, for some obscure reasons, keeps forgetting. Perhaps she is afraid that he will not understand: "If I tell the Professor about the cactus *and* the butterfly, he will think I have made up one or the other, or both" (127, emphasis in original).

Thus, in the first weeks of analysis, a split is created between her chaotic night experiences and her relatively ordered analytic experience. The order and sequence of the analysis were created, in H. D.'s view, by the order that Freud represented, an order that felt foreign to her at times, as is most profoundly expressed in the following statement: "The Professor's explanations were too illuminating, it sometimes seemed; my bat-like thought-wings would beat painfully in that sudden searchlight" (30). Freud's beam of light represents the enlightenment of rational thought, which strives for objective, scientific explanations. At another place in the memoir, she states, "I have said earlier in these notes that the Professor's explanations were too illuminating or too depressing" (91). H. D.'s thought is presented by her as belonging to the dark world of night creatures, of bats, perhaps implying insanity.[1] The difference in views between Freud and H. D. is also expressed in their thoughts and stance toward death, a subject that is linked to the upcoming separation between them: "But he confused me. He said, 'In analysis, the person is dead after the analysis is over.' Which person? ... The Professor had said, 'In analysis, the person is dead after the analysis is over—as dead as your father'" (141). In analysis, Freud's determined views made H. D. silent and passive, a repetition of her childhood state.

One of the most salient and intense moments of dispute between H. D. and Freud is the scene involving the goddess Athena. This scene, in which Freud invited H. D. to look with him at his statue of Athena, has been read and discussed many times, especially within feminist research. "*This* is my favorite," Freud tells H. D., "She is perfect, *only she has lost her spear*" (68–69, emphasis in original). This oxymoron of an imperfect perfection perhaps serves as an allusion to the possibility of creating an innovative femininity built on the oxymoron of imperfect perfection or, as an elaboration of this idea, femininity as a combination of empowerment and fragility, castration and intensification. Or perhaps Freud's words are referring not only to femininity, but more generally to the possibility of experiencing satisfaction and joy alongside loss and pain, of accepting this imperfect perfection as a continuous existential state.

For H. D., however, the reference to Athena's lost spear seems to dispute the indisputable divine power of the great goddess. Freud's words stimulate her own conflicts with regard to her identity as a woman, especially with respect to its associations with fragility and dependence. This rouses her to a great rage, which leads her to reveal anti-Semitic views:

> He was speaking of value, the actual intrinsic value of the piece; like a Jew, he was assessing its worth; the blood of Abraham, Isaac, and Jacob

ran in his veins. He knew his material pound, his pound of flesh, if you will, but this pound of flesh was a *pound of spirit* between us.

(70, emphasis in original)

Moreover, she criticizes Freud's reference to Athena as goods while overlooking her mythic essence. H. D. then puts this dramatic dispute into a poem, one that she refuses to publish but that is published later on, in which she writes, "Woman is *perfect*" (H. D. 1981, 411, emphasis in original).

In her retrospective writing, compared with her writing during analysis, H. D. allows herself more explicit and thorough criticism. She connects Freud's materialistic stance toward the ancient gods with his views on the unconscious. Although she admires Freud for discovering the unconscious, in retrospect she finds essential differences between his views and hers in this matter. For H. D., the unconscious is a limitless sphere, holding much more depth and richness than it did, she felt, in Freud's view. Her wish, as revealed in the memoir, is to continue Freud's ideas about the unconscious, to further explore and research this mysterious realm along paths of imagination and spirituality.

Looking back on her experience as an analysand, H. D. feels that the most crucial ideas for her, which she calls "transcendental," were not treated by Freud in a satisfying way. On this deep dispute, she states dramatically, "About the greater transcendental issues, we never argued. But there was an argument implicit in our very bones" (13). She refers to Freud's expression "we had struck oil" in significant analytic moments, and criticizes his "businessman's concrete definite image" (83). Instead, she states,

> The point was that for all his amazing originality, he was drawing from a source so deep in human consciousness.... He called it striking oil, but others—long ago—had dipped into that same spring. They called it "a well of living water."
>
> (82)

Freud and H. D.: paternal and maternal transference

H. D.'s father is presented as a dark figure, closed within himself and his research and wrapped in prohibitions, mystery, and a dangerous appeal. He appears as a mythical figure from a different realm, an astronomer, creature of the night, for he used to work all night and sleep in the daytime, and he was not to be interrupted: it was forbidden to enter his study, touch his things. He arouses in his daughter both yearning and rage. The analogy between her father and Freud is woven through the memoir, the two aloof Professors, absorbed in their research, creating in her a response of both temptation and dread, curiosity and prohibition. Thus, in her transference, her paternal ambivalence is repeated, and she finds herself muted in front of Freud, "as an over-grown school-girl"

(99). In retrospect, she understands her muteness as an inability to find a voice in the presence of the paternal authority, a repeated stance from her childhood.

In H. D.'s writing, she goes back to these moments of muteness and gives herself a voice. With this new voice, the relationship is given a new translation. This is a key aspect of the text. Moreover, the challenge of creating a voice when confronting the paternal authority figure is further entangled with the oedipal aspect of the relationship. In the context of the enigmatic messages suggested by Laplanche, the confused H. D., struggling with feelings of yearning and dread, also needs to cope with enigmatic messages from Freud. These messages carry with them an erotic potential which, as she only understands in *après coup*, further deepens her helplessness and confusion in his presence. Through her retrospective writing, she retrieves these messages and invests herself in a work of translation, trying to rewrite her version of what happened and thereby extricate herself from her muteness. One example of such an enigmatic message is Freud's invitations to follow him into the "other room," discussed earlier. Another example, even more salient, is when at one point in analysis, Freud beats with his fist on the headpiece of the sofa and declares, "The trouble is—I am an old man—*you do not think it worth your while to love me*" (16, emphasis in original). She remembers herself as having been much surprised by this remark at the time. She veered around to face him, wondering "if this was some idea of *his* for speeding up the analytic content or redirecting the flow of associated images" (ibid., emphasis in original). She returns to this scene in *Advent*, writing:

> The Professor said to me today, when I entered the consulting room, "I was thinking about what you said, about its not being worthwhile to love an old man of seventy-seven." I had said no such thing and told him so. He smiled his ironic crooked smile. I said, "I did not say it was not worthwhile, I said I was *afraid*."
>
> (141, emphasis in the original)

She did not understand his anger then and speculated that it was some kind of analytic stance. In retrospect, she can articulate that he was occupied with his phallic presence, while she was occupied with other things, such as his upcoming death. Her deferred-action conclusion is one of disagreement:

> The impact of his words was too dreadful—I simply felt nothing at all. I said nothing. What did he expect me to say? Exactly it was as if the Supreme Being had hammered with his fist on the back of the couch where I had been lying. Why, anyway, did he do that? He must know everything or he didn't know anything. He must know what I felt. Maybe he did, maybe that was what this was all about. Maybe, anyway, it was just a trick, something to shock me, to break something in myself of

which I was partially aware—something that would not, must not be broken."[2]

(16)

The passion to translate Freud's enigmatic messages brings H. D. back to a scene in which she was arriving at Freud's house for a session. It was the time of the Nazi occupation, and Vienna was filled with rifles, soldiers, and swastikas; even Freud's door had been damaged. When Freud asked her why, then, she had come, she did not answer. In retrospect, she can give the following expression to her feelings: "*I am here because no one else has come.* As if again, symbolically, I must be different" (61, emphasis in original). In *après coup* she translates her coming into an answer to Freud's frustrated declaration that it was not worth her while to love him. She writes,

> Again, I was different. I had made a unique gesture, although actually I felt my coming was the merest courtesy, this was our usual time of meeting, our session, our "hour" together. I did not know what the Professor was thinking. He could not be thinking, "I am an old man—*you do not think it worth your while to love me.*" Or if he remembered having said that, this surely was the answer to it.
>
> (62, emphasis in the original)

The most prominent work of translation offered in the memoir is H. D.'s presentation of her initial meeting with Freud. This scene appears, somewhat surprisingly, toward the end of the text, which begins with her return to Freud a year after the termination of her analysis. Situating the first scene between Freud and herself toward the end of the narrative represents the transformative process of writing. There, H. D. creates a voice for the time in her life when she was the most mute, overwhelmed by meeting Freud after intense anticipation. The scene of the initial meeting commences with a reminder about her sole obligation in writing, her obligation to her inner impressions: "I have said that these impressions must take me, rather than I take them. The first impression of all takes me back to the beginning, to my first session with the Professor" (95–96).

Most of the readings that have been offered of this scene relate to the presentation of the initial meeting as an actual event, which can help us to examine the relationship between H. D. and Freud and its development (Momigliano 1987, 381; Lohser and Newton 1996, 41–42; Holland 2000, 134–136). I suggest that it is crucial to read the presentation of this scene in the sequence in which it is offered. Evidence of the significance of the context within which this scene is offered is that the same scene is presented differently in the second part of the memoir, *Advent*, and that yet a third version is offered in a letter to Bryher that H. D. wrote on the day the meeting took place (Friedman 2002, 33–35 (letter from H. D. to Bryher, January 3, 1933); a discussion about the three versions appears in Jeffrey 1995).

Although one would probably, in a memoir that presents itself as a tribute to Freud, expect a positive account of the first encounter, that first encounter is in fact presented as a confrontation between two mythical forces, two symbols. Freud is presented as an "infinitely old symbol," as the "Keeper of the Door" in the "House of Eternity" (97). H. D. is presented in the scene for the first time as "Psyche." According to Apuleius, Psyche was a human princess who fell in love with Cupid. She had to meet and overcome great and dangerous challenges imposed on her by Venus to prove herself worthy of divine love. After she had proved her courage and determination, even entering the underworld, Venus gave Psyche the drink of immortality and the approval to join her lover in sacred marriage. Inspired by the myth, H. D. presents herself as Psyche, who, after going through dreadful challenges, has proved herself worthy of receiving Freud's love.

Yet this much anticipated encounter causes H. D. disappointment:

> He is an infinitely old symbol, weighing the soul, Psyche, in the Balance. Does the Soul, passing the portals of life, entering the House of Eternity, greet the Keeper of the Door? It seems so. I should have thought the Door-Keeper, at home beyond the threshold, might have greeted the shivering soul. Not so, the Professor.
>
> (97)

In her letter to Bryher from that day, H. D. writes that as she entered the room, Freud kindly greeted her by saying, "enter fair Madame" (Friedman 2002, 34). The difference between the two versions strengthens the symbolic presentation of this scene. In her first telling of the scene in the memoir, Freud welcomes H. D. in silence, waiting for her to speak, but she remains silent for she has no voice: "Automatically, I walk through the door. It closes. Sigmund Freud does not speak. He is waiting for me to say something. I cannot speak" (96). In retrospect, H. D. thinks that Freud should have spoken to her at that point, for she had gone through so much hardship before she came to him; perhaps, indeed, following the myth, she went through all that hardship precisely in order to come to him. Looking back, she finds Freud's silence significant with respect to the question of the extent to which he understood her. In contrast with her disappointment with the personal encounter, H. D. finds the greeting that she was expecting from Freud's room instead: "But no one has told me that this room was lined with treasures. I was to greet the Old Man of the Sea, but no one had told me of the treasures he had salvaged from the sea-depth" (97).

The conflict between foreignness and intimacy, enriched by mythical intensity, finds expression in Freud's reaction to her silence:

> waiting and finding that I would not or could not speak, he uttered. What he said—and I thought a little sadly—was, "You are the only person who

has ever come into this room and looked at the things in the room before looking at me."

(97–98)

In this dramatic moment of conflict and muteness for H. D., there occurs a change, as a third figure enters the room and changes the balance. Into the room comes Freud's dog: "A little lion-like creature came padding toward me —a lioness, as it happened." H. D., despite her embarrassment and muteness, intuitively leans toward the dog. "Embarrassed, shy, overwhelmed, I bend down to greet this creature." Freud, like her father in childhood, reacts with a warning and says, "Do not touch her—she snaps—she is very difficult with strangers." H. D. objects to these determined prohibitions, the boundaries, to him calling her a stranger. In Freud's room, H. D. expresses her objection in a rebellious act, and at the time of writing, this act is given words that substantiate and articulate its meaning:

> Strangers? Is the Soul crossing the threshold a stranger to the Door-Keeper? It appears so.... Unintimidated but distressed by the Professor's somewhat forbidding manner, I not only continue my gesture toward the little chow, but crouch on the floor so that she can snap better if she wants to. Yofi—her name is Yofi—snuggles her nose into my hand and nuzzles her head, in delicate sympathy, against my shoulder.
>
> (98)

The initial encounter with Freud is presented with broad complexity. On the one hand, it is this encounter that H. D. has anticipated with such intensity and that has summed all these profound and tantalizing experiences of anticipation and overwhelming anxiety, muteness and rebellion, disappointment and excitement, foreignness and recognition. Freud's dog symbolically receives her name in the text after H. D. has welcomed her and the two have created a loving relationship. The representation of the dog as a "lion-like creature," "a lioness," evokes the biblical story of Daniel in the lion's den. This story, which appears in the book of Daniel, finds Daniel as a high minister in the kingdom of Mede, previously Babylon, after he has helped Darius the Mede overcome King Belshazzar. At that time, jealous rivals incited the king against Daniel, as he was a Jew, demanding that he either convert or be sentenced to death. The king, however, spared Daniel and ordered him to be put in the lion's den overnight, hoping that he would somehow be saved by divine providence. At dawn, the king's men were shocked to see Daniel alive in the lion's den, praying.

With regard to the theme of conversion, the memoir expresses the question in H. D.'s mind about whether Freud expected her to convert from her faith in the occult to psychoanalysis. She returns to this troubling notion in a work of mourning,

So again I can say the Professor was not always right. That is, yes, he was always right in his judgments, but my form of rightness, my intuition, sometimes functioned by the split-second (that makes all the difference in spiritual time-computations) the quicker.

(98)

For her there was always another dimension, another time, another sequence. As an analysand it was not as clear to her as it is at the time of writing, clear as a transparency held in front of a candle in a dark room. Freud is presented as the "Tree of Knowledge" with "the great giant roots" and she is "the invisible intuitive rootlet." This fragile rootlet is small but determined and has an impact. And now the rootlet is given a voice: "'If he is so wise, so clever,' the smallest possible sub-soil rootlet gives its message, 'you show him that you too are wise, are clever'" (99).

Freud is an ambivalent figure for H. D.: On the one hand, he is terra firma, the Tree of Knowledge, the Gate-Keeper, contained in the things he loves. On the other hand, his responses are often surprising, leaving her overwhelmed or confused, and she doubts whether Freud even notices that "I am really somewhat shattered. But there is no answering flareback" (18). In contrast to Freud's changing subjectivity, his room is presented as a sanctuary of stability and comfort, as an everlasting, never-changing home. So in her writing, H. D. finds the strength to speak up to Freud, to pronounce her need and choice to look at the room instead of at him. She turns to Freud and continues her "wordless challenge." In front of Freud she was indeed wordless; in writing, she puts words to her silence, yet the words do not erase the silence, they offer it a new translation:

> You are a very great man. I am overwhelmed with embarrassment, I am shy and frightened and gauche as an over-grown school-girl. But listen. You are a man. Yofi is a dog. I am a woman. If this dog and this woman "take" to one another, it will prove that beyond your caustic implied criticism—if criticism it is—there is another region of cause and effect, another region of question and answer.

(99)

The three personas, Freud, Yofi, and herself, are presented as tied together in relations of power and authority, the two feminine figures joining together to stand up to the ultimate authority of Freud: together, perhaps, they can change the relationship hierarchy and state their thoughts and beliefs.

In *Advent*, H. D.'s edited analytic diary, she also refers to this triangular relationship, but there she explicitly presents the relationship as a magical cooperation: "We make an ancient cycle or circle, wise-man, woman, lioness (as he calls his chow)!" (117). Going back to Freud's room as a "mysterious lion's den or Aladdin's cave of treasures" (132), these images express a tempting security overlaid with an obscure sense of threat. H. D. is expected to let go, to drift with her imagination, knowing that she can return to Freud's terra firma, yet some mysterious voice within her tells her that she should watch out for the lion or the hidden trap.

As to the transference relationship, H. D. states that Freud interpreted it as a maternal transference. She even states in her diary that Freud told her she forms an unusual pattern of transference relationship, an inhibition in her turn from mother to father: "The Professor said I had not made the conventional transference from mother to father, as is usual with a girl at adolescence. He said he thought my father was a cold man" (136). In the first section of the memoir, *Writing on the Wall*, she is reminded of Freud's transference interpretation and offers it new words, a new translation:

> Why had I come to Vienna? The Professor had said in the very beginning that I had come to Vienna hoping to find my mother. Mother? Mamma. But my mother was dead. I was dead; that is, the child in me that had called her mamma was dead. Anyway, he was a terribly frightening old man, too old and too detached, too wise and too famous.
>
> (17)

The sharp dichotomy created here between the yearning for the lost mother and Freud as representing the authoritative father almost overshadows the fact that it was Freud's words that summoned the yearning for the mother in the first place. Freud, the frightening paternal representation, is the one who offers her the idea that she has in fact come to Vienna hoping to find her mother. Thus, as in the contrast between Freud as person and Freud as room discussed earlier, here too the contrast between mother and father is also obscurely contained in the figure of Freud. The conflicts arise because the contrasts that Freud contains for H. D. are dialectically tied to feelings of wholeness and sanctuary and the deepest sense of loss. Although Freud is the one who offers H. D. this valuable insight about her deep affinity with her mother, the insight also evokes the mother's absence and Freud's inability to fill it. In other words, Freud gives H. D. the valuable recognition of her loss, yet along with this valuable gift the unbearable pain of loss is also revived. Analysis can offer recognition, thought, and comfort, but it cannot eliminate the pain that it arouses.

H. D.'s reference to her mother arouses the child in her: in the most direct use of the infantile language of child to mother, she calls her Mamma. Yet the mother is dead, and therefore she herself (H. D.) is dead, for the child that had called her mother Mamma is dead. The mother, H. D., and the child within H. D. are all drawn into a joint experience of death. This implies that the psychic livelihood of the subject depends upon its sustaining a lively link to the mother, or maternal representation.

This notion has implications for H. D. in terms of language and of sustaining her own voice. She gradually understands, so it seems, that in the dialog between feminine and masculine there is a power relationship, a hierarchy, of one surrendering to the other, muting itself, surrendering to the other's language. In the work of mourning done by H. D. in *après coup*, she feels that that is what she was expected to do as an analysand. Yet she has a language of her own, of silence, a wordless language that she tries in her writing to transform into words. Her distinct transference to Freud, which they both agree was maternal in its essence, is a key feature for her in her quest for lost language. She looks to find the obscure signs with which she and Freud communicated. A childhood memory arises in her, of her older half-brother lifting a log in front of her brother and herself, showing them the white slugs underneath. The two children stared "spellbound" at the "unborn things." In this context, she writes, "There were things under things, as well as things inside things" (21), as in language, and psychic life.

It is from the position of the invisible subsoil rootlet that H. D. can make her voice heard, for roots have a function regardless of their size; they thrive in the soil and create life. In her childhood reminiscence that involves her mother and brother, she writes about her mother,

> It is *she* who matters for she is laughing, not so much at us as with or over us and around us. *She* has bound music folios and loose sheets on the top of our piano. About *her*, there is no question. The trouble is, she knows so many people and they come and interrupt. And besides that, she likes my brother better. If I stay with my brother, become part almost of my brother, perhaps I can get nearer to *her*.
>
> (33, emphasis in original)

Life revolves around the mother; she contains life and attracts life, and the girl feels that her life is contained within her mother. The link drawn here between the mother and music will be given pivotal significance later on in the connection the author seeks between herself, her mother, and Freud. In *End to Torment*, the memoir H. D. wrote on Ezra Pound, she writes of the mother as the ultimate muse. Using an analogy with Helen of Troy, she writes, "But the mother is the Muse, the Creator, and in my case especially, as my mother's name was Helen" (H. D. 1979, 41).

The fantasy of the lost mother receives expression in a dream that becomes pivotal in both the analysis and the memoir: the dream of the princess. At the center of the dream there appears a feminine figure of royal grace, and it is emphasized that it is not outward features that express her high position but the fact that her unique identity as a subject shines from within, showing her to be an Egyptian princess.

> She wears no ornament, no circlet or scepter shows her rank, but anyone would know *this is a princess*.... The steps are geometrical, symmetrical and she is as abstract as a lady could be, yet she is a real entity, a real person.
>
> (H. D. 1974, 36–37, emphasis in the original)

Another characteristic of the princess's that is noted is her perfect balance and proportional movements. Her perfect pace is expressed musically: "Down, down the steps she comes. She will not turn back, she will not stop, she will not alter the slow rhythm of her pace" (36). The perfect pace and the wholeness of her figure create a perfect moment in time, a complete presence in the present: "There is no before or after, it is a perfect moment in time or out of time" (37).[3]

Although the dream creates a perfect moment in time, a certain detail distracts the dreamer from her complete attention to the princess:

> There, in the water beside me, is a shallow basket or ark or box or boat. There is, of course, a baby nested in it. The Princess must find the baby. I know that she will find this child. I know that the baby will be protected and sheltered by her and that is all that matters.
>
> (37)

The narrative of the dream gradually comes closer, in its associations, to the biblical story of Moses in the basket, who was drawn from the Nile by the princess of Egypt. As part of the dream work in analysis, Freud, who was deeply absorbed with this biblical story at the time, asks H. D. whether she identifies with the baby, Moses, or with his sister, Miriam, who does not appear in the dream but in the biblical story is hiding in the rushes. This question regarding her identity continues to trouble H. D. through the years: "Am I, perhaps, the child Miriam? Or am I, after all, in my fantasy, the baby? Do I wish myself, in the deepest unconscious or subconscious layers of my being, to be the founder of a new religion?" (37).

H. D.'s associations with the dream take her to the triangular relationship between the princess, the baby, and herself as a witness in the dream. In Freud's *Interpretation of Dreams*, he writes that when a woman dreams about the act of saving someone, especially from water, the meaning tends to be giving birth (Freud 1900, 403). Continuing the motif of saving and being saved within the context of triangular relationships, I would like to look at the dream of the princess in relation to the pair of childhood memories that H. D. brought forth earlier, proposing that the dream expresses her wish to free herself from a passive presence that she has identified and to create a new representation of a triangular relationship. In the initial triangular relationship, offered through the childhood memories, H. D. is the passive little sister, her brother's shadow, yet in the dream her stance is that of an active witness, with a determined opinion about the actions that need to be taken. The crucial distinction is between two distinct glances of the witness, between a mute and helpless glance and an active and determined one. In addition, the reproachful or self-absorbed parent of her childhood memories is replaced by a devoted and caring parental figure, an adoptive parent to the deserted baby. H. D.'s attraction to the baby also deserves attention, for she is spellbound by his presence and by the need to care for him. The baby or preadolescent child appears in H. D.'s poetics as signifying hope and the possibility of change (for example, H. D. 1979, 21, 45).

H. D.'s emotional reaction to the baby revives the memory of the child she herself was, the child whom she considered to be long dead. She writes, "The child in me has gone. The child has vanished and yet is not dead. This contact with the Professor intensifies or projects this dream of a princess, the river, the steps, the child" (38). The child who seemed to have died with the death of her mother is given a new life through the recreation of the dream of the princess in the poetic sphere.

Writing as a process of birth or rebirth is expressed through a unique section in the memoir devoted to a significant experience from H. D.'s past, an experience she calls "writing on the wall," which also gave its name to the first part of the memoir. This is an experience that H. D. had during her journey to Greece with Bryher, mentioned earlier. The central destination of the journey was the ancient temple of Delphi, which was for her a divine fantasy: "If I could only feel that I could walk the sacred way to Delphi, I know I would get well" (H. D. 1974, 50). During that time, in her stay at a hotel in Corfu with Bryher, she had experienced, or seen, a series of images on the room's wall, formed or written for her eyes only. In retrospect, she understands these enigmatic images that were written for her as a sign of her being chosen by divine forces.

> We can read my writing, the fact that there was writing, in two ways or in more than two ways.... But symptom or inspiration, the writing continues to write itself or be written. It is admittedly picture-writing, though its symbols can be translated into terms of today.
>
> (51)

Looking back, H. D. feels strongly that this pivotal, even transformative, experience did not receive its proper place in analysis, for Freud interpreted it as, "a dangerous tendency or symptom" (41). The writing of the memoir brings her back that memory from two and half decades earlier and gives the experience its deep meanings in *après coup*. In a way that is characteristic of the dialectical relationship she creates with Freud, he is presented in this context as an oppositional force who both presented this experience as a hallucination and simultaneously offered her a significant insight. "The Professor translated the pictures on the wall, or the picture writing on the wall... as a desire for union with my mother" (44). The work of memory and translation offered to this experience is presented as exhausting, yet crucial:

> I feel that my whole life, my whole being, will be blighted forever if I miss this chance. I must not lose grip, I must not lose the end of the picture and so miss the meaning of the whole, so far painfully perceived.

> I must hold on here or the picture will blur over and the sequence be lost. In a sense, it seems I am drowning; already half-drowned to the ordinary dimensions of space and time, I know that I must drown, as it were, completely in order to come out on the other side of things.... I must be born again or break utterly.
>
> (53–54)

These powerful labor pains are linked to the struggle to cling to the sequence of pictures that keeps fading away, erased by either internal or external forces. The pictures carry with them, in H. D.'s intuition, a prophecy of hope. The work of translation of the sequence of signs is presented by her as a challenge that can lead her either to rebirth or to death. The medium for this translation work is writing, for writing is a form of representation in language that gives her wings when the walls of insanity are closing in. "We ourselves are free to imagine, to reconstruct, to *see* even, as in play or film" (77, emphasis in original).

The freedom to imagine, to construct and see, takes its toll and has psychic implications. That freedom is what causes H. D. the great pain that she feels at her separation from Freud after the analysis terminates and after his death. In spite of their different views on death and life after death, she wants to save Freud from death, not only by paying him a literary tribute but also on an actual level. Perhaps it is possible, she writes, for "he himself, in his own character, has made the dead live, has summoned a host of dead and dying children from the living tomb" (74). The oxymoron of "the living tomb" expresses her opposition to the common dichotomy between life and death, for she deeply feels that death is not absolute.

Two poets, two lost children: H. D. and Mignon

H. D.'s memoir presents writing as a force that has the potential to save us from illness, insanity, the terror of war, even death. Writing is presented as a mythical force, mysterious and great. The memory of the writing on the wall is retranslated in the text as an inspiration, a mystical experience that identifies H. D. as a messenger of the Gods:

> Memories too, like the two I have recorded of my father in the garden and my mother on Church Street, are in a sense super-memories; they are ordinary, "normal" memories but retained with so vivid a detail that they become almost events out of time, like the Princess dream and the writing on the wall.
>
> (41–42)

Thus, H. D. binds together the childhood dreams with the princess dream and the experience with the writing on the wall. She creates an innovative private sequence out of them, like beads threaded on a necklace, a new translation of these experiences regarding a destiny that calls to her through the years. Once she has discovered the transformative power of writing, a forgotten poem from her childhood appears from the repressed, and she writes, "*Kennst du das Land?* Oh yes Professor, I know it very well" (85). The words in German appear in the text as a riddle, in accordance with the mysterious language she had with Freud. With no reference given for these German words, Mignon's song is woven into her text, as her pattern is woven into the Professor's.

Mignon is a pivotal figure in Johann Wolfgang von Goethe's *Wilhelm Meister's Apprenticeship* (Goethe 1795). This novel is considered to be the classic bildungsroman, telling the evolution of a protagonist until he becomes a part of culture and society. The English translator of the novel, Thomas Carlyle, writes in his preface: "The history of Mignon runs like a thread of gold through the tissue of the narrative" (Goethe 1901 [1795], xxvi). Goethe commented about the novel in retrospect, "this work is one of the most incalculable productions; I myself can scarcely be said to have the key to it. People seek a central point, and that is hard, and not even right" (Eckermann 1949 [1836–1848], 91).

I would like to look more deeply into how H. D.'s text thoughtfully weaves in allusions to the classic novel and to the mysterious and intriguing figure of Mignon. Wilhelm Meister's first impression of Mignon in the novel is described in the following way:

> He was going up-stairs to his chamber, when a young creature sprang against him, and attracted his attention. A short silk waistcoat with slashed Spanish sleeves, tight trousers with puffs, looked very pretty on the child. Its long black hair was curled, and wound in locks and plaits about the head. He looked at the figure with astonishment, and could not determine whether to take it for a boy or a girl.
>
> (Goethe 1901 [1795], 110)

Thus, Mignon is presented as a "creature," and later is shown to Meister as "the enigma" (117). Meister queries Mignon about her name, age, and origins, but the enigma remains. Mignon tells him only that "They call me Mignon"; her age is unknown, as "no one has counted"; and, regarding the identity of her father, "The Great Devil is dead" (118). Thus, Mignon is a small creature with no roots and no home, who has been purchased or stolen by a traveling rope-dancing company. Her language is broken, an odd mixture of "broken German interlaced with French and Italian" (132), her talk stuttering and her writing fragmented.

Wilhelm Meister is a young man seeking his way at the outset of mature independent life, leaving his father's business and going on a journey through different cultures and social groups. In Meister's development, Mignon represents the infantile and non-adaptive, living outside every social frame or label, without history, without any language besides the poetic (Stock 1957, 95–96; Dougherty 2002, 127–129). Poetry is presented as the only language that

Mignon has with which to express herself, and in the realm of this language she expresses herself magically. Later in the novel, it is discovered that

> from her earliest years ... she sang beautifully, and learned to play upon the cithern almost of herself. With words, however, she could not express herself; and the impediment seemed rather to proceed from her mode of thought than from her organs of speech.
> (Goethe 1901 [1795], 362–363)

Wilhelm Meister's spontaneous attraction to Mignon from the first time he looks at her remains a mystery in the novel, representing perhaps the mysterious yet powerful forces beneath the explicit layer of adaptation and apprenticeship. After their first encounter, Wilhelm Meister is witness to the maltreatment of Mignon by the master of the rope-dancing company, and Meister decides to buy her from him and take care of her. Their gradual acquaintance is described as gentle and full of excitement. Mignon is gradually revealed as a being of pure innocence and creativity.

At some point, Meister is caught in turmoil and decides to quit his travels, thereby also leaving Mignon. Mignon's reaction to the announcement is dramatic: "She looked at his eyes, glistening with restrained tears, and knelt down with vehemence before him" (173). This begins a palpitating scene, with gradually increasing violence. Meister embraces Mignon with a kiss. She seems motionless at first and then cries out and "[falls] down before him, as if broken in every joint" (174). This reaction serves as a prefiguration of her premature death. At this point, Meister is overwhelmed by her devotion, "afraid she would dissolve in his arms, and leave nothing there for him to grasp." He changes his mind about leaving and decides to stay with Mignon, who cries out with joy and gratitude and declares, in her distinctly broken language, "My father! ... thou wilt not forsake me? Wilt be my father? I am thy child!" (174). The next morning, Wilhelm awakens to the music of Mignon's *Kennst du das Land* (177).

In the second and final part of Wilhelm Meister's journey of discovery, he finds himself with the aristocratic "company of the tower," the *Turmgesellschaft*. There he is reunited with Mignon and with two other figures he has adopted along the way, an old man named the harper and a small child named Felix, later discovered to be Meister's own. As he enters the tower, Wilhelm feels mysteriously at home, and this feeling reminds him of Mignon's poem. He speaks of this notion excitedly:

> I shall recollect for life my impression yesternight, when I entered, and the old figures of my earliest days were again before me. I thought of the compassionate marble statues in Mignon's song: but these figures had not to lament about me; they looked upon me with a lofty earnestness, they brought my first years into immediate contact with the present moment.
> (285)

In other words, the poetic longing for home, as expressed by Mignon in her song, stimulates in her adoptive father his own archaic reminiscences of home and summons within him the deep notion of home as he enters the company of the tower.

In the tower, Wilhelm meets Mignon again after a period of separation. Mignon has been going through an intriguing transformation in her appearance. For the first time, she is letting her hair grow and wearing feminine clothes, yet Wilhelm is also told of a mysterious heart illness from which she has started to suffer. The doctor who is treating her tells Wilhelm, "The strange temper of the child seemed to consist almost exclusively of deep longing: the desire of revisiting her native land, and the desire for you, my friend, are, I might almost say, the only earthly things about her" (288). The longing for a home is therefore deeply attached to a longing for a father-lover figure.

This novel and, most profoundly, the figure of Mignon and her unique relationship with the protagonist become significant in H. D.'s quest for a home. The German words of Mignon's song come back to H. D. from some unknown place within her. "My mother spoke perfect German," she mentions (H. D. 1974, 115), and when she first meets Freud, she states that she feels she "had come home, in fact," and since then, she feels as though her faith had been tied to his forever: "The years went forward, then backward. The shuttle of the years ran a thread that wove my pattern into the Professor's" (9). Her associations with Freud and memories of their encounters rise and overwhelm her, resonating with events from her childhood and life crisis. Gradually, the associations weave themselves into the lyrics of Mignon's song.

Freud was always interested in H. D.'s poetic writing. In a letter to her before the analysis begins, he asks to have her books sent to him. For Freud, being deeply acquainted with H. D. is inseparable from being acquainted with her writing, and his letters to her reveal that he has continued to read her writing ever since. One of the most pivotal issues that they deal with in her analysis is her writing block.[4] A memory rises in her of a little branch that the Professor gave her on a winter's day, from a box of oranges he had received from his son in the south of France. H. D. murmurs words of thanks, but in *après coup* it becomes clear to her that this was the Golden Bough, the mythical gift of inspiration. Yet she doubts whether Freud was aware of this translation of his act, and whether he would agree with it. "Did he know, did he ever know, or did he ever not-know, what I was thinking?" (90). In retrospect, she understands that the poetic words "were there. They were singing" (90). The words that come to her are deeply linked to the words of the song:

> Thoughts are things—sometimes they are songs. I did not have to recall the words, I had not written them.... There was a song set to them.... No, not Schumann's music—lovely as it is—there was a song we sang as school-children, another setting to the words. And even the words sing themselves without music, so it does not matter that I have not been able to identify the "tune" as we lilted it. *Kennst du das Land?*
>
> (90)

The words of the song as sung by the mouth of Mignon or Goethe are retrieved from the repressed, words without music in a tune that speaks to H. D. in profound and mysterious ways. She vaguely remembers that the song had been known to her in her early childhood, that it belongs to her roots in the German-speaking Moravian community that she lilted it as a school-girl, and the memory of her school days, previously gone and dead, is now revived.

The song is presented in the memoir in full, and in German. It is presented as the answer that H. D. was looking for in order to be able to face the dread of war and to retranslate her roots, her family, her childhood, and her analysis. After the words of the song start to appear in her mind, she thinks of Freud and states that she has never been to one of the gardens of remembrance for him, "For our Garden of Remembrance is somewhere else" (95). Their distinct shared garden of remembrance is the song, Mignon's song, and here H. D. reproduces it not only in full but in German, Freud's language and her own forgotten mother tongue. With the song, innovative sequences of memory are created. The initial sequence that follows from the song consists of memories of her childhood that are connected to her mother, followed by the deep attachment to Freud as her adoptive father, and, finally, the poetic realm now rediscovered for her as a language that she was seeking from a place of silence and writing blocks. Thus, the allusion to Mignon's song is presented as the answer to the quest, for it links together broken sequences of childhood and lost home, of analysis and the relation with Freud, and of the poetic language and her search for a distinct voice. Here is the song as it is presented in the memoir (95):

Kennst du das Land, wo die Zitronen blühn,
Im dunkeln Laub die Gold-Orangen glühn,
Ein sanfter Wind vom blauen Himmel weht,
Die Myrte still und hoch der Lorbeer steht,
Kennst du es wohl?
    Dahin! Dahin
Möcht' ich mit dir, o mein Geliebter, ziehn.

Kennst du das Haus? Auf Säulen ruht sein Dach,
Es glänzt der Saal, es schimmert das Gemach,
Und Marmorbilder stehn und sehn mich an:
Was hat man dir, du armes Kind, getan?
Kennst du es wohl?
    Dahin! Dahin
Möcht' ich mit dir, o mein Beschützer, ziehn.

Kennst du den Berg und seinen Wolkensteg?
Das Maultier sucht im Nebel seinen Weg,
In Höhlen wohnt der Drachen alte Brut,
Es stürzt der Fels und über ihn die Flut;

Kennst du ihn wohl?
Dahin! Dahin
Geht unser Weg! O Vater, lass uns ziehn!

H. D.'s mysterious ties to the song gradually find associations in her thoughts and memories:

> Our Professor ... did not pretend to bring back the dead who had already crossed the threshold. But he raised from dead hearts and stricken minds and maladjusted bodies a host of living children. One of these children was called Mignon. Not my name certainly. It is true I was small for my age, *mignonne*; but I was not, they said, pretty and I was not, it was very easy to see, quaint and quick and clever like my brother.
>
> (101)

The small physical size links the forgotten child that was H. D. to the literary character of Mignon and constructs an anchor to repressed memories. H. D. remembers that she was considered little, and otherwise indistinct compared to her brother. The novel's *Mignon* and the memoir's *mignonne* perhaps signify the fragility of childhood and its delicate nature, the lack of any means of protection and the dependence on others. These names also express a lack of roots, origin, or history; in the absence of these, the name given to the two girls represents their outward appearance only. H. D. returns once again to this analogy between Mignon and herself as a child, writing,

> One of these souls was called Mignon, though its body did not fit it very well. It was small, *mignonne*, though it was not pretty, they said. It was a girl between two boys; but, ironically, it was wispy and mousy, while the boys were glowing and gold. It was not pretty, they said ... the soul was called Mignon, but, clearly, it did not fit its body. But it found itself in a song. Only the tune is missing.
>
> (106–107)

The reference to her soul as "it" emphasizes the alienation H. D. as a writer feels in relation to her childhood self, and perhaps also the alienation the child felt from her surroundings. The fact that the soul does not fit its body is presented as a pivotal attribute of Mignon's figure in the novel, and a distinct feature that contributes to Wilhelm's mysterious attraction to her. In the novel, Wilhelm is intrigued by Mignon, as if she were a riddle waiting to be deciphered:

> Wilhelm could not satisfy himself with looking at her. His eyes and his heart were irresistibly attracted by the mysterious condition of this being. He reckoned her about twelve or thirteen years of age: her body was well formed, only her limbs gave promise of a stronger growth, or else

announced a stunted one. Her countenance was not regular, but striking....
This form stamped itself deeply in Wilhelm's soul: he kept looking at her
earnestly, and forgot the present scene in the multitude of his reflections.
(Goethe 1901 [1795], 118)[5]

The lack of accordance between body and mind tells of an impeded development, of a potential that was not given the opportunity to grow in its optimal path or at its optimal pace, and these inhibitions and historic interruptions lead to Mignon's tragic death (Viëtor 1970 [1949], 125–126).

After her premature death, the true story of Mignon, unknown even to herself before then, is revealed. She was the daughter of two siblings who, not knowing of their blood connection, fell in love. After she was born, her parents discovered their family ties, abruptly gave up their daughter for adoption, and separated. The aftermath of this separation was pure tragedy for the little family. The impeded development that is apparent in Mignon is retrospectively understood as a result of the abrupt separation from her parents. In her early development, "she had displayed an extraordinary disposition. When still very young, she could run and move with wonderful dexterity" (Goethe 1901 [1795], 363). After the traumatic separation from her parents, Mignon started wearing boys' clothes, seeking adventures, and leaving home. From one of her "wild walks," she did not return, and eventually she was considered dead. Later it was revealed that the harper who had joined the group that surrounded Meister and had become close to Mignon was in fact her lost father, without either of them knowing it.

In a way that recalls Augustine's commentary at the end of his *Confessions*, H. D. ends her memoir with a commentary on Mignon's song. The lyrics are presented in German, then translated by H. D. into English. The reading follows her own sequence of impressions and associations. She links Mignon with Miriam because of Freud's question, during the work on the princess dream, about whether H. D. identifies with Moses's sister, her brother's keeper. She associates, "Miriam? Mignon?" and continues, "Miriam or Mignon, we may call her" (H. D. 1974, 108–109). The song inspires her "ritual of question and answer" and she follows some of the questions in the poem, "Do you know the Land? Do you know the House? Do you know the Mountain?" (108). She chooses first to turn to the question that opens the third section of the poem, "Do you know the mountain and its cloud-bridge?" in German and English. She chooses this question first because "the idea of mountain and bridge is very suitable to this whole *translation* of the Professor and our work together" (108, emphasis in the original). Immediately afterward, she offers her answer to the question, "There is plenty of psychoanalytic building and constructing; there are the Gods that some people read Goods. We are dealing here with the realm of fantasy and imagination, flung across the abyss, and these are a poet's lines" (108). The poet's lines, or poetic space, is found to be the missing sequence she had been looking for.

H. D.'s re-encounter with Mignon's poem, meanwhile, gives her a renewed arena of meeting with Freud, reliving their encounter as opposed to accepting its termination and Freud's subsequent death. Wilhelm Meister serves as Mignon's adoptive father and secret lover, and it is her premature oedipal love that he eventually declines. Meister is intertwined with Freud and Goethe to create for H. D. a triangle of adoptive fathers and lovers. H. D. is reunited with the persona of Mignon in order to remind herself of her own forgotten childhood, allowing H. D. to encounter herself as a lost child whom she had thought of as dead. In this way, the act of being revived through the poetic sphere serves as an answer to the demand for reconciliation with death. Inspired by Mignon, who uses a poetic gesture to change Meister's decision to leave her, H. D. offers Freud her textual tribute.

In the novel, after Meister declines her love, Mignon dies a tragic death and thereby becomes a symbol of the poetic, crowned with inspiration by the sublime muse that need not be touched by earthly drives. H. D.'s identification with Mignon relates to the erotic aspects of her transference toward Freud, which were not resolved in analysis. These aspects of the transference and countertransference between Freud and H. D. that were not thoroughly worked through find further expression in Mignon's poem. The poem was not only a precious memory for H. D. but a valuable and personal text for Freud as well, and he referred to it in several of his letters. In his letter of December 12, 1897, to Wilhelm Fliess, during his self-analysis and his insights into the impact of early sexual traumas, Freud, while describing a patient's infantile memories, quotes the dramatic words from Mignon's poem, "A new motto: 'What has been done to you, you poor child?'" (Masson 1985, 289). And in a letter to his family during his 1902 Italian tour, he again quotes from the poem, this time in order to give expression to his impressions of beautiful Italy, Mignon's homeland: "My dear ones: 'Kennst du das Land wo die Citronen blühen?' If not, I will describe to you what I can see from the terrace in front of our room" (Jones 1955, 24).

H. D.'s memoir dedicated to Freud ends with the German words of Mignon's poem, along with H. D.'s own writing in English. The different and fragmented languages are molded to one another in an ecstatic poetic moment, and a new language is created:

> But you, of all people, know it, don't you, the inquiring soul asks.... O, let's go away together, pleads the soul, the Mignon of the poet Goethe; let's go, O my dearest, she says first,
>
> *O mein Geliebter*
> Then O my guardian, my protector,
> *O mein Beschützer,*
>
> And in the end, she does not ask if she may go; or exclaim, if only we could go; but there is the simple affirmation, with the white roses—or the still whiter gardenias, as it happened—of uttermost veneration.

> *Dahin! Dahin*
> *Geht unser Weg! O Vater, lass uns ziehn!*
>
> (H. D. 1974, 111)

In Goethe's novel, after Wilhelm Meister listens to Mignon sing her song, he asks to translate it into his own language, yet during his efforts, he realizes that the words lose their mysterious magic in this translation:

> the originality of its turns he could imitate only from afar: its childlike innocence of expression vanished from it in the process of reducing its broken phraseology to uniformity, and combining its disjointed parts. The charm of the tune, moreover, was entirely incomparable.
>
> (Goethe 1901 [1795], 178)

This essence of poetry that does not surrender to common language, to coherence or rationality, is the lost language that H. D. has restored to her, empowered by her female literary companion Mignon.

Mignon is presented in the novel as constantly longing for a distant and warmer place, her long-lost home. H. D. wrote her memoir of Freud in a state of alienation from her surroundings as well, alone in London, where she had insisted on staying during the bombing. The memoir expresses the challenge of writing during a time of war, and H. D. understands this situation as a turning point, in which it will be decided whether she will "be born again or break utterly."

The memoir, and most profoundly the motif of Mignon, tell the story of a quest for a lost home. The writer looks at her analysis in *après coup* as a place where she was offered treasures and images of home, yet not all her questions were answered there. The connection made with Mignon, however, gave her further inspiration as a female poet.

In her late memoir of Ezra Pound, *End to Torment*, H. D. writes about the vicissitudes of the crises of war and the fateful choice she made then, to turn away from life and devote herself to writing.

> When I came here to Küsnacht, May 1946, after the war, I cleared out the grubby contents of my bag. Why did I tear up the pictures? Well, they were frayed and old, as I was, and I must find new talismans. I found them in my writing.
>
> (H. D. 1979, 6)

Notes

1 It is interesting to note in this context that Wilfred Bion offers an innovative understanding of psychoanalysis using representations of dark and light and sometimes even complete darkness—in a way that is relevant to H. D.'s notions on the importance of remaining in darkness—in order to find a lost source of internal light

"Instead of trying to bring a brilliant, intelligent, knowledgeable light to bear on obscure problems, I suggest we bring to bear diminution of the 'light'—a penetrating beam of darkness: a reciprocal of the searchlight.... So that, if any object existed, however faint, it would show up very clearly. Thus, a very faint light would become visible in maximum conditions of darkness" (Bion 1990, 20–21).

2 In her diary, H. D. writes about Freud, "Then he said he thought my voice was 'delicate' and added, as if there might be danger of my letting outside matters intrude, 'I am, after all, seventy-seven.'" (H. D. 1974, 118–119).

3 This perfect moment in time that is presented in the dream alludes to another notion of time that H. D. seeks, which is not obligated to the actual stream of events, to coherence, or, perhaps most important of all, to the limitations of time. The memoir opens with the turmoil involved in the experience of the limited time offered by analysis, "I had a small calendar on my table. I counted the days and marked them off, calculated the weeks. My sessions were limited, time went so quickly" (H. D. 1974, 3).

4 In *Advent*, H. D. gives expression to her thoughts about her writing block. After she forgets her bottle of smelling salts on Freud's couch, she dreams of salting her typewriter, and writes, "So I presume I would salt my savorless writing" (148). She continues to express her frustration: "My books are not so much still-born as born from detached intellect.... There is a feeling that it is only a *part* of myself here" (149, emphasis in original).

5 Further in the novel, Mignon devotes herself to writing, and this task challenges her greatly, for although she knows what she wants to write, her expression in writing, as well as speaking, is impeded: "For some time the creature had been laboring with great diligence in writing everything she knew by heart.... She was indefatigable, and of good comprehension; but still, her letters were irregular, and her lines crooked. Here, too, the body seemed to contradict the mind" (Goethe 1901 [1795], 163–164).

Chapter 8

The creation of voice in psychoanalysis and literature

The autobiographical-psychoanalytic writing of Freud's analysands summons impressions and reminiscences from the analytic process and from the writers' archaic history as revived, repeated, and reconstructed in analysis. The space of writing allows movement between narratives and points of view and playfully offers re-translations of the analytic experience and the encounter with Freud. I propose to conclude here with the essence of this distinct kind of writing in three aspects, as suggested throughout the book: writing as a work of memory, writing as a work of mourning, and writing as a translation of the message of the other in *après coup*.

Writing and psychoanalysis as a work of memory

The work of memory has intrigued psychoanalysis from its very beginning. The primary aim of psychoanalysis was always, for Freud, to "fill in gaps in memory" by overcoming "resistances due to repression" (Freud 1914a, 148). Memory is a dynamic inner entity and reminiscences are dynamically constructed, deconstructed, and reconstructed in the continuous flow of the psychic movement. In his pivotal 1914 essay on psychoanalytic technique, "Remembering, Repeating and Working Through," Freud deals with the elusive nature of memory and the work of memory. There are two groups of reminiscences—namely forgotten impressions and events that occurred in the external world, alongside fantasies and associations that occurred internally—that are shut off from the subject's awareness, yet can be retrieved under suitable circumstances. The most salient forgotten memories belonging to these two groups are the screen memories of childhood that represent the forgotten childhood years, yet in distorted forms. But there is a third group of reminiscences, and that is the experiences that have never passed through consciousness and can only be retrieved through repetition. The return of repressed memories from all three groups involves the challenge of containing these forgotten memories, from the various layers of repression, as part of the subjective history of the individual, with all the resistances involved in this process. The work of memory has to do therefore with a re-articulation of the subject's history and personal narrative.

The collection of texts brought together in this book presents a work of memory involving the distinct reminiscence of the analytic encounter and the implications and effects of this encounter on the authors' lives and evolving selves. Freud was in each case a pivotal figure in the construction of the personal narrative and a source of inspiration. The personal narratives the authors offer are strongly tied to the narrative created and constructed in the analytic process, woven by Freud's interpretations and presence.

One salient example of how a memoir presents a work of memory is Kardiner's *My Analysis with Freud: Reminiscences*, discussed in Chapter 4. At the beginning of his memoir, Abram Kardiner constructs his life story exactly as he had told it to Freud in analysis, more than 50 years earlier. He avoids any retrospective additions or après coup understanding. He even refrains from mentioning or mending any gaps in the sequence of memories that were later made whole during the analytic work. A prominent example of this is Kardiner's early experience of being a sole witness to his mother's death, which was reconstructed in the analytic work but never as a vivid memory. Kardiner refrains from mentioning this pivotal childhood event at the beginning of the text. In so doing, he invites the reader into the analytic experience in real-time, with all its resistances, obscurities, and riddles. The memoir thus invites the reader to a game of hide-and-seek, as memory constantly and dynamically plays with consciousness. Blanton's *Diary of My Analysis with Freud* and Dorsey's *An American Psychiatrist in Vienna*, meanwhile, present edited versions of the diaries they kept at the time they were in analysis. These two texts each present a relatively detailed sequence of sessions, associations, dreams, and interpretations and manifest the significant effect of Freud's presence on the writers at the time of analysis and later.

The memoir *Fragments of an Analysis with Freud*, by Joseph Wortis, is an example of a distinct work of memory in which Freud is the other. Wortis's text presents an analytic encounter missing benevolent aspects of the transference relationship. The transference to Freud in this case was highly complicated, and many questions regarding the writer's motivation for presenting Freud in such a negative light are left to be deciphered. Was this his disavowal of his dependence needs, or revenge for not gaining Freud's appraisal? Wortis's work of memory is distinctly lacking in intimacy and mourning. Perhaps one cannot mourn something that is, at least as explicitly presented, so malevolent. Wortis's one-sided work of memory is perhaps connected to the relatively early appearance of the text. The memoir was published in the mid-1950s, a comparatively short time after the analysis terminated. Moreover, Wortis describes in the memoir how he sent his written impressions of his analysis to Havelock Ellis and other American psychiatrists as soon as he separated from Freud, as evidence for their criticisms of psychoanalysis.

The analysands' works of memory in regard to Freud present the encounter with him as a turning point in their lives. The act of writing revives their memories of this encounter, from their first impression of him, through the analytic process, to their separation from him. The work of memory constructs a narrative made of reminiscences with which the writing analysands can work through various aspects of the analytic experience in retrospect. This working through is facilitated by the freedom of the literary sphere and the retrospective point of view.

Another aspect that is explicitly and implicitly worked through in the memoir is Freud's death. After his death, the analysands' writing of their own distinct memories of him becomes even more crucial, for writing becomes a literary "Garden of Remembrance" of his persona. Freud's persona, as an admired and sometimes disputed trailblazer, appears as a central motivation for writing and publishing the memoirs. His analysands present their writings as a participation in the memorial corpus created for their famous analyst. Freud's cultural significance strongly affects the personal analytic encounter with him and the work of memory for this encounter. The memoirs express awareness of the fact their texts serve the public's interest, and this awareness affects the attention given to Freud's characteristics as a man and analyst; his daily routine, residence, analytic technique, and presence; his family; and his stance on various matters as he occasionally expressed them in analysis and personal gestures. The writing about Freud by his analysands is presented as greatly motivated by the notion that they had known Freud in a way that was distinct, in various ways, from his public image. Writing memoirs about Freud is also understood as a platform for reexamining the transference relationship and its limitations and drawbacks due to the short periods of time usually given to analysis back then, as well as to the blind spots and limitations of Freud the analyst and person.

Writing and psychoanalysis as a work of mourning

The process of creating a voice in a dialectical relationship with the lost authority figure, stands at the center of the texts written by Freud's analysands. The creation of voice involves a complex work of mourning including psychic pain and guilt and has the potential to be transformed into the understanding of this creation as a continuity of the relationship with the beloved authority figure. This understanding can be regarded as a successful mourning, in contrast to the pathological condition of melancholia.

Freud, in "Mourning and Melancholia," defines mourning and compares it to the pathological condition of melancholia: "Mourning is regularly the reaction to the loss of a loved person, or to the loss of some abstraction which has taken the place of one, such as one's country, liberty, an ideal, and so on" (Freud 1917b, 243). Mourning and melancholia are both characterized by "a profoundly painful dejection, cessation of interest in the outside world, loss of the capacity to love" (244). Freud states, in regard to mourning,

Why this compromise by which the command of reality is carried out piecemeal should be so extraordinarily painful is not at all easy to explain in terms of economics. It is remarkable that this painful unpleasure is taken as a matter of course by us.

(245)

In melancholia, the condition is even more complex, for "one cannot see clearly what it is that has been lost." Even in cases where there is an actual and definable loss, the patient "knows whom he has lost but not what he has lost in him" (245). There is another pivotal distinction between mourning and melancholia:

> The melancholic displays something else besides which is lacking in mourning—an extraordinary diminution in his self-regard, an impoverishment of his ego on a grand scale. In mourning it is the world which has become poor and empty; in melancholia it is the ego itself.
>
> (246)

The conclusion is therefore that at the basis of the melancholic affinity to the object lies a conflictual love–hate relationship, a narcissistic ambivalence. After the loss of the object, facing the challenge of mourning,

> In melancholia, accordingly, countless separate struggles are carried on over the object, in which hate and love contend with each other; the one seeks to detach the libido from the object, the other to maintain this position of the libido against the assault.
>
> (256)

Freud stresses the painfulness of melancholia, for the subject experiences both the loss of the object and the deprivation of the self, for as "the ego will have succeeded in freeing its libido from the lost object" in normal mourning, "the complex of melancholia behaves like an open wound, drawing to itself cathectic energies—which in the transference neuroses we have called 'anticathexes'—from all directions, and emptying the ego until it is totally impoverished" (252–253).

For Derrida, memory, mourning, and writing are profoundly intertwined and together are presented as a promise, obligation, and invitation to the object, as part of the love for it. The relationship between the two subjects is created within the framework of the awareness of death and of the idea that one will die before the other, leaving the bereaved subject obligated to the work of memory and mourning. The realm of writing is presented as the realm of hope, evoked by the possibility of finding expression for the infinite bereavement in the loss of the object. Writing can save the bereaved subject from the threat of inner deprivation embodied in melancholy, as Freud presented it, and allow new life within and alongside the work of mourning. When a person close and dear to us dies, Derrida suggests, that person's presence no longer exists outside of us: "Upon the death of the other we are given to memory, and thus to interiorization, since the other, outside us, is now nothing" (Derrida 1986, 34). The work of mourning is deeply and profoundly tied to the work of memory, for in the work of mourning, "one *must* always begin by remembering" (35, emphasis in original). For Freud, melancholic interiorization is based on the narcissistic conflict between love and hate. For Derrida, the challenge of mourning involves the interiorization of the other, a process whereby the "possible remains impossible." On one level, there is the "faithful interiorization," which

> bears the other and constitutes him in me (in us), at once living and dead. It makes the other a *part* of us, between us—and then the other no longer quite seems to be the other, because we grieve for him and bear him *in us*, like an unborn child, like a future.
>
> (35, emphasis in original)

On another level, yet simultaneously, a different interiorization takes place, the "aborted interiorization" of "a respect for the other as other, a sort of tender rejection, a movement of renunciation which leaves the other alone, outside, over there, in his death, outside of us" (35).

These notions regarding the work of mourning gather together many of the themes that are developed throughout this book. The memoirs about Freud present a complex work of mourning, with the continuous working through of the separation from analysis and of unresolved aspects of the transference–countertransference relationship. In spite of the complexity and the inevitable ambivalence, mourning in its essence also has to do with a wish to revive reminiscences from the encounter with Freud and to recreate the analytic space as a space of security, protection, and belonging. One of the most striking impressions left by reading the memoirs is the presentation of the experience of separation from analysis and from Freud as an ongoing loss, "like an open wound," as Freud stated about melancholia.

Furthermore, the stories of analysis presented in this textual collection present variations on the experience of premature separation. This experience does not necessarily depend on the length of the analytic process, as it is present both in Pankejeff's four-and-a-half-year analysis and in H. D.'s relatively brief process. Blanton's memoir presents the experience of a premature separation that became a never-ending process, as Blanton returned to Freud time and time again in what seems to have been a deep need to practice separations and reencounters. Kardiner's memoir presents a separation process that was experienced as a re-traumatization. The abrupt separation was intensely felt because early traumatic experiences of his were retrieved in analysis, leaving him confused and lost after the analysis ended. In his retrospective writing, Kardiner offers new perspectives on his abrupt termination that involve both Freud's and his own subjectivity and limitations. Dorsey's memoir gives a late expression to the abrupt termination of analysis that left him feeling drained and depressed, though at the time he did not interpret those symptoms as a response to separation. Pankejeff's memoir presents a complex work of mourning the forced termination that was not thoroughly worked through at the time, and of the case study about him, from which he felt alienated. H. D.'s memoir expresses the refusal of the author to compromise with Freud's absence and her search for innovative realms of communication with him. Wortis's memoir is distinguished from the others in the critical narrative that it offers, which allows only limited expression to any mourning over the analysis. Nevertheless, even in this story of a negative transference relationship, there is an implicit mourning of the unfulfilled potential that analysis held for him.

The representation of separation as offered by the analysands reflects a melancholic dynamic that revolves around the internalization of the analyst as a narcissistic object and as a subject. The internalization of the analyst as a narcissistic object is characterized by the ambivalence that lies at the base of this type of internalization, as suggested by Freud, and the internalization of the analyst as a subject is based on obligation and love toward him, as emphasized by Derrida. Narcissistic internalization involves a work of mourning that gives expression to the ambivalence toward the lost object that the ego identifies with the abandoned object. In this case, as Freud beautifully articulated, "the shadow of the object fell upon the ego" (Freud 1917b, 249). Given that the essence of transference is a repetition of the infantile narcissistic relationships with the parents, the analytic process aims to decipher these archaic internalizations and transform them into a more developed form of internalization. Yet residues of the archaic internalization of the object remain in the roots of the analytic relationship.

The internalization of the other in Derrida's terms appears in the analysands' texts in the representation of Freud not only as an ambivalent transference figure but also as an enriching subject, gifted and intriguing. The internalization of Freud as a love object and a distinct subject finds expression in the rich layers of reminiscences offered of his unique figure as a person, analyst, and writer. This aspect of the work of mourning as an internalization of Freud as other creates his figure as an unborn child, which makes possible a transformative textual experience, similar to the analytic experience. In the case of H. D., the memoir is presented as a distinct and belated gift offered to Freud as a tribute in return for his gift of psychoanalysis. The text progresses from the wish to give Freud "something different" for his birthday to the symbolic gift of the text dedicated to him after his death.

Freud: paternal and maternal transference

The melancholic-narcissistic attachment to Freud touches on the transference relationship and especially on the archaic relationship with the parents. The psychoanalytic framework, with its various characteristics and most especially its intensity and asymmetry, encourages a repetition of the maternal and paternal representations.

The dominant explicit representation of Freud in the memoirs is that of an authoritative father, yet intriguingly, in more obscure forms, the maternal transference is also dominant. Freud's paternal representation appears in the memoirs in his determined figure holding the power to give meaning to obscure phenomena, raise intriguing questions and give unconventional answers, and articulate the hidden and the unthinkable. He is usually represented as expressing the language of law, rationality, and social order. His figure evokes admiration and awe, and a distinct form of attentiveness.

Wortis's memoir is the most salient and harsh expression of the conflict aroused by Freud's representation as an authoritative father figure. The ongoing dispute described between Freud and the writer is offered in the present reading as an expression of the analysand's unresolved oedipal conflict and absence of maternal representation. The creation of a phallic triangular relationship based on the writer and his two paternal representations implies an exaggerated preoccupation with the father as a compensation for the maternal absence. The reading offered here of Blanton's memoir notes that the affinity to the authoritative father figure offers a limited space for psychic transformations, as it overlooks the inhibitions created after the early loss of the mother. In Kardiner's text, in a somewhat similar fashion, the paternal figure is offered as a dominant yet conflictual figure and the maternal figure is absent due to early loss. In the reading offered here of Kardiner's memoir, the maternal representation is obscurely offered as the root of an early denied trauma, which created internal incoherence. In Dorsey's text, the transference toward Freud as a revered father figure begins at their initial encounter, and the mother is hardly mentioned. The transference dynamic presented by Dorsey fluctuates between the presence of intense dependence needs and the denial of those needs. In this text, as in the other three texts mentioned above, the paternal voice is overly potent compared to the muted maternal voice. In Pankejeff's memoir, Freud's figure is also represented as a dominant father figure and as a substitute for Pankejeff's actual father, who died shortly before he met Freud. Nevertheless, the prolonged analytic encounter evolved in the shadow of Pankejeff's deep yearning for a woman he had met shortly before the analysis began. This woman, Therese, who later became Pankejeff's wife, was a main theme in the analysis, as Freud strongly advised against the fulfillment of the love relationship before analysis terminated. The reading offered in the present book of Pankejeff's memoir presents his passion for the absent woman as a pivotal motivation for him.

In reading this collection of memoirs today, the dominance of the paternal representation in the transference relations developed with Freud becomes obvious and the maternal representation is salient for its absence. An examination of the memoirs written by Freud's analysands in terms of dreams, interpretations, and patterns of transference yields the impression that while on the explicit level Freud offered an ordered interpretive construction, the analytic sphere also obscurely evoked a wish for regressing to archaic forms of communication. One possible explanation for the repeated overlooking of the maternal aspects of transference has to do with the cultural environment at the time the analysis took place. At that time, women were still fighting for equality and against oppression on much more explicit platforms than today. The oppressive attitude toward women is also evident in Freud's writing. Perhaps it was easier for men at that time to admit their paternal identifications than their maternal yearnings. Moreover, the challenge of admitting maternal transference was surely made even more challenging for men because it was often interpreted by Freud as a passive homosexual inhibition of the male subject.

It is H. D., perhaps because she is a woman, who allows herself to offer the most explicit expression of her yearning for the mother, and this is explicitly recognized by Freud in analysis. The maternal transference is discussed in H. D.'s analysis in the most intriguing way. First, she admits in her diary that "the Professor's surroundings and interests seem to derive from my mother rather than from my father, and yet to say the 'transference' is to Freud as mother does not altogether satisfy me" (H. D. 1974, 146). The awkwardness involved in H. D.'s recognition of her transference as maternal deepens with Freud's honest response to the matter: "And—I must tell you (you were frank with me and I will be frank with you), I do *not* like to be the mother in transference—it always surprises and shocks me a little. I feel so very masculine" (146–147, emphasis in original). H. D. asks him whether others besides her tend to develop "this mother-transference," and Freud answers, "ironically and I thought a little wistfully, 'O, *very* many'" (147, emphasis in original).

In the memoirs written by male patients, the maternal transference is much more obscure. In Blanton's memoir, for example, as I suggested earlier, there is a gradual transition from the representation of Freud as the authoritative paternal figure in the first analytic chapter to Blanton's growing acquaintance with the maternal aspects of the transference in the subsequent analytic sequences, as expressed for example in his dream about the queen of England.

The maternal representations of Freud, as offering a womb-like space and a soft presence, are presented in the various memoirs as taking place in channels that are external to the analytic work per se. First of all, the analytic setting itself offers the patients security and serenity. It is described as a home and a refuge. During the sessions, the analysands form a strong attachment to Freud's room, his antiques, the quiet atmosphere, and the many books he wrote and the books he cherished. His patients also become attached to his conduct between the sessions, which involves informal gestures and remarks about his life, dogs, and health condition. This informality is also occasionally expressed in queries from Freud about his patients' general well-being, occupations, and faraway relatives. Although these gestures are not considered by Freud to be part of the analytic process, they are given significance from the analysand's point of view.

As articulated in *Unorthodox Freud* (Lohser and Newton 1996, 169–176), it is quite striking to see that although Freud discovered the phenomenon of transference and was brave enough to articulate its pivotal importance, he worked with it in somewhat simplified and theoretical ways. The impression created from reading the analysands' memoirs is that Freud remained quite reserved about various aspects of the transference, such as Wortis's envy or Kardiner's and Dorsey's regression to dependence. Nor does his line of interpretation touch on his own countertransference at all, although its various forms seem quite apparent. His responses sometimes seem too reserved and aloof, while at other times he exhibits direct, even impulsive, responses, such as when he grasps Blanton's hand, or when he asks Wortis to leave analysis after Wortis has outraged him. This does not mean that these gestures are necessarily experienced as errors; sometimes it is quite the opposite. Yet it seems that Freud does not invest much thinking into an analysis of the distinct transference–countertransference patterns that are created with his various patients.

In his retrospective writing, Kardiner is explicitly and harshly critical of Freud's unsatisfactory working through of the transference. After his analysis terminated, Kardiner met Freud and asked him what he thought of himself as an analyst. Freud's reservations about working through the vicissitudes of the transference relations are expressed quite clearly: "I have no great interest in therapeutic problems. I am much too impatient now. I have several handicaps that disqualify me as a great analyst. One of them is that I am too much the father" (Kardiner 1977, 68–69). Nevertheless, Freud's stance toward the transference relations is distinctly different in H. D.'s case. Freud seems much more sensitive and responsive to transferential issues with her and does not hide his curiosity about her. His apparent interest in her before, during, and after analysis is shown in various ways in the memoirs as well as in the letters he addresses to her. Freud's responsiveness to H. D. contains what is experienced by her as enigmatic messages concerning obscure erotic aspects of the transference-countertransference relations.

Translating the enigmatic messages of the other

Enigmatic messages in the psychoanalytic space that repeat the archaic relationship with the parents and summon an *après coup* translation bring us to the thinking of Jean Laplanche and his general theory of the primal seduction and theory of translation. In Laplanche's thinking, translation is offered as the basis for unconscious processes and the psychoanalytic dialog. The communication between the parent and the child is inevitably constructed from libidinal messages that remain unconscious to both participants at the time of occurrence. Translation is the effort of the child to tie together aspects of these messages in links that will give them meaning. This process of translation is ongoing and inevitably partial, and the aspects of these messages that remain unknown become the building blocks of the child's unconscious.

Laplanche, in his essay *Interpretation Between Determinism and Hermeneutics* (1999a), points to the deterministic and hermeneutic aspects of psychoanalysis: deterministic in terms of the construction of the present through the examination of the past; hermeneutic in terms of the interpretation of the past through the examination of the present. The distinction lies in the direction of the research, whether past to present or vice versa, and also in the difference between a relatively certain construction and manifold potential interpretations. The subject constantly interprets what he or she experiences, and thus it is impossible to retrieve history as is. The subjective experience, which includes the construction of the past, lies in the space between perceptive reality and psychological reality. The subjective narrative is constructed by a mysterious mixture of the actual and the fantasized.

The most innovative part of Laplanche's theory is that in addition to external and internal realities, he offers a third reality, which he considers to be the most significant one for analytic work. This aspect is the message of the other:

> With the *message*, there is the idea that an existing, pre-existing sense is offered to the subject, of which, however, he is not the master and of which he can become the master only by submitting to it. With the concept of *enigma*, a break in determinism appears: to the extent that the originator of the enigmatic message is unaware of most of what he means, and to the extent that the child possesses only inadequate and imperfect ways to configure and theorize about what is communicated to him, there can be no linear causality between the parental unconscious and discourse on the one hand and what the child does with these on the other.
>
> (Laplanche 1999a, 160)

The other expresses three constructs: the infantile other, meaning the enigmatic messages perceived in childhood and their interpretations at that time; the inner other, which is unconscious and constructed from those particles of the messages that were impossible to translate and were therefore internalized as such; and the analyst as other, for the communication with him as a transferential figure also contains enigmatic messages.

The messages that come from the psychoanalyst and their translation in the psychoanalytic space are understood as repetition, i.e., a re-translation in *après coup* of the historic messages the analysand interiorized as a child. In addition, these messages are translated as part of an innovative communication system between analyst and analysand. The concept of translation is more accurate than interpretation for the process of deciphering the enigmatic messages because translation embodies both the hermeneutics of interpretation and the determinism of the historic message: "What is *translated*, specifically, is not a natural, or even an historic sign, but a message, a signifier or a sequence of signifiers. In order for there to be translation, someone must have meant something" (157, emphasis in original).

The analytic interpretations are offered as de-translations, for they examine and deconstruct the previously offered translations of the enigmatic historic messages from childhood. Transference is thus understood as the analysand's attempt to decipher the enigmatic messages of the analyst in their present occurrence as well as in a continuous series of *après coup* attempts at translation. The importance of the *après coup* lays in the notion that the ability to decipher the other is inevitably limited. The enigmatic quality creates a passion for knowledge and the repeated, even endless, process of translation allows a gradual creation of meaning. The translation processes always take place in *Nachträglichkeit*, or *après coup*, as discussed in Chapter 1 (Laplanche 1999b, 260–265).

These notions regarding translation are part of Laplanche's general theory of primal seduction, which is inspired by Freud's early seduction theory. Although Freud neglected seduction theory early on, preferring to concentrate on internal fantasies, Laplanche argues that seduction theory never really disappeared from psychoanalytic thought. In *The Interpretation of Dreams*, Freud discusses the child's inevitable yet bewildering encounter with adult sexuality,

> It is, I may say, a matter of daily experience that sexual intercourse between adults strikes any children who may observe it as something uncanny and that it arouses anxiety in them. I have explained this anxiety by arguing that what we are dealing with is a sexual excitation with which their understanding is unable to cope and which they also, no doubt, repudiate because their parents are involved in it, and which is therefore transformed into anxiety.
> (Freud 1900, 585)

Laplanche returns to these ideas and is intrigued not only by the child's response to the adult's sexuality but also by the adult who unconsciously and inevitably transfers to the child messages concerning the adult's sexuality.

Another significant point in Freud's seduction theory, which Laplanche points to and develops, is the passivity of the child in its relationship with the adult. The early seduction challenges the child in two phases, the first phase taking place during the event of seduction and the second phase taking place after its occurrence. In the first phase, the child is helpless against the enigmatic messages and cannot reject or otherwise defend itself against their implications. Therefore, these messages are not repressed but are encapsulated in memory. The second phase always occurs in *après coup*, after certain defensive mechanisms have developed in the child. The child then finds itself attacked from within by the encapsulated messages and their potential meanings, possibly triggered by an external event. The event itself is not necessarily pathogenic or traumatic, it only becomes that way because it resonates with associations from the internalized enigmatic messages. The second phase contains the advantage of retrospection and the potential for finding psychic translation in *après coup*.

The *après coup* in the psychoanalytic context means that certain events echo the early seduction during their occurrence. This resonance stimulates an inner chain of responses that allows the subject to give these events meaning in the form of translation. Laplanche refers to this as translation and not as interpretation because, as already noted, he wishes to emphasize the communicative quality of the situation. The communicative aspect of the message from the other challenges the subject to decipher it, because "someone wanted to say something to someone." These are messages that concern the great riddles of life and death, not as abstract ideas but as actual events that stimulate fantasies and are communicated to the child, as for example in the message, "You will be getting a little brother," or in the message that someone dear to the child has died.

Enigmatic messages revolve around the primal scene and castration and involve curiosity, anxiety, stimulation, and the mourning processes (Laplanche 1999a, 169–173). The enigmatic messages that were internalized in early childhood remain enigmatic for both the child who incorporates the message and the adult who delivers it. The reason for their enigmatic quality is their libidinal aspects, which can therefore be expressed as a symptom, a parapraxis. The libidinal aspects of the messages make them seductive to the child, a seduction that is both threatening and pleasant. This seduction is the basis for the continuous passion to translate, de-translate, and retranslate in *après coup* as a never-ending process of the birth, mourning, and rebirth of messages and meanings.

The passion to translate is at the base of the motivation to write and, even more saliently, to write memoirs. Whether the *après coup* takes place a couple of hours after the session in a diary or a couple of decades later in retrospective writing, the texts written by analysands collected here can be seen as works of translation of their analytic experience and evolution as subjects. They all present an encounter that is characterized by a dialectic of familiarity and foreignness. The transference relationship with Freud summoned enigmatic messages that were repetitions of their early seductions, which then went through deconstruction and retranslation in the analytic setting. The encounter with the intriguing figure of Freud created innovative enigmatic messages that the analysands were passionate to translate. The writing of these memoirs about Freud expresses this passion for translation as an endless work of creation and mourning, with an effort to find new meaning in the memories of analysis and early history and a recognition, apparent in the texts, of aspects of the experience that remain forever enigmatic and untranslatable in the encounter with the other and with oneself.

The work of translating enigmatic messages from the other is woven throughout the collection of memoirs. Smiley Blanton's memoir presents a retranslation of Freud's surprising gesture of grasping Blanton's hand when they met again. There is also a retranslation offered of their scenes of separation, with Freud waving to Blanton from the window. And finally, a retranslation of the transference–countertransference relations is offered through the presentation of Freud's and Blanton's evolving discourse throughout the years about dogs. Abram

Kardiner's memoir presents a translation of Freud's request of Kardiner toward the termination of his analysis that he visit Freud's grandchildren and son-in-law after the death of Sophie, Freud's daughter. This occurs after Freud admits to Kardiner that he suffers from depression as a response to her untimely death. Pankejeff implicitly offers in his memoir an après coup retranslation of Freud's case study about him, a complex task that involves conflictual feelings of love and hate, familiarity and foreignness, and even trust and betrayal.

H. D.'s memoir offers the most profound and richest expression of her quest or work of translation through historic enigmatic messages from her past and the dialog that these messages create with enigmatic messages communicated to her from Freud. An image offered in Mignon's song, "*Kennst du den Berg und seinen Wolkensteg?*" speaks of H. D. as it represents her passion for translation. In the memoir, H. D. first translates the words into English, then wonders about the accuracy of the translation, and then finally decides that the words of her incomplete and imperfect translation are a perfect image for analysis: "'Do you know the mountain and its cloud-bridge?' is an awkward enough translation but the idea of mountain and bridge is so very suitable to this whole *translation* of the Professor and our work together" (H. D. 1974, 108, emphasis in original). It is the notion of translation that brings H. D. to conclude, at this point in the text, that within the context of "psychoanalytic building and constructing" and "the Gods that some people read Goods," the message waiting to be deciphered is the "poet's lines" she has found, Mignon's poem written by Goethe, within "the realm of fantasy and imagination" (108). For H. D., writing the memoir is offered as a work of translation of repressed messages, as in her writing she constantly challenges her own perception of the professor and the professor's perception of her. While she feels deep admiration and love for Freud, she also dares to ask to what extent he has understood her, especially as a spiritual person and as a woman.

The figure of Mignon and H. D.'s rediscovery of her as a source of identification implicitly refer to denied erotic aspects of her transference. In the transference, Freud becomes in her fantasy not only a parental figure but also a lover. H. D. raises questions about Freud's stance toward her, as expressed in his furious response to his own notion that he is too old for her to love him, or in their mutual passion for travels to Rome, her knowledge of secret love for gardenias, and his remark that they met in their love of antiquity. In Goethe's *Bildungsroman*, the protagonist Wilhelm Meister is Mignon's adoptive father, who becomes her forbidden lover. Mignon and her elusive relationship with Meister are gradually woven into H. D.'s text as a retranslation of her relationship with Freud. In hindsight, she presents Freud as her parental figure, both father and mother, and also, through various images and allusions, as her lover. The realm of fantasy and imagination offered through writing allows her the relatively free movement of retrieving enigmatic messages from her relationship with Freud and offering a retranslation of them inspired by the relationship between Mignon and Meister. This literary model represents a relationship between a lost child and an adoptive father as well as between the literary creation or muse and the poet. Writing or creativity is presented as a possibility for rebirth after mourning.

Reading this collection of memoirs about Freud as creations that offer various works of translation of the analytic experience makes evident the playful space offered by psychoanalysis and literature, the free movement among times, identifications, translations. Unresolved aspects of each writer's relationship with Freud, their separation from him, and his enigmatic messages are given a retranslation through writing. Memoir writing is presented here as a space of movement among archaic history, the re-experience of history in psychoanalysis, the encounter with the other, and, finally, the retranslation of these transformative experiences in *après coup*. The memoirs we have looked at in this book offer a narrative of the analytic experience with Freud: its deterministic reconstruction of the past, hermeneutic aspects of interpreting the past based on transference, and the work of translation of enigmatic messages from the archaic past and of the intensity of the analytic encounter. These three aspects provide the prolonged inspiration and passion for experiencing and deciphering the past.

The continuous effort to remember, mourn, and translate is an expression of our inherent passion to understand ourselves and the world. In reading these analysands' memoirs we see their striving to decipher the other and translate the enigmatic messages the other delivers, while the uncanniness and foreignness with which those messages challenge us are presented as cornerstones in our continuous quest to know and to love.

Epilogue
Psychoanalysis terminable and interminable

As a concluding note to this book, which offers a reading of a collection of memoirs written by Freud's analysands, I want to return to a distinct scene that was presented along the way. This is the scene of Blanton's separation from Freud after their re-encounter in the summer of 1935, five years after the first analysis terminated. Blanton offers a vivid description of these moments of separation, as we saw:

> I left from the garden at the rear side of the house and came around to the street gate. It was unlatched, so I stepped out and turned to close it. To my surprise, I saw Freud standing at one of the windows of the consultation room that looks on the street. The house is about forty feet from the street. As I looked up, he waved to me good-bye. I waved back and took off my hat. I closed the gate, and when I looked again, he was gone.
> (Blanton 1971, 81–82)

The analysand says farewell to his analyst and leaves the clinic, which in many ways has become his home. He walks out the door and out of the house. At the street gate, he raises his head to look at the familiar window, supposedly for the last time. Until this point, this is an expected separation scene from analysis. Yet there is a transformation in the expected scene, revolving around Freud's surprising appearance at the window. That appearance, and the fact that his eyes meet Blanton's, can be interpreted as the expression of a mutual wish to postpone the inevitable separation and to remain, even for just one more moment, in the protective timelessness offered by the analytic sphere. After analysis terminates, its setting and essence continue to follow the analysand as an internal space that has been opened or created there. Termination involves a work of mourning for the cessation of the analytic sessions and the end of the analyst's presence in the analysand's life. These challenges tend to bring up earlier experiences of separation from the analysand's history. Termination also involves a working through of the analytic process in terms of its achievements and limitations. Thus, the work of mourning usually involves both longing and analyzing.

This moment after separation from analysis that Blanton describes in the farewell at the window suggests that separation is a significant moment not only for the analysand, who is taking the first steps on his new, independent, post-analysis path. Freud's surprising appearance at the window presents him not only as a subject, or self-object, who offers his attunement and skills to his analysand's needs. His appearance attests to his desire. His standing in the window after the formal farewell while Blanton is looking up from below expresses the mutual desire of analysand and analyst. The analyst is asking for one last glance at his analysand, for he is also expecting a work of mourning. This deviation from the regular analytic setting initiated by Freud possibly serves as a seductive message for his analysand, yet not in a malignant way.

This act tells the story, not often told, of the analyst's desire for his analysand and of the analytic relationship as constructed on mutual passion, "the happiness of the quest," as H. D. called it. This aspect of the analytic relationship, as formed by mutual desire, was not given much thought by Freud. Nevertheless, the collection of memoirs written by Freud's patients tells the story of the very dominant presence of their analyst. The collection shows that Freud was by no means an abstinent or neutral analyst. His patients witnessed and accompanied his life routine, connections with family and friends, medical procedures, summer holidays, exile from Vienna, and opinions on various subjects. Freud seems from the memoirs to be a direct and straightforward person, who understood the principles of neutrality and abstinence in his own personal way. It also appears that he tended to overlook the way in which his subjective presence affected his patients. He seems to have been ambivalent about the degrees of freedom he lost within these intense transference patterns: as he told Kardiner, "I am too much the father." Freud's dominant presence as a person and as a persona deeply affected the transference relationship from its very beginning. Starting an analysis with Freud was a distinctly different experience from starting any other analysis, and the very act of writing signifies it. His dominance, both before analysis as a persona and writer, and as a person in the actual analytic encounter, created a redundancy of his presence as subject.

The analysand naturally experiences curiosity toward the subjectivity of the analyst. The subjectivity of the analyst or parental figure has an erotic aspect and is experienced, as Laplanche suggests, as enigmatic seductive messages. The analyst's interest in the analysand can be experienced as seductive in itself, arousing questions, either explicitly or implicitly, about that interest. These questions might include: why is the analyst interested in me? What strengthens this interest and what weakens it? What does he get from this interest? What are the limitations of this interest? Analysands tend to fear changes in the analyst's interest in them, as a repetition of their childhood patterns of dependency. They fear that the analyst will lose interest in them and also fear a redundancy of interest from the analyst that will reveal his subjectivity in terms of desire. As a repetition of the analysand's childhood dependency on their parental figures, the redundancy of enigmatic messages from the analyst's side makes their incorporation by the analysand impossible and leads to repression. The repressed messages create an urge for translation.

Freud, who was not adequately aware of this redundancy, presented his patients with a challenge that was complicated by the fact that it was not recognized as such. In contrast to the challenge of free association, for instance, which was explicitly presented to the analysand as a challenge, the challenge of Freud's dominant presence as an analyst was overlooked by Freud himself. This redundancy, to my understanding, is the heart of what continued to occupy his patients and created a stronger motivation for writing as a space for continual works of translation.

The ties among psychoanalysis, writing, and translation are a recurring theme in the present book's reading of this collection of memoirs written by Freud's patients. I want to conclude with an image of the psychic apparatus offered by Freud that seems significant for the notions presented here. I am referring to the image of the mystic writing pad (*Der Wunderblock*). In a short 1925 paper, Freud proposes this multi-layered device, which usually functions as a playful writing instrument for children, as a metaphor for the multi-layered psyche (Freud, 1925b).

Freud describes in detail the different layers that make up the writing pad, as well as the process that enables writing on it. To write on the mystic/magical pad, one scratches on the external celluloid portion in a process similar to ancient writing methods, with no need for other materials. One simply writes on the celluloid portion of the covering-sheet, which rests on the wax slab. No pencil or chalk is necessary, since the writing does not depend on material being deposited on the receptive surface. The erasure of the writing is also presented as simple: "If one wishes to destroy what has been written, all that is necessary is to raise the double covering-sheet from the wax slab by a light pull, starting from the free lower end" (229). Nevertheless, a close examination of the internal layers of the device shows that nothing that was written is ever completely erased:

> The Pad provides not only a receptive surface that can be used over and over again, like a slate, but also permanent traces of what has been written, like an ordinary paper pad: it solves the problem of combining the two functions *by dividing them between two separate but interrelated component parts or systems*. But this is precisely the way in which, according to the hypothesis which I mentioned just now, our mental apparatus performs its perceptual function.
>
> (230, emphasis in the original)

The marvel (*Wunder*) of the writing pad is seemingly located in the disappearance of the engraved writing from the apparent layer, carried out with "a light pull." Yet Freud points to a different, more obscure marvel that he finds much more intriguing, the marvel that is revealed only to someone who searches deep inside the internal layers of the device. This wise researcher is destined to find that none of the writing ever really disappears. The engraving leaves "permanent traces of what has been written" on the innermost layer of the device.

Psychic life is constructed of manifold layers that move at different paces and in different directions. The image of the magical writing pad challenges us not to seek psychic transformation in the outermost, apparent layer of the psyche but to tunnel deep into the innermost layers, where apparently lost traces are revealed. The reminiscences and traces of significant experiences that seem to have been forgotten and therefore lost remain in fact forever present and archived in our psychic apparatus. Nothing significant is lost, only the path leading to it.

The notion of the unconscious as a reservoir of libidinally cathected reminiscences and experiences allows us to conceive of psychic development as a playful movement through different layers of consciousness, above boundaries of time and otherness, with consciousness being constantly enriched by mysterious flickerings from the unconscious. This playful movement broadens psychic space and allows us to simultaneously write and erase, remember and forget.

Freud concludes his comparison of the magical writing pad and memory with a slight adjustment to the image, a wish perhaps:

> If we imagine one hand writing upon the surface of the Mystic Writing Pad while another periodically raises its covering-sheet from the wax slab, we shall have a concrete representation of the way in which I tried to picture the functioning of the perceptual apparatus of our mind.[1]
>
> (232)

> Transformation in some of the layers of the psyche affects the other layers at different paces, in different directions, and in a complex back-and-forth movement. Sometimes the regression to past symptomatology is pathological; on other occasions it is an inevitable part of the gradual process of change.

Psychic life is analogous to the magic writing process in that they both include engraving, erasing, and rediscovering. One important difference, however, is that in contrast to the writing pad (where the hidden layer never appears on the external layer, and the writing engraved on it usually remains obscure, as a forever unfulfilled potential), in the psyche memories are libidinally charged and therefore continually insist on their presence in manifold ways. This is an expression of the mysterious essence of the psyche, which refuses and yet is inevitably drawn to speak its own voice. The individual voice of the subject is bound to find expression within the limitations or prohibitions of the censor. The text eventually created is the product of this internal struggle. The text expresses not the engraving of the outer layer of the writing device but the allusiveness of psychic life, of the movement between layers of consciousness, internal entities, and time. Stories, as articulated by Walter Benjamin, will always embody enigmatic traces, impossible to grasp and decipher, yet continuously intriguing (1997 [1925]).

Freud begins his essay on the magic writing pad with the idea that writing assists him in the work of memory, as he writes what he wishes to remember and fears to forget. The text carries his thoughts more safely than does his memory. Memory, Freud argues, is not as reliable as a sheet of paper; memory is as elusive as the mystical writing pad. The characterization of the writing pad as "mystical" further contributes to the presentation of memory as a realm of mysterious interplay. Psychoanalysis aims to enable a better flow of impressions from the unconscious to consciousness and vice versa. Writing, as an engraving of these impressions, penetrates all the manifold layers of the psyche and, in spite of the elusive nature of memory, gives permanence to the impressions.

Psychoanalysis and writing are spaces that make it possible to discover reminiscences from the various layers of the psyche. This process can be presented as the experience of listening to an ancient riddle, which echoes memory-traces from the archaic roots of childhood, prior to the formation of conscious memory. The most significant riddle awaiting translation is the riddle of love and seduction in the parent–child relationship. This is the relationship that invites the subject into the world, where it is destined to adapt to the laws of morality and social order and accept the limitations that those imply. Yet fantasized aspects of this relationship continue to evolve in the unconscious, with a repeated effort to translate the other's enigmatic messages. The work of translation involves a work of memory and of mourning in relation to self and other and a continuous striving for love as a potential and an actuality. Love, our mysterious longing for otherness, is bound to remain an everlasting secret.

Note

1 Freud raises an intriguing idea here that is, regrettably, not further developed, namely the idea of the gaps between perception and consciousness as forming the basis of the notion of time. "This discontinuous method of functioning of the system *Pcpt.-Cs.* lies at the bottom of the origin of the concept of time" (1925b, 231). Freud is referring here to the notion of temporality created in the context of the system of perception and consciousness, which constantly involves the elusiveness of the unconscious.

References

Abraham, N. and Torok, M. (1986 [1976]). *The Wolf Man's Magic Word: A Cryptonymy.* Translation: Nicholas Rand. Minneapolis, MN: University of Minnesota Press.

Amir, D. (2014). *Cleft Tongue: The Language of Psychic Structures.* Translation: Mirjam Hadar. London: Karnac.

Amir, D. (2018). *Bearing Witness to the Witness: Four Modes of Traumatic Testimony.* Translation: Mirjam Hadar. London and New York, NY: Routledge.

Anderson, L. (2001). *Autobiography.* New York, NY: Routledge.

Anzieu, D. (1986 [1975]). *Freud's Self-Analysis.* Translation: Peter Graham. Madison, CT: International Universities Press, first published 1959.

Appignanesi, L. and Forrester, J. (1992). *Freud's Women.* London: Weidenfeld & Nicolson.

Armstrong, R. H. (2005). *A Compulsion for Antiquity: Freud and the Ancient World.* Ithaca, NY: Cornell University Press.

Aron, L. (1996). *Meeting of Minds: Mutuality in Psychoanalysis.* Hillsdale, NJ: Analytic Press.

Atkins, S. (1978). "The New York Psychoanalytic Society and Institute: Its Founding and Development." In J. M. Quen and T. E. Carlson (eds.), *American Psychoanalysis: Origins and Development.* New York, NY: Brunner/Mazel, 73–86.

Augustine, J. (1998). "Introduction." In *The Gift by H. D.: The Complete Text.* Gainesville, FL: University Press of Florida, 1–28.

Benjamin, W. (1968 [1955]). "The Task of the Translator." In *Illuminations.* Translation: Harry Zohn. London: Collins-Fontana Books, 69–82.

Benjamin, W. (1997 [1925]). "Goethe's *Elective Affinities.*" In *Selected Writings, Volume 1 1913–1926.* Cambridge and London: Belknap Press, 297–360.

Berman, A. (1984). *L'Èpreuve de l'étranger.* Paris: Editions Gallimard.

Berman, E. (1996). "The Ferenczi Renaissance." *Psychoanalytic Dialogues* 6, 391–411.

Berman, E. (1999). "Sándor Ferenczi Today: Reviving the Broken Dialectic." *American Journal of Psychoanalysis* 59, 303–313.

Bieber, I. (1982). "In Memory of Abram Kardiner (1891–1981)." *Journal of the American Academy of Psychoanalysis* 10 (2), 285–287.

Bion, W. R. (1967). *Second Thoughts: Selected Papers on Psychoanalysis.* London: Karnac.

Bion, W. R. (1990). *Brazilian Lectures: 1973, São Paulo; 1974, Rio de Janeiro/São Paulo.* London and New York, NY: Karnac.

References

Birksted-Breen, D. (2010). "Is Translation Possible?" *International Journal of Psychoanalysis* 91 (4), 687–694.

Blanton, S. (1940). "Analytic Study of a Cure of Lourdes." *Psychoanalytic Quarterly* 9, 348–362.

Blanton, S. (1971). *Diary of an Analysis with Sigmund Freud*. New York, NY: Hawthorn Books.

Blanton, S. and Peale, N. V. (1940). *Faith Is the Answer: A Psychiatrist and a Pastor Discuss Your Problems*. New York, NY: Abingdon–Cokesbury Press.

Blum, H. P. (1974). "The Borderline Childhood of the Wolf Man." *Journal of the American Psychoanalytic Association* 22, 721–742.

Breger, L. (2000). *Freud: Darkness in the Midst of Vision*. New York, NY: John Wiley& Sons.

Breuer, J. and Freud, S. (1895). *Studies in Hysteria. Standard Edition* (vol. 2).

Brooks, P. (1984). "Fictions of the Wolf Man: Freud and Narrative Understanding." In *Reading for the Plot: Design and Intention in Narrative*. New York, NY: Alfred A. Knopf, 264–285.

Buirski, P. and Haglund, P. (1998). "The Wolf Man's Subjective Experience of His Treatment with Freud." *Psychoanalytic Psychology* 15, 49–62.

Cohn, D. (1999). "Freud's Case Histories and the Question of Fictionality." In *The Distinction of Fiction*. Baltimore, MD and London: John Hopkins University Press, 38–57.

Deleuze, G. and Guattari, F. (1986 [1975]). *Kafka: Toward a Minor Literature*. Translation: Dana Polan. Minneapolis, MN: University of Minnesota Press.

Derrida, J. (1987[1980]). "To Speculate—on 'Freud'". In *The Post Card: From Socrates to Freud and Beyond*. Translation: Alan Bass. Chicago, IL and London, University of Chicago Press, 257–409.

Derrida, J. (1986). *Memoires for Paul de Man*. Translation: Cecile Lindsay, Jonathan Culler and Eduardo Cadava. New York, NY: Columbia University Press.

Derrida, J. (2001 [1967]). *Writing and Difference*. Translation: Alan Bass. London and New York, NY: Routledge.

Dimock, G. (1995). Anna and the Wolf Man. *Representations* 50, 53–75.

Dorsey, J. M. (1976). *An American Psychiatrist in Vienna, 1935–1937, and His Sigmund Freud*. Detroit, MI: Center of Health Education.

Dorsey, J. M. (1980). *University Professor John M. Dorsey*. Detroit, MI: Wayne State University Press.

Dougherty, W. P. (2002). "Mignon in Nineteenth-Century Song: Text, Context, and Intertext." *Words and Music Studies* 19, 123–141.

Dufresne, T. (1996). "An Interview with Joseph Wortis." *Psychoanalytic Review* 83, 589–610.

Duplessis, R. B. and Friedman, S. S. (1981). "'Woman Is Perfect': H. D.'s Debate with Freud." *Feminist Studies* 7 (3), 417–430.

Eckermann, J. P. (1847). *Gespräche mit Goethe in den letzen Jahren seines Lebens*. Halle A. S.: Verlag von Otto Hendel.

Eckermann, J. P. (1930 [1836–1848]). *Conversations of Goethe with Johann Peter Eckermann*. Translation: John Oxenford. Introduction: Havelock Ellis. Da Capo Press (first published in English at 1901).

Eckermann, J. P. (1949 [1836-1848]). *Words of Goethe: Being the Conversations of Johann Wolfgang von Goethe*. Translation: John Oxenford. Tudor Publishing, New York.

Ellis, H. (1897–1928). *Studies in the Psychology of Sex* (six volumes). New York, NY: Random House.
Ellis, H. (1919). "The Mechanism of Sexual Deviation." *Psychoanalytic Review* 6, 229–267, 391–423.
Frankland, G. (2000). *Freud's Literary Culture*. Cambridge: Cambridge University Press.
Freud, S. (1900). *The Interpretation of Dreams*. Standard Edition (vol. 4–5).
Freud, S. (1905a). "Fragment of an Analysis of a Case of Hysteria." *Standard Edition* (vol. 7, 1–124).
Freud, S. (1905b). "Three Essays on the Theory of Sexuality." *Standard Edition* (vol. 7, 124–243).
Freud, S. (1913a). "On Beginning the Treatment (Further Recommendations on the Technique of Psychoanalysis I)." *Standard Edition* (vol. 12, 121–144).
Freud, S. (1913b). "The Theme of the Three Caskets." *Standard Edition* (vol. 12, 289–302).
Freud, S. (1914a). "Remembering, Repeating and Working Through (Further Recommendations on the Technique of Psycho-Analysis II)." *Standard Edition* (vol. 12, 145–156).
Freud, S. (1914b). "On Narcissism." *Standard Edition* (vol. 19, 67–102).
Freud, S. (1917a). "A Childhood Recollection from *Dichtung und Wahrheit*." *Standard Edition* (vol. 17, 145–156).
Freud, S. (1917b). "Mourning and Melancholia." *Standard Edition* (vol. 14, 239–258).
Freud, S. (1918). "From the History of an Infantile Neurosis." *Standard Edition* (vol. 17, 1–124).
Freud, S. (1920a). *Beyond the Pleasure Principle*. Standard Edition (vol. 18, 1–64).
Freud, S. (1920b). "A Note on the Prehistory of the Technique of Analysis." *Standard Edition* (vol. 18, 263–265).
Freud, S. (1925a). "An Autobiographical Study." *Standard Edition* (vol. 20, 1–74).
Freud, S. (1925b). "A Note upon the 'Mystic Writing-Pad.'" *Standard Edition* (vol. 19, 225–232).
Freud, S. (1927). *The Future of an Illusion*. Standard Edition (vol. 21, 1–56).
Freud, S. (1930). "The Goethe Prize." *Standard Edition* (vol. 21, 205–214).
Freud, S. (1933). "Sándor Ferenczi." *Standard Edition* (vol. 22, 225–230).
Freud, S. (1937). "Analysis Terminable and Interminable." *Standard Edition* (vol. 23, 216–254).
Freud, S. (1938). "An Outline of Psychoanalysis." *Standard Edition* (vol. 23, 144–208).
Friedman S. S. (1981). *Psyche Reborn: The Emergence of H. D.* Bloomington, IN: Indiana University Press.
Friedman S. S. (1986). "A Most Luscious 'Vers Libre' Relationship: H. D. and Freud." *Annual of Psychoanalysis* 14, 319–344.
Friedman S. S. (1990). *Penelope's Web: Gender, Modernity, H. D.'s Fiction*. Cambridge and New York, NY: Cambridge University Press.
Friedman S. S. (2002). *Analyzing Freud: Letters of H. D., Bryher, and Their Circle* (ed.). New York, NY: New Directions.
Frink, H. W. (1918). *Morbid Fears and Compulsions: Their Psychology and Psychoanalytic Treatment*. New York, NY: Moffat, Yard & Company.
Frosch, J. (1991). "The New York Psychoanalytic Civil War." *Journal of the American Psychoanalytic Association* 39 (4), 1037–1064.

Gardiner, M. M. (1971a). *The Wolf-Man and Sigmund Freud* (ed.). London: Hogarth Press and the Institute of Psycho-Analysis.

Gardiner, M. M. (1971b). "The Wolf-Man in Later Life." In Muriel Gardiner (ed.), *The Wolf-Man and Sigmund Freud*. London: Hogarth Press and the Institute of Psycho-Analysis, 309–366.

Gardiner, M. M. (1983). *Code Name: 'Mary': Memoirs of an American Woman in the Austrian Underground*. New Haven, CO and London: Yale University Press.

Gay, P. (1988). *Freud: A Life for Our Time*. New York, NY and London: W. W. Norton.

Gay, P. (1990). *Reading Freud: Explorations & Entertainments*. New Haven, CO and London: Yale University Press.

Gibbs, W. (1955). "A Couch of My Own." *New Yorker*, February 19, 1955.

Ginsburg, L. M. (1999). "To the Editor." *Journal of the American Academy of Psychoanalysis and Dynamic Psychiatry* 36, 379–381.

Goethe, J. W. (1795). *Wilhelm Meisters Lehrjahre*. Husum: Hamburger Lesehefte Verlag.

Goethe, J. W. (1901 [1795]). *Wilhelm Meister's Apprenticeship*. Translation: Thomas Carlyle and Nathan Haskell Dole. Boston, MA: Francis A. Niccolls & Company.

Gonzalez S. P. E. (2002). "The Textual Unconscious and Its Effects: Aggression and Reparation in H. D.'s Work, 1935–1948." *Atlantis* 24(1), 205–224.

Gray Blanton, M. (1971a). "Preface." In *Diary of an Analysis with Sigmund Freud*. New York, NY: Hawthorn Books, 5–10.

Gray Blanton, M. (1971b). "Biographical Notes and Comments." In *Diary of an Analysis with Sigmund Freud*. New York, NY: Hawthorn Books, 119–135.

Grinker, R. R. (1973). "Reminiscences of a Personal Contact with Freud." In Hendrik M. Ruitenbeek (ed.), *Freud As We Knew Him*. Detroit: Wayne State University Press, 180–185.

Grosskurth, P. (1980). *Havelock Ellis: A Biography*. New York, NY: Alfred A. Knopf.

Greenacre, P. (1973). "The Primal Scene and the Sense of Reality." *Psychoanalytic Quarterly* 42: 10–41.

Guest, B. (1984). *Herself Defined: H. D. and Her World*. Tucson: Schaffner Press.

H. D. (Hilda Doolittle). (1973). *Trilogy: The Walls Do Not Fall/Tribute to the Angels/The Flowering of the Rod*. New York, NY: New Directions.

H. D. (Hilda Doolittle). (1974). *Tribute to Freud*. Boston, MA: Godine.

H. D. (Hilda Doolittle). (1979). *End to Torment: A Memoir of Ezra Pound*. New York, NY: New Directions.

H. D. (Hilda Doolittle). (1981). "The Master." *Feminist Studies* 7(3), 407–416.

H. D. (Hilda Doolittle). (1998). *The Gift by H. D.: The Complete Text*. Gainesville, FL: University Press of Florida, first published 1949.

Hadar, D. (2012). "The Wolf Man's Novel." *American Imago* 69(4), 559–578.

Holland, N. N. (1973). *Poems in Persons: An Introduction to the Psychoanalysis of Literature*. New York, NY: Norton.

Holland, N. N. (2000). *Poems in Persons: A Psychology of the Literary Process* (Revised Edition). Cybereditions.

Jeffrey, W. D. (1995). "'Lazarus Stand Forth': H. D. Encounters Freud." *Psychoanalytic Study of the Child* 50, 397–417.

Jones, E. (1953). *The Life and Work of Sigmund Freud, Volume 1: The Formative Years and the Great Discoveries 1856–1900*. London: The Hogarth Press.

Jones, E. (1955). *The Life and Work of Sigmund Freud, Volume 1: The Formative Years and the Great Discoveries 1856–1900*. London: The Hogarth Press.

Jones, E. (1957a). *The Life and Work of Sigmund Freud, Volume 3: The Last Phase 1919–1939*. London: The Hogarth Press.

Jones, E. (1957b). "Tribute to Freud by H. D." *International Journal of Psychoanalysis* 38, 126.

Kardiner, A. (1939). *The Individual and His Society: The Psychodynamics of Primitive Social Organization*. New York, NY: Columbia University Press.

Kardiner, A. (1941). *War Stress and Neurotic Illness*. New York, NY: Hoeber.

Kardiner, A. (1945). *The Psychological Frontiers of Society*. New York, NY: Columbia University Press.

Kardiner, A. (1965). *Reminiscences of Abram Kardiner (manuscript)*. Bluma Swerdloff (ed.), Psychoanalytic Movement Project, Oral History, Special Collection, Rare Book and Manuscript Library, Columbia University.

Kardiner, A. (1977). *My Analysis with Freud: Reminiscences*. New York, NY: Norton & Company.

Kardiner, A. and L. Ovesey. (1962). *The Mark of Oppression: Explorations in the Personality of the American Negro*. Cleveland and New York, NY: Meridian Books.

Langs, R. (1976). "The Misalliance Dimension in Freud's Case Histories: I. The Case of Dora." *International Journal of Psychoanalytic Psychotherapy* 5, 310–317.

Laplanche, J. (1999). *Essays on Otherness*. Edited by John Fletcher. London and New York, NY: Routledge.

Laplanche, J. (1999a). "Interpretation between Determinism and Hermeneutics." In *Essays on Otherness*. Edited by John Fletcher. London and New York, NY: Routledge, 138–165.

Laplanche, J. (1999b). "Notes on Afterwardness." In *Essays on Otherness*. Edited by John Fletcher. London and New York: Routledge, 260–265.

Laplanche, J. and Pontalis, J. B. (1973 [1967]). *The Language of Psycho-Analysis*. Translated by Donald Nicholson-Smith. London: The Hogarth Press and the Institute of Psycho-Analysis.

Lev Kenaan, V. (2019). *The Ancient Unconscious: Psychoanalysis and the Ancient Text*. Oxford: Oxford University Press.

Little, M. I. (1990). *Psychotic Anxieties and Containment: A Personal Record of an Analysis with Winnicott*. Northvale, NJ: Aronson.

Lohser, B. and Newton P. M. (1996). *Unorthodox Freud: The View from the Couch*. New York, NY and London: Guilford Press.

Looney, T. J. (1920). *'Shakespeare' Identified in Edward De Vere, 17th Earl of Oxford*. New York, NY: Frederick A. Stokes.

Loughman, C. (1984). "Voices of the Wolf Man: The Wolf Man as Autobiographer." *Psychoanalytic Review* 71, 211–225.

Mack Brunswick, R. (1928). "A Supplement to Freud's 'History of an Infantile Neurosis.'" *International Journal of Psychoanalysis* 9, 439–476.

Mack Brunswick, R. (1971). "A Supplement to Freud's 'History of an Infantile Neurosis.'" In M. Gardiner (ed.), *The Wolf-Man and Sigmund Freud*. London: Hogarth Press and the Institute of Psycho-Analysis, 63–307.

Mahony, P. J. (1984). *Cries of the Wolf Man*. New York, NY: International Universities Press.

Masson, J. M. (1985). *The Complete Letters of Sigmund Freud to Wilhelm Fliess 1887–1904* (ed. And translation). Cambridge, MA and London: Harvard University Press.

Momigliano, L. N. (1987). "A Spell in Vienna—But Was Freud a Freudian?—An Investigation into Freud's Technique Between 1920 and 1938, Based On the Published Testimony of Former Analysands." *International Review of Psychoanalysis* 14, 373–389.

Nägele, R. (1987). *Reading after Freud: Essays on Goethe, Hölderlin, Habermas, Nietzsche, Brecht, Celan, and Freud.* New York, NY: Columbia University Press.

Obholzer, K. (1982 [1980]). *The Wolf-Man Sixty Years Later: Conversations with Freud's Controversial Patient.* Translation: Michael Shaw. London, Melbourne, and Henley: Routledge & Kegan Paul.

Offenkrantz, W. (1973). "Problem of the Therapeutic Alliance: Freud and the Wolf Man." *International Journal of Psychoanalysis* 54, 75–78.

Ogden, T. H. (1998). "A Question of Voice in Poetry and Psychoanalysis." *Psychoanalytic Quarterly* 67, 426–448.

Ogden, T. H. (2005). "On Psychoanalytic Writing." *International Journal of Psychoanalysis* 86, 15–29.

Ogden, T. H. (2009). "Reading Harold Searles." In *Rediscovering Psychoanalysis: Thinking and Dreaming, Learning and Forgetting.* London and New York, NY: Routledge, 133–153.

Pankejeff, S. C. (1971a). "The Memoirs of the Wolf-Man." In M. Gardiner (ed.), *The Wolf-Man and Sigmund Freud.* London: Hogarth Press and the Institute of Psycho-Analysis, 3–132.

Pankejeff, S. C. (1971b). "My Recollections of Sigmund Freud." In M. Gardiner (ed.), *The Wolf-Man and Sigmund Freud.* London: Hogarth Press and the Institute of Psycho-Analysis, 135–152.

Priel, B. (2003). "Psychoanalytic interpretations: Word-music and translation." *International Journal of Psychoanalysis* 84, 131–142.

Ricoeur, P. (2006 [2004]). *On Translation.* Translation: Eileen Brennan. London and New York, NY: Routledge.

Roazen, P. (1995). *How Freud Worked: First-Hand Account of Patients.* Northvale and London: Jason Aronson.

Stock, I. (1957). "A View of Wilhelm Meister's Apprenticeship." *PMLA* 72, no. 1 (Mar 1957), 84–103.

Taylor, G. (2001). *H. D. and the Public Sphere of Modernist Women Writers, 1913–1946: Talking Women.* New York, NY: Oxford University Press.

Tolpin, M. (1991). "'She Is Perfect… Only She Has Lost Her Spear': The Goddess Athene, Freud, and H. D." *Annual of Psychoanalysis* 19, 33–49.

Trosman, H. (1965). "Freud and the Controversy over Shakespearean Authorship." *Journal of the American Psychoanalytic Association* 13, 475–498.

Tzur Mahalel, A. (2017). "'For Our Garden of Remembrance Is Somewhere Else': Narratives of Separation through the Eyes of Freud's Patients." *International Journal of Psychoanalysis* 98 (6), 1719–1739.

Tzur Mahalel, A. (2018). "Memory, Mourning and Writing: Abram Kardiner's Memoir of Freud." *Psychoanalytic Review* 105 (4), 397–424.

Tzur Mahalel, A. (2019). "The Wolf Man's Glückshaube: Rereading Sergei Pankejeff's Memoir." *Journal of the American Psychoanalytic Association* 67 (5), 789–813.

Viëtor, K. (1970 [1949]). *Goethe the Poet.* Translation: Moses Hadas. New York, NY: Russel & Russel.

Wagner, R. (1914). *The Flying Dutchman by Wagner*. Retold by Oliver Huckel. New York, NY: Thomas Crowell Company.

Weissberg, L. (2012). "Patient and Painter: The Careers of Sergius Pankejeff." *American Imago* 69: 163–183.

Werbert, A. (1998). "Where the Horsetails Grow as High as Palms: The Case of the Wolf Man." In Iréne Matthis and Imre Szecsödy (eds.), *On Freud's Couch: Seven New Interpretations of Freud's Case Histories*. Northvale: Jason Aronson, 185–212.

Wilder, T. (1927). *The Bridge of San Luis Rey*. New York, NY: Albert & Charles Boni.

Winnicott, D. W. (1949). "Mind in Its Relation to the Psycho-Soma." In *Through Pediatrics to Psycho-Analysis*. New York, NY: Basic Books, 243–254.

Winnicott, D. W. (1960). "Ego Distortion in Terms of True and False Self." In *The Maturational Processes and the Facilitating Environment: Studies in the Theory of Emotional Development*. London: Hogarth Press, 140–152.

Wortis, J. (1940). "Freudianism and the Psychoanalytic Tradition." *American Journal of Orthopsychiatry* 10, 814–820.

Wortis, J. (1950). *Soviet Psychiatry*. Baltimore, MD: Williams & Wilkins.

Wortis, J. (1954). *Fragments of an Analysis with Freud*. New York, NY: Simon and Schuster.

Wortis, J. (1984). *Fragments of an Analysis with Freud* (New Edition). New York, NY and London: Jason Aronson.

Index

abstinence 1, 25, 48, 66, 179, 188
afterwardsness *see Nachträglichkeit*
aggression, *see also* love–hate relationship: in dreams 30, 52, 75, 125
American Psychiatrist in Vienna, 1935–1937, and His Sigmund Freud, An (Dorsey) 111, 174, 178–179; introduction 90–93; representation of a muted termination 101–105; telling a story in psychoanalysis and in writing 105–111
analysis, *see also* psychoanalysis: *specific topics*; aims of 25, 173, 191; didactic 8–9, 72, 74; Kardiner's portrayal of 81
"Analysis Terminable and Interminable" (Freud) xi, 130, 132
analytic narratives *see* case studies
analytic setting, Freud's 5, 35–36, 40–41, 43–44, 74, 81, 150, 180, 184; boundaries of and intrusions on xvi, 35–36, 39–40, 43–44, 81, 82, 179, 182, 188; *see also* gifts; structure of xvi, 92
analytic stance 48; *see also* analytic setting; Freud, Sigmund
analytic state of mind 37
Anderson, Linda 10
après coup see Nachträglichkeit translation
Apuleius, Lucius 156
Aron, Lewis xvi, xvii
art criticism 134; *see also* beauty and the beautiful
Athena 152, 153

beauty and the beautiful: death and 126, 127; nature of 118, 127; Pankejeff and 123; Pankejeff's mother and 126–127; and the veil 118–119, 123, 127, 134; Walter Benjamin on 118–119, 127, 134
Benjamin, Walter 112; on materiality and the beautiful 118–119, 127, 134; on stories 191; on translation 13; on truth 112, 118, 127; on the veil 112, 118–119, 127, 134
Berman, Emanuel 13
Beyond the Pleasure Principle (Freud) 86–87, 122
Bible 51, 55, 100, 157, 158, 161
Bion, Wilfred R. 89n3, 171n1
birth, *see also* womb: in a *Glückshaube* (caul) 112, 117, 132, 135n3; premature 46, 65, 81, 117, 132
Blanton, Smiley, *see also Diary of My Analysis with Sigmund Freud*: areas of dispute between Freud and 52–57; and boundaries of the analytic setting 40–41; criticism of psychoanalysis 44, 53; dreams 39, 41–44, 52, 53, 58, 59–61, 67; dream about Queen Victoria 63–64; dream of porcupine and his dog (Bobs) 45–48, 65, 67; on Freud 49; and Freud as authoritative father 179, 180; Freud's grasping the hand of 181, 184; grandmother 63–64; *The Interpretation of Dreams* and xi, 49–51, 58; Jews and 49, 53, 55; life history 40; in Lourdes 53, 54; mother 63–65, 179; death of 40, 64, 65; science and 42, 49, 54; separations from and re-encounters with Freud 177, 184, 187, 188; Shakespeare and 46–47, 51, 52, 56, 57, 61; submissiveness and compliance with Freud xi, xii; termination 65, 187; narrative of separation 58–61; transference 42–43, 52, 56–57, 64, 68,

Index

69, 180, 184; crisis in transference relationship 56–57
Blum, Harold P. 117
boundaries *see under* analytic setting
Bryher (Annie Winfred Ellerman) 138

cancer 26
Carlyle, Thomas 164
case studies, psychoanalytic xiv; *see also specific cases*; analytic narratives from patient's point of view 5–11; psychoanalytic writing and 3–4; texts written by analysands as autobiographical xv, 3
caul (*Glückshaube*), birth in a 112, 117, 132, 135n3
Christianity 40, 48, 53–55
communism 29
concealing *see* veil
consciousness 190; bringing the unconscious to 11–12, 14, 25, 104, 191; movement between layers of 190; time, perception, and 191n1
container, *see also* womb: analytic setting as a 81; *see also* analytic setting
Conversations with Goethe (*Gespräche mit Goethe*) 32–36, 38n3; Freud and 32; Wortis and 30, 32–36, 38n3
couch, analytic 28
countertransference 120; Freud's 34–35, 81, 82, 170, 177, 181, 184
Cries of the Wolf Man (Mahony) 135n7
crown-prince fantasy, Ferenczi's xii
Cupid and Psyche 156

Daniel (biblical figure) 157
darkness and light 143–144, 151–152, 171n1
death and dying, dreams about 26, 95
deferred action *see Nachträglichkeit*
Deleuze, Gilles xvi–xvii, 7, 8
democracy, Freud, and psychoanalysis 55, 56
depression, *see also* melancholia: Freud's 86, 185; Kardiner's 71, 73–75, 80, 84, 88; Pankejeff's 89n5, 114, 115, 121, 124, 127
Derrida, Jacques 64, 176–178
diaries of analytic patients xiii, 17n1
Diary of My Analysis with Sigmund Freud (Blanton) 9, 41, 174, 179; *see also* Blanton, Smiley; disruptions and changes in the analytic setting 39–40, 43–44; *see also under* analytic setting; material omitted from 41, 49, 59; publication 9, 40, 69; search for the fragmented voice 61–65; writing 9
didactic analysis 8–9, 72, 74
dogs: Blanton and 41, 45–48, 59, 60, 65, 67–68, 184; Freud's 28–29, 41, 45, 46, 67–68, 157, 158
Doolittle, Gilbert (brother) 142–145, 160, 169; as chosen son 144, 145; death in World War I 138, 142, 144–145; H. D. in the shadow of 142–144, 160, 161, 168; *see also* Miriam; H. D. replacing 144–145; oedipal conflicts and 144–145
Doolittle, Hilda (H. D.) i: background 137; bell jar experience 150–151; diary 137–138, 158, 180; *see also Tribute to Freud: Part II* (*Advent*); *End to Torment: A Memoir of Ezra Pound* 139, 160, 171; English language and 169, 170, 185; Freud criticized by 153; Freud's countertransference toward 170, 181; Freud's death and 163; Freud's disputes with 152; gardenias and 147, 148, 170, 185; German language and 146, 164, 166, 167, 169; on Jews 152–153; in Küsnacht 137, 138, 171; mother ("Mamma") 138, 143–145, 159, 160, 166, 167, 180; death of 159, 162; mourning 163; music and 160, 165–167; as poet 9, 137–139, 141, 143, 153, 162, 164, 166, 167, 171; *see also under* Mignon; psychotic break and hospitalization 137; re-encounter with Freud 142; self-image 144; termination 139, 163, 169–170, 177; return to Freud following premature 141–142; transcendental ideas and issues 153; transference 181; erotic aspects of 170, 181, 185; paternal and maternal 153–163, 180; translation and 137, 139, 142–144, 154, 155, 157, 158, 162–164, 166, 169, 171; writings 138; *see also Tribute to Freud*; *The Gift* 137, 139
Dora, Freud's case of 30, 31, 36
Dorsey, John Morris x–xii; analysis with Heinz Hartmann 90, 91, 102, 103; diary 90–92, 96, 97, 102–105, 159, 172n2, 174; *see also American Psychiatrist in Vienna, 1935–1937, and His Sigmund Freud*; dreams 95, 96, 101; finances 101, 102; free association and 94, 96,

98, 102, 106, 108, 110; on Freud 93; Freud's analytic stance toward 97, 98, 106; on Freud's technique 103–104; life history and overview 91; mother 94, 179; "my Sigmund Freud" xi, 103, 109–111; poetry 100–101; science and 93–94, 100–101, 109–110; self-analysis 91, 97–98, 103, 109–111; termination 108–109, 111; representation of a muted termination 101–105; transference 92, 103, 106, 109, 179, 181; enchantment and separation in 93–101
dreams: aggression in 30, 52, 75, 125; Bion and 89n3; childhood 95; Freud appearing in patients' 31, 43–44, 59–60, 67; Freud on 89n7; Freud's interpretations of patients' 26, 44, 47, 75–78, 83, 88, 122; sexuality in 31, 75, 116; in termination phase 29–30; transference 26, 42–43, 59, 64

Eckermann, Johann Peter 35, 36; Goethe and 32–34; memoir. *see Conversations with Goethe*
Eissler, Kurt R. 115
ellipsis/elliptic essence 64
Ellis, Havelock: Freud and 19–22, 25, 26, 28, 37; overview 19–20; psychoanalysis and 19–21, 25; Wortis and 18–21, 25, 26, 28, 37, 38n1, 38n3, 174
English language: Freud and 15, 30, 34, 37, 72, 93; H. D. and 169, 170, 185
Exodus 161

false self and true self 17n1, 89n2
Ferenczi, Sándor: analysands 82; Blanton and 47, 48, 69n2; childhood 69n2; *Clinical Diary* xiii; crown-prince fantasy xii; fixed termination date and 135n9; Freud and xii 47, 48; Freud on 69n2; on his relationship with Freud xii; outward posture of compliance and internal critical awareness xii; personality and psychopathology 47, 70n2; psychoanalytic writings and contributions 47–48, 69n2
Fichtl, Paul (Freud's housemaid) 31, 51, 65
fixed termination date, *see also* forced termination of Pankejeff: Ferenczi on 135n9
Fliess, Wilhelm: Freud's letters to 12, 170

flowers, *see also* gardenias: Freud and 146–148
Flying Dutchman, The (Wagner) 145–147
"Fool's Prayer, The" (Dorsey) 100–101
forced termination of Pankejeff 88, 130, 177; Freud's decision regarding 130; reasons for 118, 131–132; mourning and 178; Pankejeff's negative feelings around 130; separation from Freud as analyst and biographer 128–131; termination from an interminable analysis 131–134; termination phase of analysis 117; ways of viewing the 130
forced termination technique, *see also* fixed termination date: time-limited analysis; Freud on 131–132
Fragment of an Analysis of a Case of Hysteria (Freud) 30
Fragments of an Analysis with Freud (Wortis) 9, 18–22, 174, 178, 179; *see also* Wortis, Joseph; impasse and a momentary encounter 36–38; looking for an unattainable object 27–30; publication 18; resistances in the analytic encounter 22–27
free association xii, 37; *see also* stream of consciousness; Blanton, Freud, and 42, 44; Freud on 106; Freud's invention of 108, 110; John Dorsey and 94, 96, 98, 102, 106, 108, 110; Pankejeff, Freud, and xii
free will 132
Freud, Sigmund 2; American culture and 15, 29, 48, 55–57, 106, 107; American patients/analysands x, xv, 8–9, 15, 56, 72; analytic stance 24–25, 31, 66, 82, 97, 98, 106; *see also* analytic setting; anger 23, 34–35; attitudes toward patients xii, 15, 72; being the mother in transference 180; birthday 146–148, 178; books and 2; characterizations of 22, 23, 49; as Christ 55; countertransference 34–35, 81, 82, 170, 177, 181, 184; criticism of xii, 31, 78, 85–86, 153, 181; cynicism about psychoanalytic treatment xii; death 17, 36, 120, 163, 175; depression 86, 185; discouraged patients from keeping analytic journal 17n1; dogs 28–29, 41, 45, 46, 67–68, 157, 158; as father figure 22, 153–154, 159; *see also* transference: paternal and maternal;

favoritism xi; flowers and 146–148; German language and 15, 51, 79, 93, 105, 146, 164, 167, 169, 170; grasping the hand of Blanton 181, 184; health problems 106, 111n1; cancer 26; hearing difficulties 63; on homosexuality 180; lack of interest in psychoanalytic treatment 81; letters to Wilhelm Fliess 12, 170; literature and 2–3; personality xi, xii, 23, 36, 55, 108, 188, 189; authoritativeness 22, 31, 36, 41, 42, 44, 72, 95, 98, 130, 133, 153–154, 158–159, 175, 179, 180; *see also* Freud: as father figure; wit x–xi; political ideologies and 29; relation to his father and father figures 38n2; resistance and 21, 23, 24, 32, 44, 113, 118, 122, 128, 133; response to transferences 181; self-assessment as analyst 181; self-disclosure 86, 185; summer house in Grinzing 59–61, 65, 105; swayed by his patients' attitudes xi; on transference 25, 181; as Tree of Knowledge 158; as writer 10; writings of 2–3, 31; *see also specific writings*; case studies 10; *see also* case studies; *specific cases*; oppressive attitude toward women in the 180

Freud, Sophie (daughter) 86, 87; death 86, 87, 185

Frink, Horace W.: analysis of Kardiner 72, 74–78, 82, 88; analysis with Freud 72, 74, 81, 82, 89n6; Freud and 78, 82; Kardiner on 82, 89n6; *Morbid Fears and Compulsions* 74; overview and life history 81–82; as paternal figure to Kardiner 82; psychotic breakdown 81–82, 89n6

From the History of an Infantile Neurosis (Freud) 9, 115; retranslation of 121–127

Future of an Illusion, The (Freud) 53–54, 97, 99–100, 104

"Garden of Remembrance" 167, 175
gardenias 147, 148, 170, 185
Gardiner, Muriel M.: life history 114; Pankejeff and 9, 113, 114, 119, 120, 126, 134, 135n2; publications 9, 113, 135n2; *see also Wolf Man and Sigmund Freud*; Ruth Mack Brunswick and 114
German language: Dorsey and 93, 105; Freud and 15, 51, 79, 93, 105, 146, 164, 167, 169, 170; H. D. and 146, 164, 166, 167, 169

Gibbs, Wolcott 27, 33
gifts: from patients to Freud 146–148, 178; *see also under Tribute to Freud*; that Freud gave to patients 2, 126
Goethe, Johann Wolfgang von, *see also Conversations with Goethe*: death 36; Freud and 2–3, 33–35, 38n2, 170; Wortis and 34, 35; writings 185; *see also Wilhelm Meister's Apprenticeship*; *Elective Affinities* 112, 118, 134
Goethe's Elective Affinities (Benjamin) 112, 118, 134; *see also* Benjamin, Walter
Gray Blanton, Margaret: background 40; editing of *Diary of My Analysis with Sigmund Freud* 39, 41; mourning 69; publication of *Diary of My Analysis with Sigmund Freud* 9, 40, 69; relationship with Smiley Blanton 40, 53, 54, 69; on Smiley Blanton 49, 62–63; writing 39, 59, 62–63, 69
Grinzing, Austria 60, 61; Freud's summer house in 59–61, 65, 105
Grosskurth, Phyllis 20
Guattari, Félix xvi–xvii, 7, 8
Guggenbühl, Anna xiii

H. D. *see* Doolittle, Hilda
Hamlet (Shakespeare) 46–47
Hartmann, Heinz 90–91, 102, 103; Freud and 91, 102, 103; John Dorsey on 103; overview 90–91
hermeneutic aspects of psychoanalysis 12, 16, 182, 186
hermeneutic readings of case studies 4, 10
holding environment *see* container womb
homosexuality: Kardiner and xi 85; "unconscious homosexuality as part of everyone's analysis" xi, 85; Wortis and 18–19, 21
hypnoidal atmosphere 80
hypnoidal states 80, 85
hysteria, hypnoidal 80

incest 135n6; *see also* seduction; sibling. *see under* Pankejeff, Anna
incestuous dream 75
interiorization 177
interminable analysis 57–58; self-analysis as interminable 104; termination from an 131–134

internalization: Dorsey and 92, 97, 99; of enigmatic messages 182–184; of Freud 97, 178; mourning and 178; narcissistic 178
interpretation, *see also under* dreams: Kardiner, Abram: mother; transference; premature 31
Interpretation of Dreams, The (Freud) 57, 161, 183; Blanton and xi 49–51, 58; Freud as writer of 49–52
intertextual allusions 122, 133
intertextual contexts 146; the work of memory and mourning in 30–36

Jackson, Edith 45, 69n1
Japanese gardener, story of the x, 160
Jews and Jewishness 157; Blanton and 49, 53, 55; Freud and 38n4, 48, 53, 55, 152–153; Wortis and 37, 38n4, 49
Jones, Ernest 47, 59
Judaism 85; *see also* Bible
Julius Caesar (Shakespeare) 46, 61

Kafka, Franz 7, 8
Kardiner, Abram i, *see also under* Frink, Horace: criticism of Freud xii, 78, 85–86, 181; "dark ages" of his childhood 73, 80, 83; depression 71, 73–75, 80, 84, 88; dissociation 80; domestic violence witnessed by 77, 85; dreams 75–78, 83, 88; father 77; Kardiner's fear of xi; and Freud as paternal figure 179, 181, 188; Freud's analytic stance toward 82; homosexuality and xi, 85; loyalty to Freud 89n6; mask (and wax figure) phobia 83–85; mother ; absence of 77, 82–88; death of 73, 84, 85, 88, 174; Freud's interpretations regarding 83–84, 87; Kardiner's amnesia about 73, 83–85; Kardiner's dreams about 83, 88; Kardiner's identification with 83–85; Kardiner's interactions with 83–84; Kardiner's memories regarding 83–85, 88; outward posture of compliance and internal critical awareness xi–xii; portrayal of analysis 81; reconstruction of the past 74–75, 83–84, 88, 174; regression to dependence 181; repressed memories 80, 83–84, 88; sexuality 75, 83; sister 73, 84; stepmother 73, 75, 77, 83, 85; termination 81, 177, 181, 185;

termination phase of analysis 78–82, 86, 88; transference of 78, 79, 88; Freud's response to the xi–xii, 78, 81, 82, 181, 188; negative xi–xii; toward Frink 74–76
Koellreuter, A. xiii

language, *see also* translation: voice; created in analytic setting 5; transference and the quest for lost 160
Laplanche, Jean: on deterministic and hermeneutic aspects of psychoanalysis 182; on erotic aspect of analyst's subjectivity 188; on the message of the other 182; on *Nachträglichkeit* 12–13; theory of primal seduction 181, 183–184; on translation (communication) 16–17, 122, 181, 183
life's essence (truth content) vs. biographical events (material content) 112
listening 1
literature, *see also* minor literature: *specific topics*; Freud and 2–3; psychoanalysis and 139
Little, Margaret I. 17n1
Lohser, Beate x, xiv 11, 40, 90, 181
love–hate relationship 176, 177

Macbeth (Shakespeare) 46, 47
Mack Brunswick, Ruth 114; analysis of Muriel Gardiner 114; analysis of Pankejeff 113–115, 135n8; Freud and 114, 115; on Pankejeff 135n8; Pankejeff and 114, 135n4; writings about Pankejeff 113
material content (biographical events) vs. truth content (life's essence) 112
material womb *see* womb
materiality (the beautiful) 134; *see also* beauty and the beautiful
maternal transference *see* transference: paternal and maternal
melancholia, *see also* depression: vs. mourning 175–177
memory, *see also* reconstruction: screen memories; Freud on 173, 191; resistance and 15, 173; schizophrenic patient's loss of 75, 77, 89n3; writing and psychoanalysis as a work of 173–175
memory and mourning, the work of: in intertextual contexts 30–36; through writing 86–88

memory-traces 12, 191
Meyer, Adolf 19, 26
Mignon (character in *Wilhelm Meister's Apprenticeship*) 164–165, 172n5; death 169, 170; and erotic aspects of H. D.'s transference 170, 185; H. D. and Mignon as poets and lost children 163–171; H. D.'s identification with 170, 171; and H. D.'s passion for translation 185; oedipal issues 170, 185; overview 164; separation from parents 169; Wilhelm Meister and 164–166, 168–170, 185–186; writing 172n5
Mignon's Song (Goethe) 139, 165–169, 171; H. D. and 139, 164, 166–169, 185
minor literature xvi, xvii, 7–8, 140; *see also* muted voices: literature that gives voice to; defined xvi–xvii; vs. major literature 7, 8
minor texts 9, 39, 69
Miriam (biblical figure) 161, 169
Moses: Freud and 96, 161, 169; Miriam and 161, 169
mother, death of 87; *see also under* Blanton, Smiley; Doolittle, Hilda; Kardiner, Abram
mother transference *see* transference: paternal and maternal
mourning 175–177, 186; Blanton and 41, 49, 69, 188; the challenge of 176, 177; definition and nature of 175–176; Derrida on 176, 177; Dorsey and 102, 103, 105; Eckermann's memoir and 35, 36; enigmatic messages and 184; H. D. and 157–158, 160; internalization and 178; Kardiner and 74, 78–81, 85–88; vs. melancholia 175–177; Pankejeff and 115, 120, 123–125, 127, 131, 178; remembering and 174; *see also* memory and mourning; termination and 102, 103, 187; forced 131, 133, 178; transference and 16, 17, 36, 88, 178; Wortis and 30, 35–38, 174, 178; writing and psychoanalysis as a work of 175–178
"Mourning and Melancholia" (Freud) 175–176
muted termination, representation of a 101–105
muted voices 179; analysts giving patients voice when they feel mute 58; liberating the analysand's inner xvi; literature that gives voice to xvi–xvii, 7, 8, 10, 114; muted maternal voices 179
muteness: of analysand xvi; *see also* muted voices; of H. D. 144, 153–155, 157, 161
My Analysis with Freud: Reminiscences (Kardiner) 9, 71–72, 174, 177, 179, 184–185; *see also* Kardiner, Abram; compared with Ferenczi's *Clinical Diary* xii
mystic writing pad 189–191
mythology 136n10, 149, 152, 153, 156; *see also* Flying Dutchman

Nachträglichkeit (deferred action/afterwardsness) 12–13, 17, 116, 122, 183; concept and meaning of 12–13; defined 12; Freud's use of the term 12
narcissistic relationships 178
neutrality, analytic 66, 188
New York Psychoanalytic Society 54, 55
Newton Peter M. x, xiv, 11, 40, 90, 181

Obholzer, Karin xi, xii 115–116
oedipal conflicts: Freud and xi 99, 126; H. D. and 144, 154; *Hamlet* and 47; of Kardiner 74, 75, 83; of Mignon 170, 185; Pankejeff and 127, 135n5; of Wortis 179
Ogden, Thomas H. 5
orchids and Freud 147

Pankejeff, Anna (sister) 125, 127, 135n6; influence on Wolf Man 135nn 5–6; seduction of Wolf Man 125–127, 134, 135n6; suicide 114, 120, 123–124, 126, 127, 134; Wolf Man's dream about 125–126
Pankejeff, Sergei Constantinovich ("Wolf Man") i, xi 9, 88, 113–114; *see also* forced termination of Pankejeff; *Wolf Man and Sigmund Freud*; as an unsolved riddle 112, 113; analytic relationship with Freud 130; biography 114–115; birth in a caul (*Glückshaube*) 112, 117, 132, 135n3; criticism of Freud xii; criticism of psychoanalysis 116; dreams 125–126; wolf dream 115, 116, 122, 131; family 179; *see also* Pankejeff, Anna; free association and xii; Freud as biographer of 113; Freud on 118; Freud's case study about 185; *see also*

Index

From the History of an Infantile Neurosis; health problems 114–115, 124; identity 135–136nn 10–11; impasse in analysis 128; lack of empathy 125, 134, 135n8; Mack Brunswick and. *see under* Mack Brunswick, Ruth; mother 126–127; music and 122–123; nanny (Nanya) 114, 125, 127; primal scene and xii, 116, 121–122, 131, 135n7; psychopathology 115, 116; borderline personality 117; depression 89n5, 114, 115, 121, 124, 127; "manic-depressive insanity" 121; symptom of a veil in front of his eyes 112, 117; *see also under* veil; relations with women 179; relationship with Therese (wife) 115, 127, 134, 179; mourning her death 115, 120, 123–126, 135n2; religion and 53–55; resistances 113, 118, 128, 133; sexuality 116, 119, 120–125, 127, 134; *see also under* Pankejeff, Anna; primal scene; psychosexual development 124, 135n6; suicide attempt 89n5; transference 116, 118, 120, 122, 128, 134; use of the name "Wolf Man" 115; and the veil 112, 114, 116–121, 123–126, 131–134

Pankejeff, Therese (wife): burial ceremony 126, 129, 131; relationship with Wolf Man 115, 127, 134, 179; suicide of 115, 120, 123–127, 134, 135n2; Wolf Man's mourning the 115, 123–126

paternal transference *see* Freud: as father figure transference: paternal and maternal

Peale, Norman Vincent 40, 54
perfection 14, 152, 153, 161
poetic relationship between H. D. and Freud 139
poetic space 162, 167, 169, 170
poetry and the poetic 32, 171; *see also Mignon's Song; Wilhelm Meister's Apprenticeship*; Blanton and 46, 52; Freud and xv, 2, 3, 101, 166; Goethe and the 3
poets, *see also* Doolittle, Hilda: Eckermann, Johann Peter; Goethe, Johann Wolfgang von; Freud and 2; H. D. and 138
poet's pen 52, 56
Pontalis, Jean-Bertrand 12–13
Pound, Ezra 138

premature birth 46, 65, 81, 117, 132
premature termination 177; *see also* Doolittle, Hilda: termination; forced termination of Pankejeff; of Blanton 59, 65; *see also* Blanton, Smiley: termination; of Dorsey 103, 105; of Kardiner 81; *see also* Kardiner, Abram: termination; of Wortis 35, 36; *see also* Wortis, Joseph: termination
primal scene: Freud on xii, 116, 121–122, 131; Pankejeff and xii, 116, 121–122, 131, 135n7
Psyche 156
psychiatry, biological 19
psychoanalysis, *see also* analysis: *specific topics*; criticism of 25, 29, 44, 53, 116
psychoanalytic movement 2; *see also specific topics*
psychoanalytic training 8–9; *see also* didactic analysis
psychotic breakdowns 81–82, 89n6, 137
Putnam, James Jackson 106

reconstruction (of the past) 9–10, 17, 163, 173, 186; *see also* repressed memories; Kardiner's 74–75, 83–84, 88, 174; and re-creation 4, 10
religion, *see also* Bible: Christianity; mythology; Blanton and 40, 52–57; Dorsey and 95, 99, 101, 104; Freud and 55, 101, 104; Freud on 52–57, 99–101; *see also Future of an Illusion*; psychiatry and 40; psychoanalysis and 53, 99; science and 54, 100–101, 149
religious faith 101; Blanton on 40; Freud on 54, 99, 100
remembering *see* memory reconstruction repressed memories
repetition 173, 184
repressed memories, recovery and reconstruction of 80, 83–84, 88, 121, 168, 173; *see also* reconstruction
resistance(s): Freud and 21, 23, 24, 32, 44, 113, 118, 122, 128, 133; memory and 15, 173; Paul Ricoeur on translation and 13–14; repression and 173; Wortis's 21–27, 32, 38
Rickman, John 89n4
Ricoeur, Paul 13–16
riddles 148–149, 191; *see also under Wolf Man and Sigmund Freud*; existential 134

schizophrenic patient's loss of memory 75, 77, 89n3
Schmideberg, Walter 140
science: Blanton and 42, 49, 54; case studies and 10; Freud on 3–4; Dorsey and 93–94, 100–101, 109–110; Freud and 20, 22–23, 25, 49, 101, 149, 152; Freud on 100; Freud on psychoanalysis as a 43; Freud's writings and 2, 3; Havelock Ellis and 20; psychoanalysis and 2–5, 20, 22, 43, 93–94, 118; religion and 54, 100–101, 149; Wortis and 20, 22–26
scientific attitude, Freud on 24–25
scientific community, Freud and the 25–26
scientific manner of Freud 42
scientist: Freud as 11, 20, 49; *see also under* science; Wortis as 19
screen memories 73, 84, 85, 89n7, 144
secularism: Dorsey and 101, 104; Freud and 99–100, 104
seduction: childhood 127, 134, 135n6, 170; as challenging the child in two phases 183–184; repetition of, in transference 184; Laplanche's general theory of primal 181, 183
seduction theory 12, 183; *see also* Laplanche, Jean: theory of primal seduction
self-analysis, *see also* Dorsey, John: self-analysis: Freud on 104; meanings of the term 97–98; writing as 140
self-consciousness 101, 103–104, 109, 110
separation: from mother 86–87; premature 105, 177; *see also* premature termination
sexual abuse *see* seduction
sexuality 31; *see also* homosexuality; oedipal conflicts; primal scene; Freud's writings about 31; language about 31–32
Shakespeare, William: Blanton and 46–47, 51, 52, 56, 57, 61; Freud and 52, 56, 57; quotes from 25, 46, 52, 61
Shakespeare authorship question 56, 57
Sill, Edward Rowland 100, 101
Strachey, James 12, 72, 89n4
stream of consciousness 108, 139; *see also* free association

termination 6, 111; *see also* mourning: termination and; abrupt. *see* Dorsey, John: termination forced termination of Pankejeff premature termination; Freud's interactions with analysands following 30, 86, 105, 147, 181, 185; nature of 187; separation and 16
termination phase of analysis 17, 101, 117; final session 29–30; Kardiner's 78–82, 86, 88
time: perfect moment in 161; temporality and 191n1
time-limited analysis 79; *see also* forced termination of Pankejeff; Kardiner, Abram
training analysis *see* didactic analysis
transcendental 149, 153
transference 16; enigmatic messages and 181–184; Freud on positive 25; Freud overlooking and failing to interpret xi–xii, 25, 56, 78, 81, 82, 109, 174, 181; Freud's interpretation of 76, 159; negative 36, 52, 120, 178; paternal and maternal 153–163, 178–181; *see also see* Freud: as father figure; writing memoirs and 175, 186
transference dreams 26, 42–43, 59, 64; *see also* dreams: Freud appearing in patients'
translation: H. D. and 137, 139, 142–144, 154, 155, 157, 158, 162–164, 166, 169, 171; Jean Laplanche on 16–17, 122, 181, 183; as metaphor for psychoanalytic work 12; *Mignon's Song* and 171; mourning and 13–17, 88, 184, 191; *Nachträglichkeit/après coup* (deferred action/afterwardsness) and 16, 124, 133, 142–144, 148, 154, 155, 173, 181–186; perfect and imperfect 14, 185; psychoanalysis, writing, and 163, 173, 189, 191; repressed images and 189; theories of 13–17, 122, 181; translating the enigmatic messages of the other 181–186; Walter Benjamin on 13; the work of 191
Tribute to Freud, A (H. D.) 9–10, 137–139; *see also* Doolittle, Hilda; the gift of the memoir 146–150; *Mignon's Song* and 139; Part I (*Writing on the Wall*) 137, 159; Part II (*Advent*) 138, 151, 154, 155, 158–159, 172n4; *see also* Doolittle, Hilda: diary; as a tribute to Freud 156
truth 119, 123–125, 127, 133; behind/ beyond the veil 112, 116, 118, 120; in

psychoanalysis 5; unveiling 120; in the veil 118; veiled 112, 125, 127, 133, 134; Walter Benjamin on 112, 118, 127
truth content (life's essence) vs. material content (biographical events) 112

unconscious 190; *see also under* consciousness
United States, *see also under* Freud, Sigmund; Freud's trip to 15, 47, 56, 106, 107, 111n1; psychoanalysis in xv 8–9, 55–56, 81

van der Leeuw, J. J. 142, 146
veil 117; beauty, the beautiful, and the 118–119, 123, 127, 134; and dialectic of revealing and concealing 119; Freud and the 112, 116, 117, 121, 125, 133–134; lifting the 112, 114, 116–121; Pankejeff and the 112, 114, 116–121, 123, 124, 126, 131–134; in Pankejeff's dreams 125, 131; psychoanalysis and the 112, 117, 132; of semblance 118–119; tearing off 125, 132; unity of the veiled and the 112, 119, 124, 127, 134; Walter Benjamin on the 112, 118–119, 127, 134; womb and the 117, 132–134
Venus 156
Victoria, Queen: Blanton's dream of 63
voice 5, 158–160; *see also* muted voices; of analysand xiv ; creating/giving oneself a 141, 154, 155; creation of 175; Freud giving Blanton a 58; having no 156; individual 190; paternal vs. maternal 179; poetry and 164–165, 167; of poets 141; *see also specific poets*; psychoanalysis and 1; search for a distinct (literary) 7, 167; texts by analysands bringing forth their xiv–xv

Wagner, Richard 145–146
What Is This Professor Freud Like? A Diary of an Analysis with Historical Comments (Koellreuter) xiii
Wilder, Thomas 105

Wilhelm Meister's Apprenticeship (*Wilhelm Meisters Lehrjahre*) 139, 164–171, 185–186; Goethe on 164
Winnicott, Donald W. 17n1
"Wolf Man" *see* Pankejeff, Sergei
Wolf Man and Sigmund Freud, The (Pankejeff) ix, 11, 113, 114, 119, 178, 185; *see also* Pankejeff, Sergei; material absent from 119, 125; as a mysterious riddle 133; one book, four authors 114–116
Wolf-Man by the Wolf-Man, The (Pankejeff) 9; *see also Wolf Man and Sigmund Freud*
womb 75; *see also* birth; analytic setting as a 41, 81; Freud and the 41, 65, 117, 180; Pankejeff and the 117, 132–134; return to the 65, 117; and the veil 117, 132–134; writing as a 110
Wortis, Joseph 42, 181; asked Freud to read his manuscript "Observations of a Psychiatric Interne" 33–34; career in psychiatry 9; *Conversations with Goethe* and 30, 32–36, 38n3; desire to become analyst 34–35; dreams 26, 29–31, 35; feeling that Freud does not like him 28; Freud's analytic stance toward 24–25; Goethe and 34, 35; Havelock Ellis and 18–21, 25, 26, 28, 37, 38n1, 38n3, 174; on his legacy 38; homosexuality and 18–19, 21; impasse in his analysis 24, 26, 36–38; Jewishness and 37, 38n4, 49; life history 18–19; mother 18; mourning and 30, 35–38, 174, 178; resistance 21–27, 32, 38; sexuality 31–32; termination 25, 29–30; premature 35, 36; transference 26, 36, 174, 178, 181
writing, nature of 7, 163
writing and psychoanalysis 7, 108; *see also specific topics*; as a work of memory 173–175; as a work of mourning 175–178
Writing on the Wall (H. D.) 137, 159; *see also Tribute to Freud*
"writing on the wall" (H. D.) 162–163
writing pad, mystic 189–191

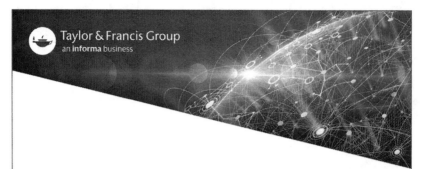

Taylor & Francis eBooks

www.taylorfrancis.com

A single destination for eBooks from Taylor & Francis with increased functionality and an improved user experience to meet the needs of our customers.

90,000+ eBooks of award-winning academic content in Humanities, Social Science, Science, Technology, Engineering, and Medical written by a global network of editors and authors.

TAYLOR & FRANCIS EBOOKS OFFERS:

- A streamlined experience for our library customers
- A single point of discovery for all of our eBook content
- Improved search and discovery of content at both book and chapter level

REQUEST A FREE TRIAL
support@taylorfrancis.com